Mastering RStudio – Develop, Communicate, and Collaborate with R

Harness the power of RStudio to create web applications, R packages, markdown reports and pretty data visualizations

Julian Hillebrand

Maximilian H. Nierhoff

[PACKT] open source ✳
PUBLISHING   community experience distilled

BIRMINGHAM - MUMBAI

Mastering RStudio – Develop, Communicate, and Collaborate with R

First published: November 2015

Production reference: 1251115

Published by Packt Publishing Ltd.
Livery Place
35 Livery Street
Birmingham B3 2PB, UK.

ISBN 978-1-78398-254-7

www.packtpub.com

Credits

Authors
Julian Hillebrand
Maximilian H. Nierhoff

Reviewer
Nicholas A. Yager

Commissioning Editor
Kartikey Pandey

Acquisition Editor
Tushar Gupta

Content Development Editor
Anish Dhurat

Technical Editor
Mohita Vyas

Copy Editor
Angad Singh

Project Coordinator
Harshal Ved

Proofreader
Safis Editing

Indexer
Rekha Nair

Graphics
Abhinash Sahu

Production Coordinator
Melwyn Dsa

Cover Work
Melwyn Dsa

About the Authors

Julian Hillebrand studied international business marketing management at the Cologne Business School in Germany. His interest in the current questions of the business world showed him the importance of data-driven decision-making. Because of the growing size of available inputs, he soon realized the great potential of R for analyzing and visualizing data. This fascination made him start a blog project about using data science, especially for social media data analysis, which can be found at `http://thinktostart.com/`. He managed to combine his hands-on tutorials with his marketing and business knowledge.

Julian is always looking for new technological opportunities and is also interested in the emerging field of machine learning. He completed several digital learning offerings to take his data science capabilities to the next level.

Maximilian H. Nierhoff is an analyst for online marketing with more than half a decade of experience in managing online marketing channels and digital analytics. After studying economics, cultural activities, and creative industries, he started building online marketing departments and realized quickly that future marketing forces should also have programming knowledge. He has always been passionate about everything related to the topics of data, marketing, and customer journey analysis. Therefore, he has specialized in using R since then, which is his first-choice language for programming, data science, and analysis capabilities. He considers himself a lifelong learner and is an avid user of MOOCs, which are about R and digital analytics.

About the Reviewer

Nicholas A. Yager is a biostatistician and software developer researching statistical genomics, image analysis, and infectious disease epidemiology. With an education in biochemistry and biostatistics, his experience in analyzing cutting-edge genomics data and simulating complex biological systems has given him an in-depth understanding of scientific computing and data analysis. Currently, Nicholas works for a personalized medicine company, designing medical informatics systems for next-generation personalized cancer tests. Aside from this book, Nicholas has reviewed *Unsupervised Learning with R, Packt Publishing*.

I would like to thank my friends, Lauren and Matt, and my mentor, Dr. Gregg Hartvigsen, for their help in reviewing this book.

www.PacktPub.com

Support files, eBooks, discount offers, and more

For support files and downloads related to your book, please visit www.PacktPub.com.

Did you know that Packt offers eBook versions of every book published, with PDF and ePub files available? You can upgrade to the eBook version at www.PacktPub.com and as a print book customer, you are entitled to a discount on the eBook copy. Get in touch with us at service@packtpub.com for more details.

At www.PacktPub.com, you can also read a collection of free technical articles, sign up for a range of free newsletters and receive exclusive discounts and offers on Packt books and eBooks.

https://www2.packtpub.com/books/subscription/packtlib

Do you need instant solutions to your IT questions? PacktLib is Packt's online digital book library. Here, you can search, access, and read Packt's entire library of books.

Why subscribe?

- Fully searchable across every book published by Packt
- Copy and paste, print, and bookmark content
- On demand and accessible via a web browser

Free access for Packt account holders

If you have an account with Packt at www.PacktPub.com, you can use this to access PacktLib today and view 9 entirely free books. Simply use your login credentials for immediate access.

Table of Contents

Preface

Data analysis, visualization, and the handling of complex statistical issues was reserved just for universities and very few organizations for a long time. In fact, an easy-to-use and free environment to make the concept of data analysis available to a broader audience was not available.

But in the early nineties, R saw the light of day, and since then, it has been on a meteoric rise. R has shaped the landscape of data science in recent years like no other programing language. Because of its open source nature, it became widely known and is often referred to as the lingua franca of data analysis. Another reason for this huge success is the availability of a sophisticated Integrated Development Environment (IDE) named RStudio.

The development of RStudio started in 2010, and now, it is the de facto, go-to IDE for everybody working with R. The mission statement of RStudio is *"to provide the most widely used open source and enterprise-ready professional software for the R statistical computing environment."*

But RStudio offers more than just a handy way to create R scripts; it grew to a real ecosystem by providing a variety of functionalities like package, application, interactive reporting creation, and more. Walking this way, RStudio has managed to bring data analysis to a broader audience. And because of its continuous desire to innovate R and its possibilities, it can be seen as a further development of the R language. RStudio combines the strong statistical power of R, the community, and open source spirit with cutting edge technologies of user interface development.

This made RStudio more than just a tool for statisticians; it became the platform for everybody who wants to generate insights from data and share them with others.

Therefore, we will hereafter guide you to develop, communicate, and collaborate with R by mastering RStudio.

What this book covers

Chapter 1, The RStudio IDE – an Overview, describes how to install RStudio, and gives a general overview of its user interface.

Chapter 2, Communicating Your Work with R Markdown, shows how to create R Markdown documents and presentations with the help of the concept of reproducible research.

Chapter 3, R Lesson I – Graphics System, gives an introduction to the landscape of plotting packages in R and the basic process of plot creation with different packages for interactive graphs.

Chapter 4, Shiny – a Web-app Framework for R, describes how to create web applications with the Shiny framework by explaining the basic concept of reactive programming.

Chapter 5, Interactive Documents with R Markdown, explains how to create interactive R Markdown documents with the Shiny framework and other R packages.

Chapter 6, Creating Professional Dashboards with R and Shiny, introduces the concept of dashboards, and how to build a professional dashboard with the `shinydashboard` package.

Chapter 7, Package Development in RStudio, describes the basic process of package development in R, and how to create R packages with RStudio.

Chapter 8, Collaborating with Git and GitHub, shows the fundamentals of Git and GitHub, and how to use them with RStudio.

Chapter 9, R for your Organization – Managing the RStudio Server, describes how to install R, RStudio, and the Shiny Server on a cloud server to create a fully flexible programming environment.

Chapter 10, Extending RStudio and Your Knowledge of R, explains where you can find additional resources to improve your work with R and RStudio.

What you need for this book

To fully apply the knowledge learned in this book, you will need a computer with access to the Internet, and the ability to install the R environment as well as the RStudio IDE. The first chapter will guide you through this process.

Who this book is for

This book is aimed at R developers and analysts who wish to work on R statistical development while taking advantage of RStudio's functionality to ease their development efforts. Experience with R programming is assumed, as well as being comfortable with R's basic structures and a number of functions.

Conventions

In this book, you will find a number of text styles that distinguish between different kinds of information. Here are some examples of these styles and an explanation of their meaning.

Code words in text, database table names, folder names, filenames, file extensions, pathnames, dummy URLs, user input, and Twitter handles are shown as follows: "You can also export the `analysis.R` script as a report in the HTML, PDF, or MS Word format, and you will then find the report in your `code` folder."

A block of code is set as follows:

```
gaToken <- GoogleApiCreds(
            userName = "your@email.com",
            list(
              client_id = "your client ID",
              client_secret = "your client secret")
            )

save(gaToken, file = "auth/gaToken")
```

Any command-line input or output is written as follows:

```
$ sudo apt-key adv –keyserver keyserver.ubuntu.com –recv-keys E084DAB9
```

New terms and **important words** are shown in bold. Words that you see on the screen, for example, in menus or dialog boxes, appear in the text like this: "Therefore, just click on the **Publish** button and RStudio will guide you through the process."

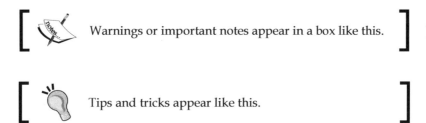

Warnings or important notes appear in a box like this.

Tips and tricks appear like this.

Reader feedback

Feedback from our readers is always welcome. Let us know what you think about this book—what you liked or disliked. Reader feedback is important for us as it helps us develop titles that you will really get the most out of.

To send us general feedback, simply e-mail `feedback@packtpub.com`, and mention the book's title in the subject of your message.

If there is a topic that you have expertise in and you are interested in either writing or contributing to a book, see our author guide at `www.packtpub.com/authors`.

Customer support

Now that you are the proud owner of a Packt book, we have a number of things to help you to get the most from your purchase.

Errata

Although we have taken every care to ensure the accuracy of our content, mistakes do happen. If you find a mistake in one of our books—maybe a mistake in the text or the code—we would be grateful if you could report this to us. By doing so, you can save other readers from frustration and help us improve subsequent versions of this book. If you find any errata, please report them by visiting `http://www.packtpub.com/submit-errata`, selecting your book, clicking on the **Errata Submission Form** link, and entering the details of your errata. Once your errata are verified, your submission will be accepted and the errata will be uploaded to our website or added to any list of existing errata under the Errata section of that title.

To view the previously submitted errata, go to `https://www.packtpub.com/books/content/support` and enter the name of the book in the search field. The required information will appear under the **Errata** section.

Piracy

Piracy of copyrighted material on the Internet is an ongoing problem across all media. At Packt, we take the protection of our copyright and licenses very seriously. If you come across any illegal copies of our works in any form on the Internet, please provide us with the location address or website name immediately so that we can pursue a remedy.

Please contact us at `copyright@packtpub.com` with a link to the suspected pirated material.

We appreciate your help in protecting our authors and our ability to bring you valuable content.

Questions

If you have a problem with any aspect of this book, you can contact us at questions@packtpub.com, and we will do our best to address the problem.

The RStudio IDE – an Overview

1

The number of users adopting the R programming language has been increasing faster and faster in the last few years. It is not just used for smaller analyses, but also for bigger projects, and often, several people collaborating on the same project. The functions of the R console are limited when it comes to managing a lot of files, or when we want to work with version control systems. This is the reason, in combination with the increasing adoption rate, why a need for a better development environment arose. To serve this need, a team of R fans began to develop an **integrated development environment (IDE)** to make it easier to work on bigger projects and to collaborate with others. This IDE has the name, **RStudio**. We will introduce you to this fantastic software and show you how to take your R programming to the next level. Mastering the use of RStudio will help you solve real-world problems faster and more effectively.

In this chapter, we will introduce you to the RStudio interface and build the foundation for more advanced topics in the following chapters.

This chapter covers the following topics:

- Downloading and installing RStudio
- Getting to know the RStudio interface
- Working with RStudio projects

Downloading and installing RStudio

Before installing RStudio, you should install R on your computer. RStudio will then automatically search for your R installation.

Installing R

RStudio is based on the R framework and it requires, at least, R version 2.11.1, but we highly recommend that you install the latest version. The latest version of R is 3.2.2, as of September 2015.

We assume that most readers are using Windows or Mac OS systems. The installation of R is pretty simple. Just go to http://cran.rstudio.com, download the proper version of R for your system, and install it using the default setting.

We would like to leave more space to talk about installing R on different Linux distributions. As there are a huge number of different Linux distributions out there, we will focus, in this book, on the most used one: Ubuntu.

For Ubuntu

CRAN hosts repositories for Debian and Ubuntu. To install the latest version of R, you should add the CRAN repository to your system.

The supported releases are: Utopic Unicorn (14.10), Trusty Tahr (14.04; LTS), Precise Pangolin (12.04; LTS), and Lucid Lynx (10.04; LTS). However, only the latest **Long Term Support** (LTS) is fully supported by the R framework development team.

We will take Ubuntu 14.04 LTS as an example. Perform the following steps:

1. Open a new terminal window.
2. Add the repository for Ubuntu 14.04 to the file /etc/apt/sources.list:

   ```
   $ sudo sh -c "echo 'deb http://cran.rstudio.com/bin/linux/ubuntu
   trusty/'>>/etc/apt/sources.list
   ```

3. The Ubuntu archives on CRAN are signed with a key, which has the key ID, E084DAB9. So, we have to add the key to our system:

   ```
   $ sudo apt-key adv –keyserver keyserver.ubuntu.com –recv-keys
   E084DAB9
   ```

4. Update the system and repository:

   ```
   $ sudo apt-get update
   ```

5. Install R with:

   ```
   $ sudo apt-get install r-base
   ```

6. Install the developer package:

   ```
   $ sudo apt-get install r-base-devInstalling RStudio
   ```

Installing RStudio on Windows and Ubuntu is pretty much the same, as RStudio offers installers for nearly all platforms. The steps are listed as follows:

1. Go to `http://www.rstudio.com/products/rstudio/download/`.
2. Download the newest installer for your system.
3. Install RStudio using the default settings.

Using RStudio with different versions of R

As R updates continuously, it is possible that you have, even after a short time, several versions of R installed on your system. Sometimes, you also have projects that require an older version of R to run properly.

Windows

When R is installed on Windows, it automatically writes the version being installed into the registry as the current version of R. And this will also be the version that RStudio uses. You can choose the version of R that you want to use by holding the *Ctrl* key during the launch of RStudio.

Ubuntu

On Linux, you can use a command with R to see which version of R, RStudio uses. If you want RStudio to use another version of R (maybe you want to use an older version or because you had to install R in your `Documents` folder because of missing admin rights) you can overwrite the settings with the following export: `RSTUDIO_WHICH_R=/usr/local/bin/R`. This line has to be added to your `~/.profile` file.

Updating RStudio

Updating RStudio is as easy as installing it. If you want to check if an update is available, navigate to **Help | Check for Updates**.

If an update is available, you can download the newest version and just install it. As RStudio saves all user information in the user's home directory, they will still be there after the update.

Getting to know the RStudio interface

Now, we can take a look at RStudio's user interface.

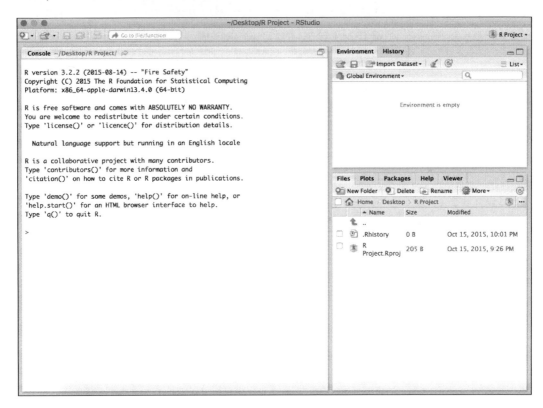

The four main panes

When you start RStudio for the first time, you will see four main panes. If you want to customize the four main panes, you can do it by navigating to **Tools | Global Options | Pane Layout**.

We will explain their use, but first we need to create a new R script file by clicking on **File | New File | R Script**.

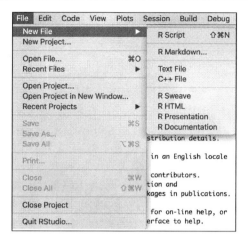

The new R script file is opened in a new pane and is named Untitled1.

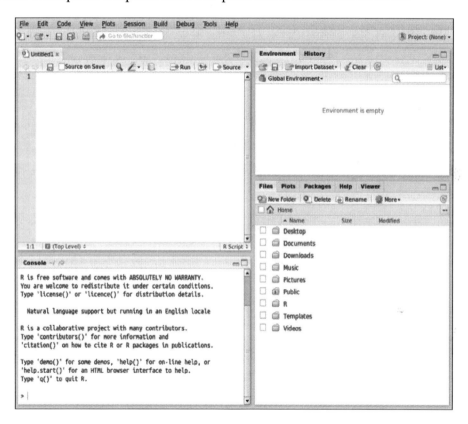

You can see that we now have four panes. They are named as follows:

- The **Source editor** pane
- The **Environment** and **History** pane
- The **Console** pane
- The **Files**, **Plots**, **Packages**, **Help**, and **Viewer** pane

The Source editor pane

RStudio's source editor was developed in a fully functional R editor over the last few years. It has a powerful syntax highlighter that works with not only every format connected to R development, such as R Scripts, R Markdown, or R documentation files, but also C++, JavaScript, HTML, and many more.

We've already created a new R script file and can now demonstrate some of the code editor's functions. You can also open an existing R document by clicking on **File | Open File**, or by using the shortcut, *Ctrl + O*.

The code editor works with tabs, which gives you the possibility of opening several files at the same time, as you can see in the following screenshot. If there are unsaved changes in a file, their names will be highlighted in red and marked with an asterisk.

If you have several files opened, you will see a double arrow in the menu of the source code editor. This will open a small menu showing you an overview of all the opened files. You can also search for a specific file.

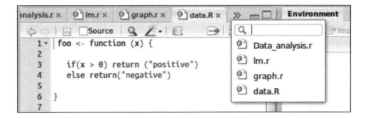

Under the tabs with the opened files, you can see a toolbox with tools for the code editor. For example, you have the **Source on Save** checkbox. This is a really handy tool especially when you are working on a reusable function. If activated, the function is automatically sourced to the global environment and we do not have to source it manually again after editing the code.

Another function you can find in the toolbox is the search and replace tool. This is known from a lot of text editors and helps you find existing code and replace it. RStudio also offers different options for your search, such as **In selection**, to just search in the code you selected in the editor or **Match case**, to make the search case-sensitive. This is demonstrated in the following screenshot:

```
1   par(mfrow=c(3,2))
2
3   plot(density(runif(100)), lwd=2)
4   text(x=0, y=0.2, "100 uniforms")
5   abline(h=0, v=0)
6
7   x=seq(0.01,1,0.01)
8   par(col="blue")                        # default colour to blu
9
10  plot(x, sin(x), type="l")
11  lines(x, cos(x), type="l", col="red")
12
13  plot(x, exp(x), type="l", col="green")
14  lines(x, log(x), type="l", col="orange")
15
16  plot(x, tan(x), type="l", lwd=3, col="yellow")
17
```

Syntax highlighting

RStudio highlights parts of your code according to the R language definition. This makes your code much easier to read. The default settings are:

- The R keywords being blue
- The text strings being green
- Numbers being dark blue
- Comments being dull green

Code completion

One of the most important menus in the source editor is what you find when you click on the magic stick. If you forgot what exact arguments the selected function needs, just hit the *Tab* button and you will see a list of available arguments with a description, if available:

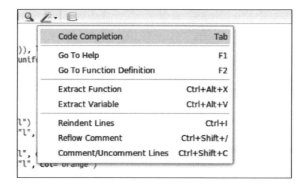

You can then scroll through the list and select the argument you want to use. This is especially useful when you have functions that can be called with a lot of different arguments; it would be very time-consuming to open the package documentation for every function call.

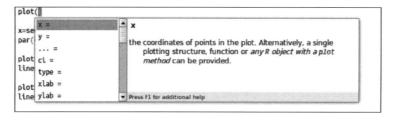

You can also find direct links to the help or function definition, which shows you where the current function is defined.

After that, you can find the functions, **Extract Function** and **Extract Variable**. These functions help you in creating functions. When you click on **Extract Function** or use the shortcut, *Ctrl + Alt + X*, RStudio creates a function from your selection and inserts it in the source code.

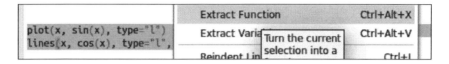

After executing the command, your code will look like this:

```
plot_sin_cos <- function (x) {
  plot(x, sin(x), type="l")
  lines(x, cos(x), type="l", col="red")
}
```

The next button is the **Compile Notebook** button. This helps you compile your currently opened source file into a notebook with the format, HTML, PDF, or MS Word:

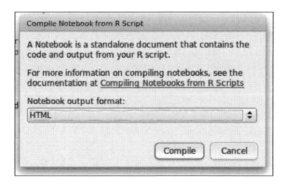

The compiled report will then open in a new window.

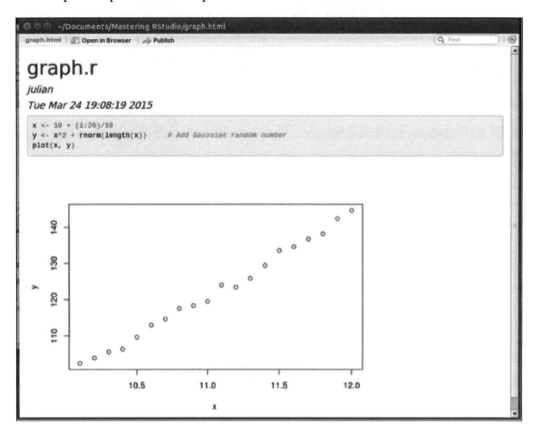

This is the code we used for the preceding example; if you want to reproduce it, type the following code:

```
x <- 10 + (1:20)/10
y <- x^2 + rnorm(length(x))
plot(x, y)
```

Executing R Code from the source pane

On the extreme right of the source code menu, you will find the buttons needed to run the code. These buttons are:

- The **Run** button executes a single line and the shortcut is *Ctrl + Enter*
- To re-run the previous region (*Ctrl + Shift + P*)
- The **Source** button executes the entire source file (*Ctrl + Shift + Enter*)

Code regions are foldable regions of code in the code editor. We will explain later how you can create them.

If you want to execute a single line, or rather, if you want to run the current line where your cursor is, you can use the **Run** button or the shortcut, *Ctrl + Enter*. After the execution, the cursor will jump to the next line in the source file.

If you want to execute several lines of code, you can select the lines and press the **Run** button.

Code folding

RStudio supports both automatic and user-defined folding for regions of code. This is a very handy feature, especially when you work with functions and larger scripts. It lets you hide and show blocks to make the code easier to navigate.

RStudio automatically folds the following regions in the source editor:

- Braced regions (function definitions, conditional blocks, and so on)
- Code chunks within R Sweave or R Markdown documents
- Code sections (user-defined)

The output looks like this:

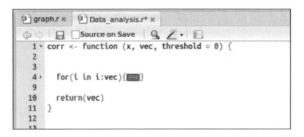

To define a code section on your own and to make it easier to navigate in larger source files, you can use three methods:

- # Section One ----------------------
- # Section Two =============
- ### Section Three #############

So, the line can start with any number of pound signs (#), but is has to end with at least four or more -, =, or # characters. RStudio then automatically defines the following code as the section. To navigate between code sections, you can use the **Jump To** menu at the bottom of the editor.

The menu at the bottom, on the right-hand side lets you choose the file format of the currently opened source file. Normally, RStudio chooses the right format automatically. If you change it manually, the code completion and the syntax highlighting will adapt to the new settings.

Debugging code

RStudio offers visual debuggers to help you understand code and find bugs and problems. Therefore, it uses the debugging functions of R but integrates them seamlessly into the RStudio user interface. You can find these tools in the **Debug** tab of the menu, or by pressing *Alt + D*:

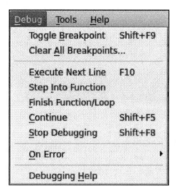

You can set breakpoints right in the source editor by clicking on the number of the line, or by pressing *Shift + F9*:

```
 1 ▾  foo <- function (x) {
 2
 3      if(x > 0) return ("positive")
●4      else return("negative")
 5
 6  }
 7
 8
 9 ▾  bar <- function () {
●10     foo(1:5)
 11  }
 12
 13  bar()
```

Global Environment ▾

Functions

| ● bar | function () |
| ● foo | function (x) |

The debugger output can help you find bugs in your code in a better way. In this example, the debugger output is `debug.R:10`. This means that we should look into the tenth line of the source file:

```
  8
 9 ▾  bar <- function () {
➔10     │ foo(1:5)
 11  }
 12
 13  bar()
```

Traceback   ☐ Show ═

➔ bar() at debug.R:10

    [Debug source] at debug.R:13

The Environment and History panes

With the default settings, this pane consists of the tabs, **Environment** and **History**. You can use the shortcut, *Ctrl + 8*, to switch to the **Environment** browser, and *Ctrl + 4* to switch to the **History** window:

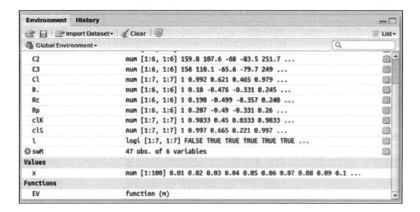

The **Environment** pane is one of the biggest advantages of RStudio. It gives you an overview over all objects currently available in an environment. So, you can see a list of all data, values, and functions.

The **Environment** browser shows you the number of observations and the number of variables in the second column. If you want to get a better overview of a dataset, you can click on the table symbol at the end of the row.

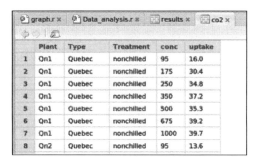

When you click on the blue and white arrow next to the name of an object, you will see its structure. This is basically the output of the str() function, but in a more structured way.

The **Import Dataset** button offers you an easy way to import data. It basically uses the read.csv() function but offers you a graphical interface to set the parameters for the import. You can either import the dataset from a local file, or you can choose an import from a URL.

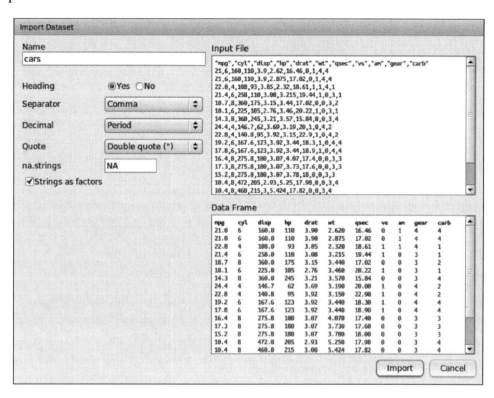

Furthermore, the Environment pane gives you the possibility of clearing the environment, which will delete all defined variables and also all sourced functions.

History pane

The **History** pane shows all the commands you entered in the console, and it also lets you send the selected command back from the history directly to the console with the **To Console** button or back to the opened source code file with the **To Source** button. You can also delete commands from the history by selecting them and pressing the paper icon with the red close sign above the history. Or you can clear the whole history by clicking the broom icon:

```
Environment   History                                                    ─□

   🖥 🖫 | 🖳 To Console  📑 To Source   ✖ 🧹                          🔍 |

y <- x^2 + rnorm(length(x)) # Add Gaussian random number
plot(x, y)
var(1:10) # 9.166667
var(1:5, 1:5) # 2.5
## Two simple vectors
cor(1:10, 2:11) # == 1
## Correlation Matrix of Multivariate sample:
(Cl <- cor(longley))
## Graphical Correlation Matrix:
symnum(Cl) # highly correlated
## Spearman's rho and Kendall's tau
symnum(clS <- cor(longley, method = "spearman"))
symnum(clK <- cor(longley, method = "kendall"))
## How much do they differ?
i <- lower.tri(Cl)
cor(cbind(P = Cl[i], S = clS[i], K = clK[i]))
## cov2cor() scales a covariance matrix by its diagonal
```

Console pane

The console pane is basically an R console but it is enhanced with some RStudio functions. This includes the command completion known from the source editor, and a history popup, which shows you the recent commands you used.

The keyboard shortcuts for the console pane are:

- **Command completion**: *Tab*
- **Command history popup**: *Ctrl* + arrow up
- **Clear console**: *Ctrl* + *L*
- **Go through historical command**: arrow up

The Files, Plots, Packages, Help, and Viewer panes

This pane is, like the name says, divided into five sub panes: **Files**, **Plots**, **Packages**, **Help**, and **Viewer**.

The Files pane

This pane is one of RStudio's biggest enhancements in comparison to the normal R console. The **Files** pane shows you all the files in the current working directory. It includes information about the file size and when the data was last modified. Clicking on an item will open it with the appropriate application.

The Plot pane

The **Plot** pane in RStudio handles all of your graphics output. This makes working with graphical output much easier than in the regular R console, as it opens a new window for every graphic.

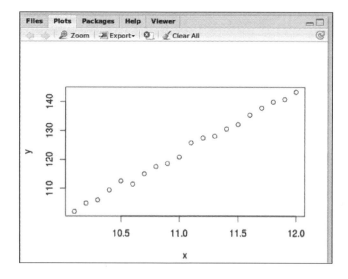

Furthermore, the **Plot** pane gives some more tools. These tools include the option to zoom into a graphic. This will open a new window with a bigger version of the current plot. This plot will then arrange itself to the current window size.

You can also export the current plotted graphic with the **Export** button. The **Export** menu has three options:

- To save the plot as an image
- To save the plot as a PDF
- To copy the plot to the clipboard

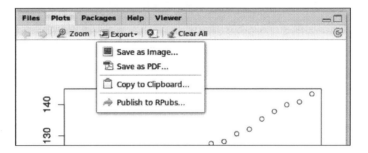

When you choose the **Save as Image...** option, RStudio will open a popup that lets you define the export image format, the directory, and the file name, as well as the width and height.

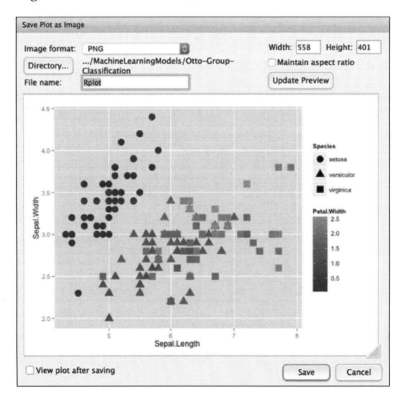

The **Save as PDF...** option will create a single page PDF document with your plot. Based on the width and height settings, it will be either in the landscape or portrait format.

RStudio also offers the option to publish your plots on RPubs. This is a free and very simple web service from the makers of RStudio to upload R graphics and R Markdown documents, which will then be publicly available on the web and you can share the link. We will talk about the possibilities of R markdown in a later chapter.

When you click on the **Publish** button, a window will open and guide you through the process.

After clicking on **Publish**, a new browser window will open and show your uploaded report:

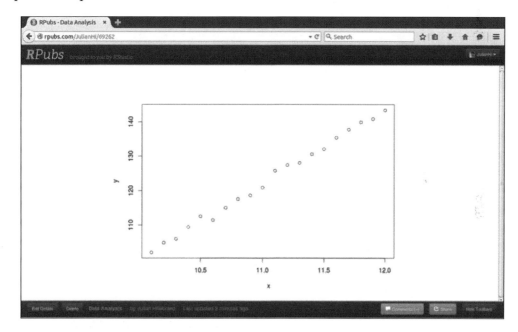

The Packages pane

The **Package** pane helps you install, update, or load packages. It gives you an overview about all installed packages, a short description, and the installed version.

If you tick a checkbox in front of a package, it will automatically be loaded, and if you remove the tick again, RStudio will automatically detach it from the environment. So, it basically unloads it again.

The **Packages** pane also provides a handy tool to install new packages with the help of a graphical interface. We just have to click on the **Install** button and we will be guided through the installation process. The **Install packages** dialog also allows us to install packages that we have saved locally on our computer:

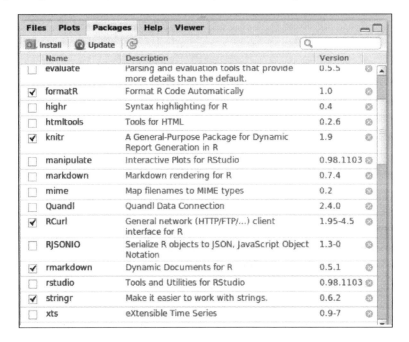

You can see next what RStudio does in the R console:

```
> library("RCurl", lib.loc="~/R/x86_64-pc-linux-gnu-library/3.1")
Loading required package: bitops
> detach("package:RCurl", unload=TRUE)
>
```

The Help pane

A big advantage of the R language is that every package on CRAN will come with package documentation. You can find these files on the CRAN website but RStudio bundles them in a handy **Help** pane. You can search the help through the search bar, or you can just press *F1*:

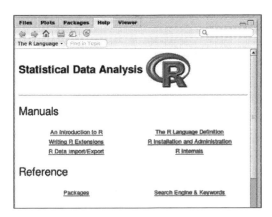

The Viewer pane

The **Viewer** pane in RStudio can be used to view local web content, such as web graphics created with packages such as rCharts, googleVis, and others. It can also show local web applications created with Shiny or OpenCPU.

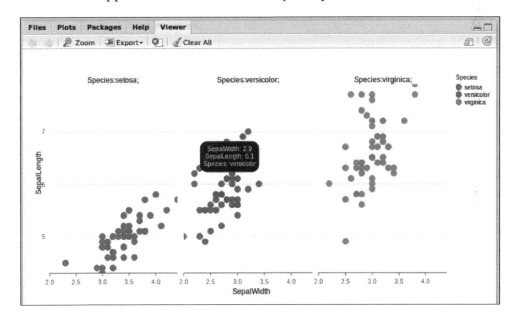

Now, we will click on **Save as Web Page...** in the **Export** menu.

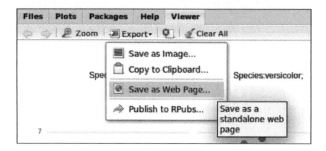

The export menu of the viewer pane offers, basically, the same option to export your work but replaces the **Save as image** option with **Save as Web Page**. This creates a standalone web page.

Customizing RStudio

The default options of RStudio are the best for most people, but you can also change the appearance and the pane layout completely according to your needs and wishes. We can open the **Options** menu by clicking on **Tools | Global Options**:

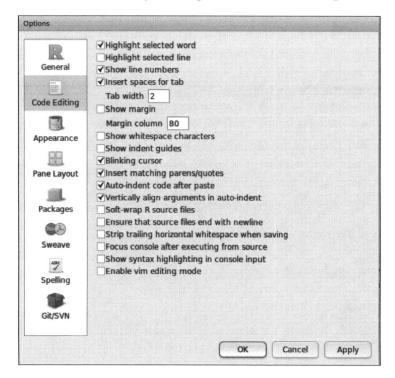

RStudio offers a lot of ways to personalize the code editing. We can, for example, set the spaces that will be inserted when we use the *Tab* key, or change the diagnostics information shown. You also have the **Appearance** tab, as shown next:

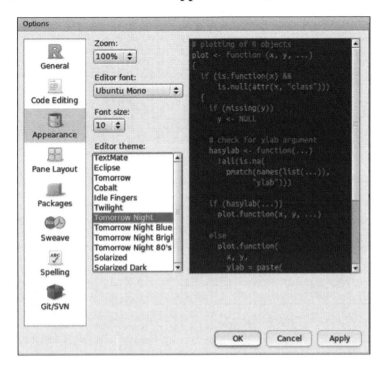

Here you can edit, for example, the font used in the code editor, or the editor theme. This way, you can make RStudio look the way you want it to.

And the **Pane Layout** tab: In this pane, we can change the content of the four main panes in the **Pane Layout** tab. You can make each of them a source, a console, or an individualized pane. So, the last option means that you can easily add elements to the pane with the help of the checkboxes.

Using keyboard shortcuts

The fastest way to use RStudio is by using it with keyboard shortcuts. In the previous text, we already mentioned some of them. But we put the most important ones together in a table, which is as follows:

Description	Windows and Linux	Mac
Move the focus to the Source editor	Ctrl + 1	Ctrl + 1
Move the focus to console	Ctrl + 2	Ctrl + 2
Move the focus to **Help**	Ctrl + 3	Ctrl + 3
Show the **History** pane	Ctrl + 4	Ctrl +4

Description	Windows and Linux	Mac
Show the **Files** pane	*Ctrl + 5*	*Ctrl +5*
Show the **Plots** pane	*Ctrl + 6*	*Ctrl + 6*
Show the **Packages** pane	*Ctrl + 7*	*Ctrl + 7*
Show the **Environment** pane	*Ctrl + 8*	*Ctrl + 8*
Open the document	*Ctrl + O*	*Command + O*
Run the current line/section	*Ctrl + Enter*	*Command + Enter*
Clear the console	*Ctrl + L*	*Command + L*
Extract the function from the selection	*Ctrl + Alt + X*	*Command + Option + X*
Source the current document	*Ctrl + Shift + Enter*	*Command + Shift + Enter*
Toggle the breakpoint	*Shift + F9*	*Shift + F9*

Working with RStudio and projects

In the times before RStudio, it was very hard to manage bigger projects with R in the R console, as you had to create all the folder structures on your own.

When you work with projects or open a project, RStudio will instantly take several actions. For example, it will start a new and clean R session, it will source the .Rprofile file in the project's main directory, and it will set the current working directory to the project directory. So, you have a complete working environment individually for every project. RStudio will even adjust its own settings, such as active tabs, splitter positions, and so on, to where they were when the project was closed.

But just because you can create projects with RStudio easily, it does not mean that you should create a project for every single time that you write R code. For example, if you just want to do a small analysis, we would recommend that you create a project where you save all your smaller scripts.

Creating a project with RStudio

RStudio offers you an easy way to create projects. Just navigate to **File | New Project** and you will see a popup window with the following options:

- **New Directory**
- **Existing Directory**
- **Version Control**

These options let you decide from where you want to create your project. So, if you want to start it from scratch and create a new directory, associate your new project to an existing one, or if you want to create a project from a version control repository, you can avail of the respective options. For now, we will focus on creating a new directory.

The following list will show you the next options available:

- **Empty Project**
- **R Package**
- **Shiny Web Application**

We will look in the categories, **R Package** and **Shiny Web Application** later in this book, so for now we will concentrate on the **Empty Project** option.

Locating your project

A very important question you have to ask yourself when creating a new project is where you want to save it? There are several options and details you have to pay attention to especially when it comes to collaboration and different people working on the same project.

You can save your project locally, on a cloud storage or with the help of a revision control system such as Git.

Using RStudio with Dropbox

An easy way to store your project and to be able to access it from everywhere is the use of a cloud storage provider like Dropbox. It offers you a free account with 2 GB of storage, which should be enough for your first project.

Preventing Dropbox synchronization conflicts

RStudio actively monitors your project files for changes, which allows it to index functions and files to enable code completion and navigation. But when you use Dropbox at the same time to remotely sync your work, it will also monitor your files and this can cause conflicts. So you should tell Dropbox to ignore the `.Rproj.user` directory in your RStudio project.

To ignore a file in Dropbox, navigate to **Preferences** | **Account** | **Selective Sync** and uncheck the **.Rproj.user** directory.

Dropbox also helps you with version control, as it keeps previous versions of a file.

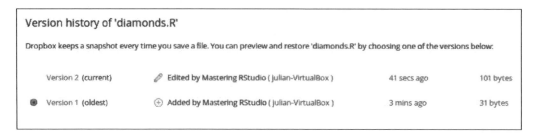

Creating your first project

To begin your first project, choose the **New Directory** option we described before and create an empty project. Then, choose a name for the directory and the location that you want to save it in. You should create a `projects` folder on your Dropbox.

The first project will be a small data analysis based on a dataset that was extracted from the 1974 issue of the Motor Trend US magazine. It comprises fuel consumption and ten aspects of automobile design and performance, such as the weight or number of cylinders for 32 automobiles, and is included in the base R package. So, we do not have to install a separate package to work with this dataset, as it is automatically loaded when you start R.

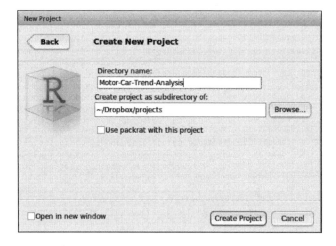

As you can see, we left the **Use packrat with this project** option unchecked. **Packrat** is a dependency management tool that makes your R code more isolated, portable, and reproducible by giving your project its own privately managed package library. This is especially important when you want to create projects in an organizational context where the code has to run on various computer systems, and has to be usable for a lot of different users. This first project will just run locally and will not focus on a specific combination of package versions.

Organizing your folders

RStudio creates an empty directory for you that includes just the file, `Motor-Car-Trend-Analysis.Rproj`. This file will store all the information on your project that RStudio will need for loading. But to stay organized, we have to create some folders in the directory. Create the following folders:

- `data`: This includes all the data that we need for our analysis
- `code`: This includes all the code files for cleaning up data, generating plots, and so on
- `plots`: This includes all graphical outputs
- `reports`: This comprises all the reports that we create from our dataset

This is a very basic folder structure and you have to adapt it to your needs in your own projects. You could, for example, add the folders, raw and processed, in the data folder. Raw for unstructured data that you started with, and processed for cleaned data that you actually used for your analysis.

Saving the data

The Motor Trend Car Road Tests dataset is part of the `dataset` package, which is one of the preinstalled packages in R. But, we will save the data in a CSV file in our data folder, after extracting the data from the `mtcars` variable, to make sure our analysis is reproducible:

```
#write data into csv file
write.csv(mtcars, file = "data/cars.csv", row.names=FALSE)
```

Put the previous line of code in a new R script and save it as `data.R` in the `code` folder.

Analyzing the data

The analysis script will first have to load the data from the CSV file with the following line:

```
cars_data <- read.csv(file = "data/cars.csv", header = TRUE, sep = ",")
```

Correcting the path for report exporting

If you want to create a report from your R script, you have to specify the relative path to the data file, beginning with two dots:

```
cars_data <- read.csv(file = "../data/cars.csv", header = TRUE, sep = ",")
```

Next, we can take a look at the different variables and see if we can find any correlations on the first look. We can create a `pairs` matrix with the following line:

```
pairs(cars_data)
```

We can then save the created matrix with the export function of the **Plots Pane** option. Then, we can save it as an image in the `plots` folder:

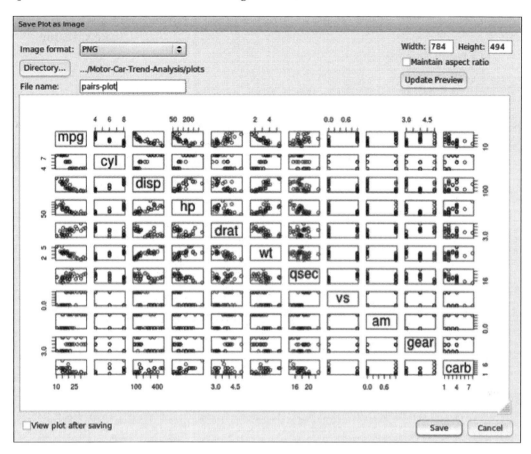

As you can see, we can expect a lot of different variable combinations, which could correlate very well. The most obvious one is surely **weight of the car (wt)** and **Miles per Gallon (mpg)**: a heavy car seems to need more gallons of fuel than a lighter car.

We can now test this hypothesis by calculating the correlation and plotting a scatterplot of these two variables. In addition, we can also do a linear regression and see how it performs:

```
cor(cars_data$wt, cars_data$mpg)
```

```
install.packages("ggplot2")
require(ggplot2)
```

```
ggplot(cars_data, aes(x=wt, y=mpg))+
  geom_point(aes(shape=factor(am, labels = c("Manual","Automatic"))))+
  geom_smooth(method=lm)+scale_shape_discrete(name = "Transmission
Type")

firstModel <- lm(mpg~wt, data = cars_data)
```

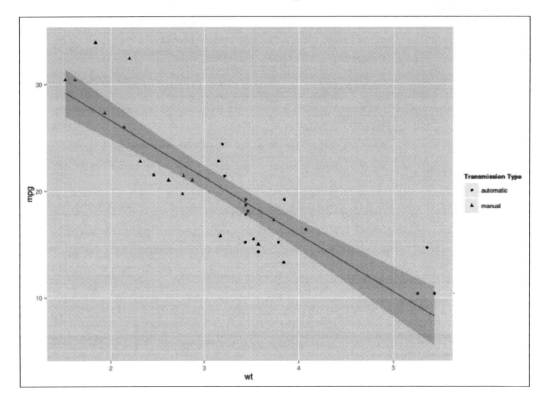

We can see more details with:

```
summary(firstModel)$coef

[1] -0.8676594

print(c('R-squared', round(summary(firstModel)$r.sq,2)))

[1] "R-squared"  "0.75"
```

We can see that there is a high negative correlation between these two variables, and the first model is a pretty good fit with an R-squared value of 0.75.

But we also have to test other combinations and see how they perform. And what we basically do is test all the correlations and use the best model.

We will not explain the statistical functions behind this approach, as it would be out of the scope of this chapter:

```
#Test other correlations
completeModel <- lm(mpg ~., data=cars_data)
stepSolution <- step(completeModel, direction = "backward")

#get the best model
bestModel <- stepSolution$call
bestModel
```

The output will look like this:

```
> bestModel
lm(formula = mpg ~ wt + qsec + am, data = cars_data)
```

The best model now has the following formula:

```
mpg ~ wt + qsec + am
```

So, we will create a final model with this formula and see how it performs:

```
finalModel <- lm(mpg~wt + factor(am) + qsec, data = cars_data)
summary(finalModel)$coef
print(c('R-squared', round(summary(finalModel)$r.sq,2)))
```

	Estimate	Std. Error	t value	Pr(>|t|)
(Intercept)	9.617781	6.9595930	1.381946	1.779152e-01
wt	-3.916504	0.7112016	-5.506882	6.952711e-06
factor(am)manual	2.935837	1.4109045	2.080819	4.671551e-02
qsec	1.225886	0.2886696	4.246676	2.161737e-04

```
[1] "R-squared"   "0.85"
```

As we can see, the final model also includes the variable, qsec, which is the time the car needs for a quarter mile, and am, which is the type of transmission (automatic or manual).

But, we can also see that just the transmission type, manual, seems to play a significant role when it comes to mileage.

After you execute the analysis script, you can see that all your results are still in RStudio, which is a big advantage in contrast to the R console.

So, you can go through all the graphs you produced in the plot viewer with the arrows.

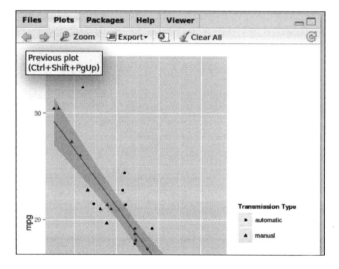

Or, you can see which variables are set in the environment. These are all the models you calculated in this analysis, as well as in your initial dataset.

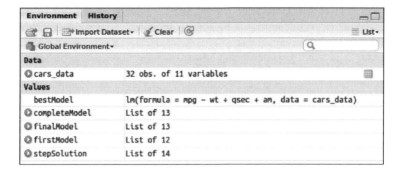

You can click on the table icon behind `cars_data` in the **Environment** pane to open the data frame in the Source pane.

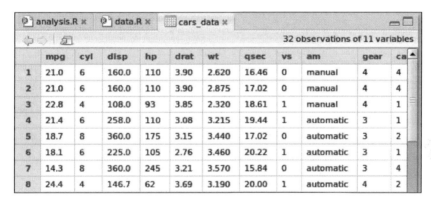

Exporting your analysis as a report

You can also export the `analysis.R` script as a report in the HTML, PDF, or MS Word format, and you will then find the report in your `code` folder. Therefore, just click on the **Publish** button and RStudio will guide you through the process.

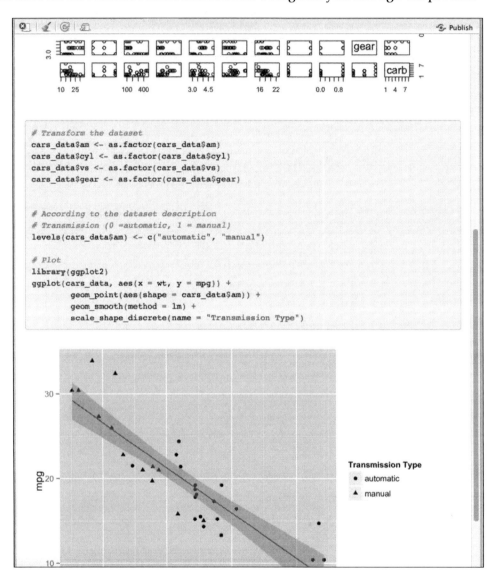

Summary

In this chapter, we learned how to install RStudio and got a general overview of its user interface. This consists of four main panes: the Source Editor pane, the console pane, the Environment and Help pane, and the Files, Plot, Help, and Viewer pane. We learned their different functions and saw what tools each pane has.

Furthermore, we learned how to create a project with RStudio in combination with Dropbox, and we started our first small data analysis.

In the next chapter, we will learn how to communicate our work with the help of R Markdown, and how to create reproducible research.

2
Communicating Your Work with R Markdown

This chapter covers the following topics:

- Reproducible research with R Markdown
- Getting started with the R Markdown interface
- Customizing R code chunks and file output
- Using templates and a custom style sheet
- Creating presentations with R Markdown

The concept of reproducible research

The possibility of replicating studies and researches is essential for strengthening the scientific evidence of the related outcomes. Especially when it comes to public trials of the influence on important social decision-making processes; it is particularly relevant to disclose all data sets, analytical methods, and related findings. By enabling such transparency, it is possible for every interested person to reproduce the results of any scientific research. With this approach, all findings can be checked for accuracy and are thus, possibly, corrected or confirmed by third-parties, even though an analysis can be reproducible and still not valid. A basic reproducible workflow could look like the following:

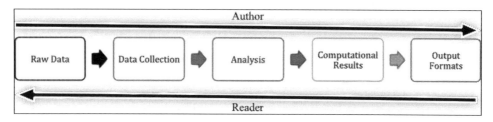

Doing reproducible research with R Markdown

Since the concepts and methods of reproducible research have their own range of topics that could easily fill several books, we would like to focus on the abilities of R Markdown in conjunction with RStudio in this chapter. But first, we will give you a few introductory statements.

What is Markdown?

> *Markdown is a text-to-HTML conversion tool for web writers. Markdown allows you to write, using an easy-to-read, easy-to-write plain text format, and then convert it to structurally valid XHTML (or HTML).*
>
> *– John Gruber, Creator of Markdown*
> (http://daringfireball.net/projects/markdown/)

This simplification, and the fact that it is akin to the markup language, enables authors to perform a fast and intuitive formatting of text. Following are some examples:

- The use of hashes will create headlines:

  ```
  # This is an H1 heading

  ## This is an H2 heading

  ### This is an H3 heading

  #### This is an H4 heading
  ```

- If you want to create an ordered list, you can use numbers with a period:

  ```
  1. Blue

  2. Green

  3. Black

  4. Yellow
  ```

- For unordered lists, you can use * (asterisks), + (plusses), and – (hyphens) as interchangeable list markers, instead of numbers.

What is literate programming?

Literate programming refers to the writing of computer programs in such as a way that they are mainly readable for human beings. Technically, it means that both the documentation and the source code of a respective program are available in a single file. The following characteristics of a literate programming system are required:

- The source code and comments can be mixed.
- The source code sections can be arranged in any order. The literate programming system automatically composes the code as machine-readable and in an executable sequence.
- The literate programming system automatically creates a human-readable document with a table of contents, references, citation, and other similar parts.

The process of creating human-readable documents is called **weaving**, while the creation of machine-readable documents is called **tangling**.

To use the principles of literate programming with R and RStudio, you can either use Sweave or the knitr package.

A brief side note on Sweave

Sweave is part of every R installation and was created by Prof. Friedrich Leisch. It uses LaTeX as documentation and R as the programming language. A heavy usage of Sweave is limited by the fact that LaTeX is a comparatively complex markup language. Furthermore, this tool lacks modern and important features such as the caching and using of various programming languages at once.

If you want to create an R Sweave document in RStudio, click on the new file button and choose **R Sweave**:

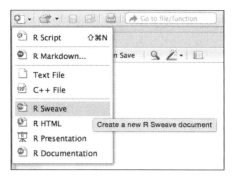

For more information about Sweave please visit: http://www.statistik.lmu.de/~leisch/Sweave/.

Dynamic report generation with knitr

> *The knitr package was designed to be a transparent engine for dynamic report generation with R, solve some long-standing problems in Sweave, and combine features in other add-on packages into one package (knitr ≈ Sweave + cacheSweave + pgfSweave + weaver + animation::saveLatex + R2HTML::RweaveHTML + highlight::HighlightWeaveLatex + 0.2 * brew + 0.1 * SweaveListingUtils + more).*
>
> *- Yihui Xie, Creator of knitr* (http://yihui.name/knitr/)

Since knitr is actively maintained and does not have the technical limitations of Sweave, we will only use this package in the following sections to create R Markdown files. Knitr uses R as the programming language, but it is also feasible to use other languages such as Python, SAS, Perl, Ruby, and others. Furthermore, it is possible to use different formats or languages such as HTML, LaTeX, AsciiDoc, and Markdown as the documentation language.

What is R Markdown?

R Markdown is the integration of plain R code and Markdown, and is based on the `knitr` package and the open-source document converter, pandoc. It further combines dynamic documents, literate programming, and reproducible research. With the help of R Markdown, you can easily use R code and Markdown to create a report with human-readable documentations along with the results of your code. As an output option, you can choose between an HTML file, PDF, Microsoft Word, ioslides, and others.

A side note about LaTeX

LaTeX is an important component of R Markdown, therefore, the following are some notes about this technology:

> *LaTeX is a document preparation system for high-quality typesetting. It is most often used for medium-to-large technical or scientific documents, but it can be used for almost any form of publishing.*
>
> *LaTeX is based on Donald E. Knuth's TeX typesetting language or certain extensions. LaTeX was first developed in 1985 by Leslie Lamport, and is now being maintained and developed by the LaTeX3 Project.*
>
> *-* (http://latex-project.org/intro.html)

Configuring R Markdown

To get started with R Markdown, you need to install and configure some required software. We assume that you already installed the latest version of R and RStudio. RStudio will automatically install the mandatory packages rmarkdown and knitr, as well as pandoc, the markup converter toolbox. Moreover, you need to install LaTeX, and also Tex for PDF, as a Markdown output format. If you want to use the output format Word, an installation of Microsoft Word or Libre Office should be installed on your computer.

Getting started with R Markdown in RStudio

Let's recapitulate, that R Markdown uses various technologies and is seamlessly embedded in RStudio.

Creating your first R Markdown document

To create an R Markdown document, perform the following steps:

1. First, click on the new file icon in RStudio and select **R Markdown....**

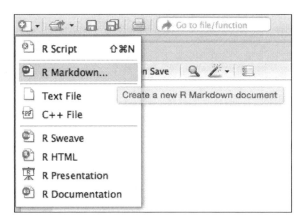

2. This will open a new popup window where you can adjust a variety of settings.

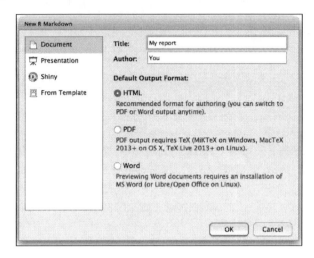

3. For our first document, we will leave all these settings as they are. You may change the **Title** and the **Author** name.

4. After hitting the **OK** button, RStudio will automatically open a new prefilled .Rmd file.

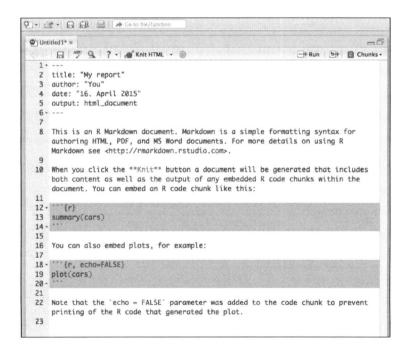

5. For a first test run, just click on the **Knit HTML** button with the small ball of yarn icon before the corresponding text.

As you can see, the knitted file opens by default in a preview window.

6. Instead of using the default option, it is recommended that you change the settings so that RStudio opens the output of a knitted .Rmd file in a dedicated viewer pane. Click on the small down-pointing arrow, to the right of the **Knit HTML** button, and check **View in Pane** to enable the pane view.

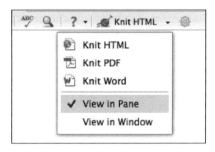

7. With this setting, it is now possible to write and generate R Markdown documents side-by-side, and that too, in a very comfortable manner:

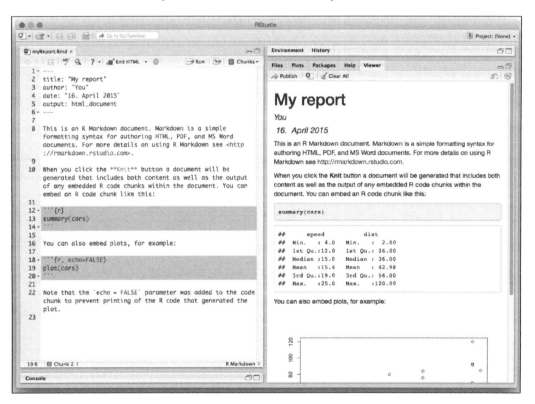

The R Markdown interface

After our first steps with R Markdown and our sample report, it is time to take a closer look at the R Markdown interface within the RStudio IDE.

Inspecting the R Markdowns panes

In the following screenshot, you can easily see that three panes play a role in the creation process of R Markdown documents:

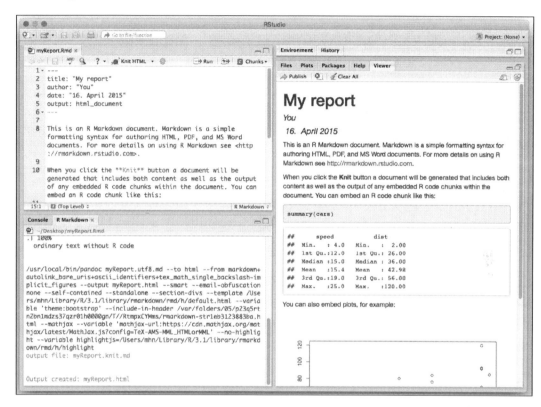

We already know the **Files** pane, where the code and text of the report can be created. As recommended, the output of the .Rmd file is shown in the **Viewer** pane. Next to the console pane is the R Markdown console, where you inspect the processing and creation of the .Rmd file. If there are any code errors in your R Markdown file, the execution will be stopped and two new buttons will appear in the right corner.

While the **Output** window shows the normal processing until reaching the first error, the **Issues** window shows only the respective errors and the associated line, where the error seems to be.

Explaining the R Markdown File pane settings

In the **File** pane, various settings can be made. The following sections explain the details in the screenshot.

File tab arrows

At the top left corner, you will see two arrows. While a click on the right-facing arrow lets you go back to the previous source location, the left-facing arrow lets you go forward to the next source location.

Saving current document

On the right-hand side, there is a button to save the R Markdown document. When you make changes to your .Rmd file in the **File** pane, hitting the **Save** button will not affect the output. To apply all the changes, you need to knit the file again. Then your output file will finally reflect the changes in your .Rmd file.

Spell check

Next you can check the spelling of your text with a click on the $^{ABC}_{\checkmark}$ icon. If there are no spelling errors, a small popup will appear; it will show that the spell check is complete. If there are any errors, another popup window will turn up and show you every word that seems to be wrong. When you are writing really long reports, the spelling check is a very handy tool.

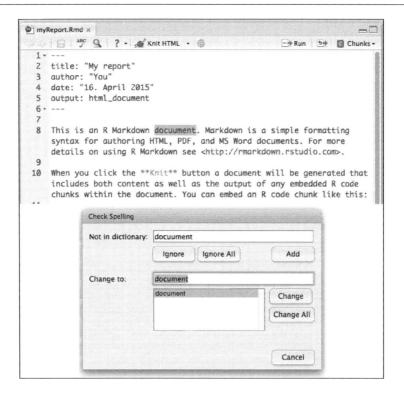

Find/replace

Next, we see a magnifier icon called find/replace. This great tool was already described in *Chapter 1, The RStudio IDE – an Overview* and it helps you find and replace text and code on the fly.

Question mark

A click on the question mark icon, **?**, will give you two more references to select:

- **Using R Markdown**: This will open a new page in your browser heading to the R Markdown reference page of RStudio (`http://rmarkdown.rstudio.com/`)

- **Markdown Quick Reference**: A click on this will open a new view in the help pane of RStudio, presenting a brief overview of the most important Markdown formatting options.

Knit HTML

As we already know, this button starts the knitting process of our R Markdown file and outputs an HTML file. A click on the down-facing arrowhead gives you the option to choose from among HTML, PDF, or Word as the output format.

Gear icon

The gear icon not only lets you edit the output format again, but also dives a lot deeper with several settings related to the chosen format.

Output Format: HTML

HTML is the standard and recommended output format. There are three areas in which settings can be made as you can see in the following screenshot:

Following is a description of the various tabs displayed in the preceding screenshot:

- In the **General** tab, you can adjust settings such as which syntax highlighting you prefer, whether you want to apply a custom CSS file to your reports, and more.

- The **Figures** tab lets you set a default height and width in inches for all the generated plots. Further, you can check whether you want to render your figures with captions.

- The **Advanced** tab gives you three more sophisticated options to check. For example, using smart punctuation will automatically produce a typographically correct output.

Output Format – PDF

PDF as an output format also offers three setting areas:

Following is a description of the various tabs displayed in the preceding screenshot:

- In the **General** tab, you can adjust the settings to include a table of contents, select a syntax highlighting, and more

- The **Figures** tab for the PDF output shows the same settings as the HTML output settings, but you can also check whether the figures should be cropped

- In the **Advanced** tab, you can select a LaTeX engine and choose whether you want to keep the Tex source file

Output Format – Word

If you like, you can also choose the output of a knitted document to be a Word file. The Word options window offers two setting areas. They are shown in the following screenshot:

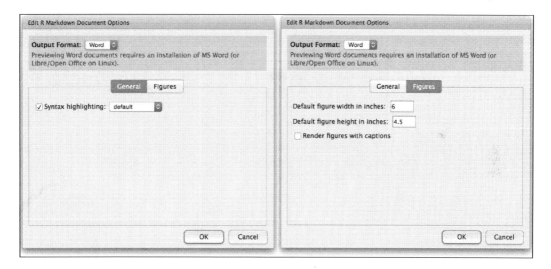

Following is a description of the various tabs displayed in the preceding screenshot:

- The **General** tab only gives you the option to select a syntax highlighting
- The **Figures** tab offers the same settings as the HTML settings

Run and re-run icons

The run and re-run icons, already known from normal .R files, allows you to run the code of a selected line, run the corresponding selection, or re-run the previous code region.

Chunks

The **Chunks** button opens a drop-down menu from where you can choose several options:

You can insert a plain R code chunk or jump between the existing chunks in your file. Moreover, you can run the previous, current, and next chunk, or you can run them all at once. The output of the chunks will be displayed in the normal console pane.

Jump to menu

The jump to menu also works for faster navigation through your code chunks. When you label each code chunk, it gets even easier to jump to the right chunk.

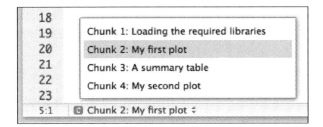

Viewer pane options

The following option is also available when you open your R Markdown output in an extra window:

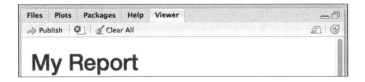

A click on the **Publish** button will make it possible to directly publish your R Markdown file on http://rpubs.com/.

Advanced R Markdown documents

After compiling our first R Markdown report, we want to go ahead and look at the advanced options for embedding code chunks with the knitr syntax. Also, you will learn how to brand your reports with custom style sheets.

Getting to know R code chunks

As we have already seen in our sample report, R Markdown uses so called *code chunks* to render R Code into reports.

This exemplary code chunk shows the most elementary way to include an R code snippet in our .Rmd file. Just three back ticks, ``` at the beginning and end of the chunk, and the letter r in curly brackets, {r}.

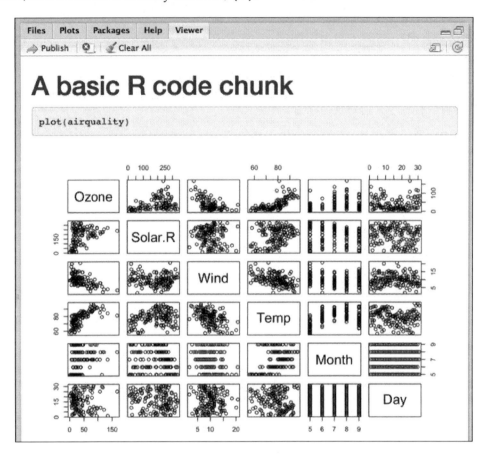

Even if it is a short code chunk, the output includes an H1 heading, the used R code, and a complete plot.

Customizing R code chunks

R Markdown offers a lot of options to customize your code chunks. This is necessary because, on the one hand, R Markdown includes all code lines and even error and warning messages by default. On the other hand, including many lines of code may distract readers from your report, especially when they are not familiar with R. Therefore, let's learn the options and arguments that help us create an easy-to-read and clean R Markdown report.

Chunk options

First, we will learn how to avoid our report showing warnings, errors, and general messages.

Avoiding errors, warnings, and other messages

In the following example, we will be loading a library, which returns a package information message that gets fully printed within our report:

```
### Chunk option example

```{r}
install.packages(forecast)
library(forecast)
```
```

Your screen will look like the following screenshot:

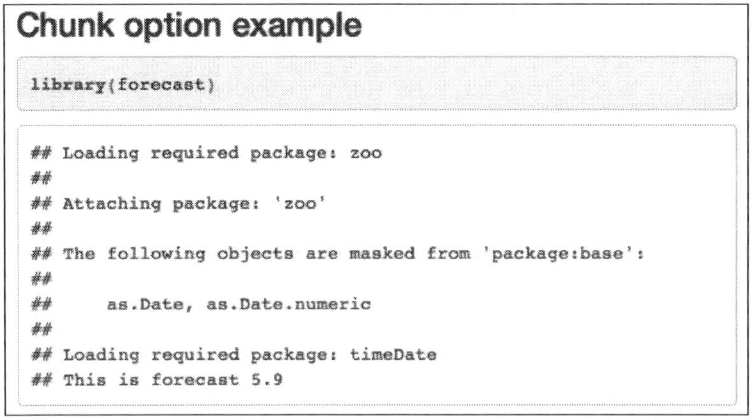

So, to prevent all these messages, we need to provide our code chunk with an argument when it's loading packages. In this case, we add the argument, `message=FALSE`, after the `r` in the curly brackets.

The code chunk looks like this:

```
### Chunk option example
```{r message=FALSE}
library(forecast)
```
```

Now, the output of our knitted file shows only the loading of the library.

Chunk option example

```
library(forecast)
```

In the same way, you can also prevent the output of warnings and errors by adding `warning=FALSE`, `error=FALSE`, or both to your code chunk. But please keep in mind that these warnings and errors are issued for a reason.

Hiding distracting lines of code

As already noted, including tons of lines of code in your report may disrupt the flow of reading and confuse people who have no idea of R code or programming. To solve this problem, a number of arguments can be added to the code chunks.

The three most popular chunk arguments are:

- `echo = FALSE`: On applying this argument, R Markdown will not print the lines of code of the chunk, but will still run the code

- `eval = FALSE`: Using this argument, R Markdown won't run the code or include the possible results, but it will show the code of the chunk

- `results = 'hide'`: With the addition of this option, R Markdown will not show any results, but will run and print the code of the chunk

```
1 ▾ ### Chunk option example
2
3 ▾ #### Without any argument
4 ▾ ```{r}
5   myNumbers <- c(12,154,124,15,23,245)
6   mean <- mean(myNumbers)
7   mean
8 ▾ ```
9
10 ▾ #### Using echo=FALSE
11 ▾ ```{r, echo=FALSE}
12   myNumbers <- c(12,154,124,15,23,245)
13   mean <- mean(myNumbers)
14   mean
15 ▾ ```
16
17 ▾ #### Using eval=FALSE
18 ▾ ```{r, eval=FALSE}
19   myNumbers <- c(12,154,124,15,23,245)
20   mean <- mean(myNumbers)
21   mean
22 ▾ ```
23
24 ▾ #### Using results='hide'
25 ▾ ```{r, results='hide'}
26   myNumbers <- c(12,154,124,15,23,245)
27   mean <- mean(myNumbers)
28   mean
29 ▾ ```
30
```

Chunk option example

Without any argument

```
myNumbers <- c(12,154,124,15,23,245)
mean <- mean(myNumbers)
mean
```

```
## [1] 95.5
```

Using echo=FALSE

```
## [1] 95.5
```

Using eval=FALSE

```
myNumbers <- c(12,154,124,15,23,245)
mean <- mean(myNumbers)
mean
```

Using results='hide'

```
myNumbers <- c(12,154,124,15,23,245)
mean <- mean(myNumbers)
mean
```

Embedding R code inline

If you want to embed R code in the text of your report, just add the `r    ` syntax. R markdown will run the code and print the results. Of course, it makes sense that you just embed results as a number, character string, or other similar things, and not as a full-blown table or something bigger.

```
1 ▾ ### Embedding R code inline
2
3 ▾ ```{r, echo=FALSE}
4   meanHp <- mean(mtcars$hp)
5   maxHp <- max(mtcars$hp)
6   minHp <- min(mtcars$hp)
7 ▾ ```
8
9 ▾ #### Motor Trend Car Road Tests
10
11 ▾ ##### Description
12
13  The data was extracted from the 1974 Motor Trend US magazine, and
     comprises fuel consumption and 10 aspects of automobile design and
     performance for 32 automobiles (1973-74 models).
14  The average gross horsepower of the given 32 automobiles is `r
     meanHp`, while the highest value lies at `r maxHp` hp and the
     lowest gross horsepower of a car in the dataset is `r minHp` hp.
```

The preceding code file results in the following R Markdown when knitted:

Embedding R code inline

Motor Trend Car Road Tests

Description

The data was extracted from the 1974 Motor Trend US magazine, and comprises fuel consumption and 10 aspects of automobile design and performance for 32 automobiles (1973–74 models). The average gross horsepower of the given 32 automobiles is 146.6875, while the highest value lies at 335 hp and the lowest gross horsepower of a car in the dataset is 52 hp.

Labeling code chunks

When you create bigger reports with lots of code chunks, it is useful to label these chunks. First of all, a label helps you know what the code chunk is doing; secondly, by adding labels you can reuse the chunks in your report.

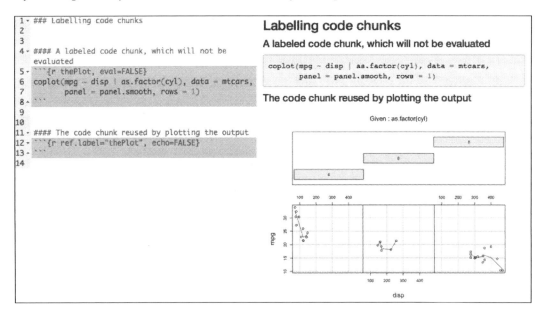

As you can see in the previous example, the first code chunk was labeled with the name, `thePlot`. Furthermore, it was given the chunk argument, `eval=FALSE`, and therefore, only the code gets shown in the final report. The second code chunk reuses the code of the first chunk by using the argument, `ref.label="thePlot"`. In the report, only the plot gets shown since the argument, `echo=FALSE`, was added to the reused code chunk.

Pandoc and knitr options

As we already know, R Markdown is a combination of many different techniques and technologies. When it comes to compiling Markdown-formatted text and code chunks into different output formats, a tool called **pandoc** is used.

> *If you need to convert files from one markup format into another, pandoc is your swiss-army knife.*
>
> *- About pandoc (`http://pandoc.org/index.html`)*

When you create a new R Markdown file in RStudio next to the prefilled text, there are also four lines of code between three dashes at the beginning of each new `.Rmd` file. After knitting the file, this so-called YAML header will not appear in the output, but R Markdown will take some information out of it.

```
1  ---
2  title: "My Report"
3  author: "Your Name"
4  date: "16. April 2015"
5  output: html_document
6  ---
7
8  ## Pandoc & knitr options
```

My Report

Your Name

16. April 2015

Pandoc & knitr options

The final HTML file takes the given title, the author name, and the date out of the YAML header and includes them in the compiled report.

Output formats

You change the output format by clicking on the down-facing arrowhead next to the Knit button, and choosing HTML, PDF, or Word; you can also change it in the YAML header. To do so, write the format after the output argument, as shown as follows:

- `output: html_document`: This creates an HTML file
- `output: pdf_document`: This produces a PDF document
- `output: word_document`: This generates a Microsoft Word file
- `output: md_document`: This outputs a Markdown file

All output formats will be saved into your existing working directory.

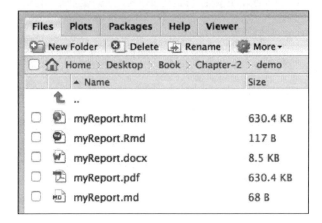

Changing the look of the output

By overwriting and adding new arguments to the YAML header, you can easily change the final look of your report. A lot of change options can be made with the help of the respective output settings.

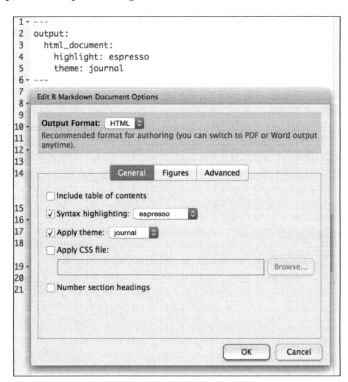

In the previous example, we changed the syntax highlighting to **espresso**, and we applied a CSS theme called **journal**. These default themes are collected from the well-known Twitter bootstrap theme. The effects of these small adjustments can be inspected in the following screenshot. On the left-hand side, we see the normal output with default syntax and the default CSS theme, and on the right-hand side is our new output with the changed syntax and theme.

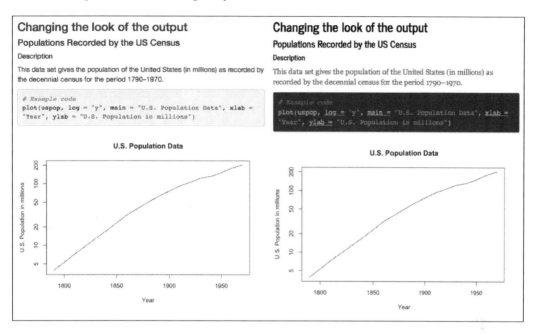

There are countless options to modify the YAML header, and hence, the output of the R Markdown file. Of course, you can change everything in the header manually, but you need to pay attention to the right indentation:

```
---
title: "My Report"
output:
  html_document:
    toc: yes
    number_sections: yes
    theme: united
---
```

The preceding header will generate a working HTML file with a table of contents and numbered headings; it uses a CSS theme called united.

The indentation for the YAML header is very strict. If you're using, for example, an incorrect indentation in the YAML header, an error message will appear in the R Markdown console. Thus, you can quickly find and fix those errors:

```
1 ---
2 title: "My Report"
3 output:
4   html_document:
5     toc: yes
6       number_sections: yes
7     theme: united
8 ---
```

The error message looks as follows:

```
Error in yaml::yaml.load(front_matter) :
  Scanner error: mapping values are not allowed in this context at
line 5, column 22
```

You can learn more about YAML at http://yaml.org/.

Using a custom CSS style sheet

As already learned, for the HTML output format, you can change the whole look by applying one of the inbuilt CSS themes. But RStudio also makes it possible to use a custom CSS file. As a result, R Markdown reports can be adapted to an existing corporate design, for example.

In the settings window of the HTML output, which opens after a click on the gear icon, you need to uncheck the **Apply theme** box and check the **Apply CSS file** box instead. Then, you can add your custom CSS file.

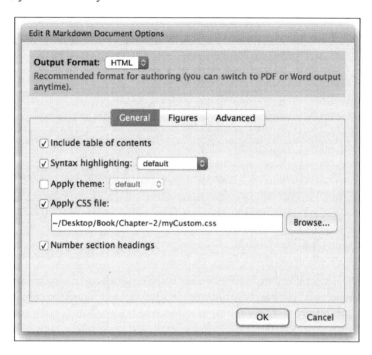

Using R Markdown templates

RStudio offers the option to use completely custom templates for R Markdown. This makes sense if you want to use a template again and again. In contrast to the possibility of applying a style sheet with its own CSS file, you can adjust basically everything with a Markdown template. So, you can adjust not only the fonts and color schemes, but also the complete formatting and the corresponding special formats. In general, these templates are installed or distributed through R packages. RStudio has installed two templates by default. One is the package vignette, and the other the so-called Tufte Handout.

You can open these templates by creating a new R Markdown file and clicking on **From Template** in the selection menu on the left-hand side.

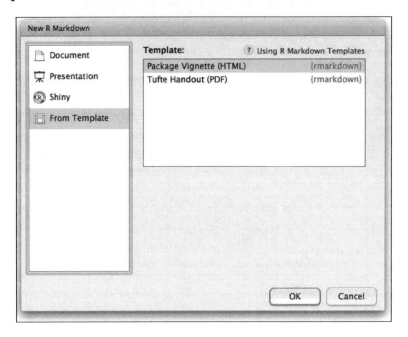

Package vignette

The Package Vignette provides an example of a format that customizes the base html_document with custom CSS and some other tweaks related to vignette authoring. The source code for the Package Vignette format and custom template is a good starting point to create your own HTML-based formats.

- R Markdown v2 Guide
(http://rmarkdown.rstudio.com/developer_document_templates.html)

The package `vignette` file also comes prefilled with Markdown-formatted text and example code chunks. It looks like this:

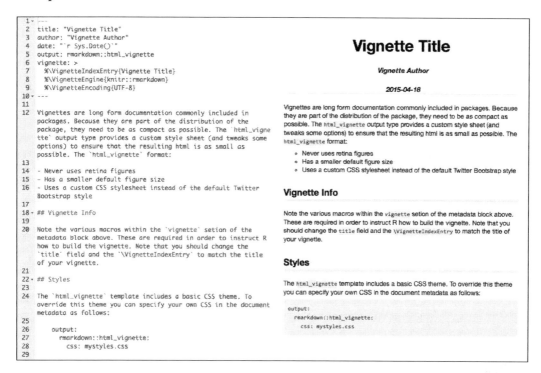

The Tufte handout

Edward Tufte is a statistician and artist, and Professor Emeritus of Political Science, Statistics, and Computer Science at Yale University. He wrote, designed, and self-published 4 classic books on data visualization.

- EdwardTufte.com (http://www.edwardtufte.com/tufte/)

The Tufte handout is adapted to the style that the famous statistician used in his well-known books. This refers to fonts, typography, the overall graphics integration in running text, and also the wide use of side notes are implemented in the prefilled template. When you knit the template, a PDF file is the output.

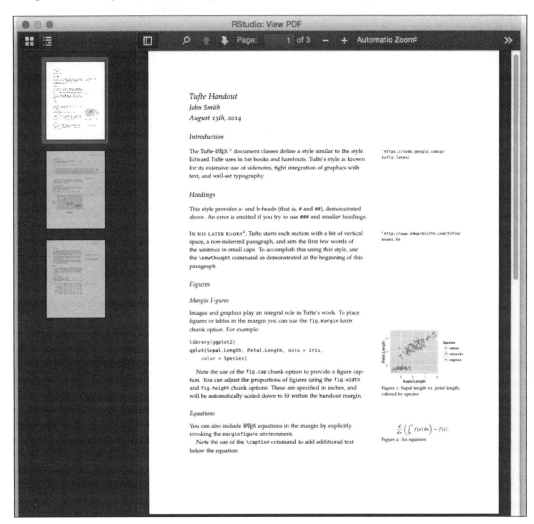

Compiling R Notebooks

R Markdown also offers a quick way to render a so-called **R Notebook**, which is in fact equal to the normal HTML output of a knitted .Rmd file. Just type rmarkdown::r ender("yourfilename.R") into the RStudio console and an HTML version of your R script will be generated.

Generating R Markdown presentations

In conjunction with R Markdown, RStudio also offers the possibility of building presentations. When you click on **New File** and choose **R Markdown...**, you need to select the item called **Presentation** in the popup window. RStudio offers three default output formats to choose from.

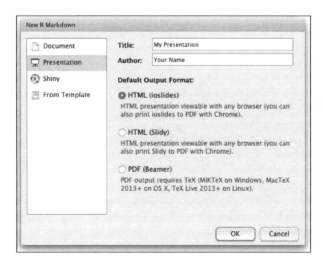

But you can also change the YAML header of existing R Markdown documents from this:

```
---
title: "My Report"
author: "Your Name"
output: html_document
---
```

To the following header, which for example, creates a `slidy` presentation:

```
---
title: "My Report"
author: "Your Name"
output: slidy_presentation
---
```

The same applies to `beamer_presentation` and `ioslides_presentation`. All R Markdown presentations will not open in the **Viewer** pane, but in a new window.

ioslides

An ioslides presentation is an HTML document, and to start a new slide, you use the # hash sign. If you use one hash sign to start a new slide, the background of the slide will be dark, and if you use two hash signs, the background looks bright. The content of the first slide will be taken from the YAML header. The following lines demonstrate this in code:

```
This will be the content of your first slide:
--
title: "My Report"
author: "Your Name"
output: ioslides_presentation
--

# Next slide (background will be dark)
… content …

## Next slide (background will be bright)
… content …

# Next slide (background will be dark)
… and so on …
```

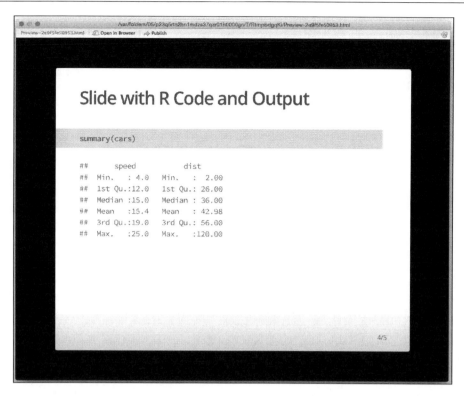

Slidy

Slidy presentations are also HTML documents after knitting, but they are somewhat more sophisticated than ioslides. For example, slidy offers an inbuilt table of contents from the beginning. Moreover, you can see the number of total slides, and so, it is no blind flight for the viewers.

Again, you use hash signs to create a new slide. But, this time, you need to decide if you use one hash sign or two hash signs. Also, the background is always bright.

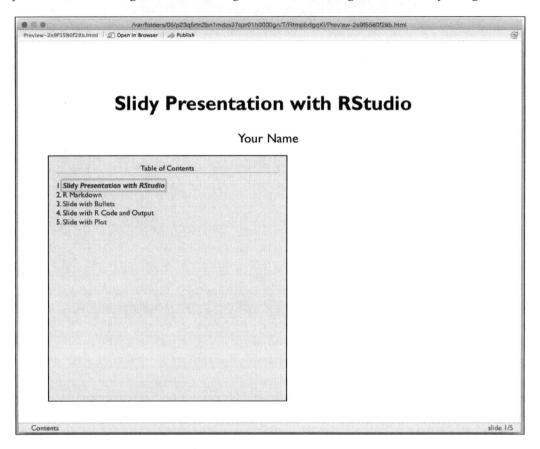

Beamer

Beamer presentations are compiled to PDF. To start a new slide or sheet, you use one or two hash signs, as we already know from slidy presentations. Beamer Presentations allow a lot of customizations with LaTeX, such as macros and others.

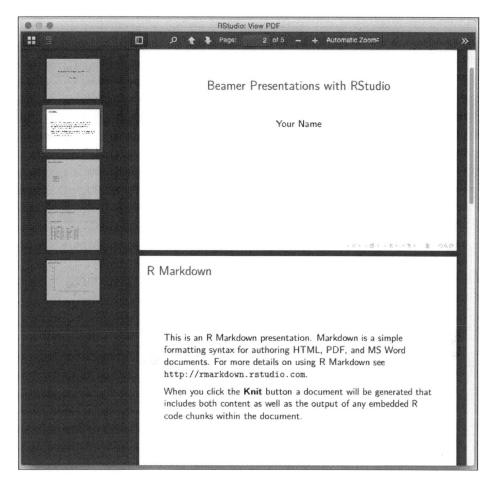

Summary

In this chapter, we learned how to create R Markdown documents and presentations. At the beginning of the chapter, we familiarized ourselves with the basics of the concept of reproducible research and how to accomplish this approach with R Markdown and the RStudio IDE. This includes setting up R Markdown and installing all the requisite packages.

We continued by studying the R Markdown interface in the RStudio IDE, and got to know all the relevant functions and how to use them. In addition to writing Markdown and integrating R code correctly, we also learned about the different output formats such as HTML, PDF, and Word. We are now able to create advanced R Markdown documents and presentations.

In the next chapter, we will focus our attention on ways to visualize our data with R, RStudio, and relevant graphical packages. For this purpose, we will dedicate ourselves mainly to the the `ggplot2` and `ggvis` packages after the introduction of the base graphics system, Lattice. We will also take a look at innovative libraries to create interactive data visualizations.

3
R Lesson I – Graphics System

This chapter covers:

- The R graphic system and the graphic devices
- Using the base plotting system
- Creating charts with the lattice system
- The grammar of graphics and ggplot2
- Using the `ggplot2` package for simple and advanced graph creation
- Introducing the `ggvis` package
- Building interactive plots with different R packages

The graphic system in R

Everywhere in our daily lives and in almost all professional fields, plots surround us. Most people find it very difficult to detect and understand the cause-effect relationships in mere numerical tables. Visualizing data helps humans quickly capture relationships between one or more variables. Therefore, the graphical system is an integral part of R.

An introduction to the graphic devices

When you visualize data, the resulting plot appears on a graphical device. There are three different types of devices:

- File devices, also called vector output, including PDF, PostScript, xfig, pictex, SVG, and win.metafile.
- Bitmap devices, including the formats PNG, JPEG, TIFF, and BMP.

Screen devices, which in turn are the services of the different platforms. For Mac OS X, it is `quartz()`, for Windows, it's `windows()`, and for Linux/Unix, the screen device is launched by `x11()`.

When you create a plot, this graphic will be sent to your screen device. There is only one screen device per operating system, and of course, you cannot launch `quartz()` on a Windows machine. For quick and easy data visualization, the screen device is most useful, which is also the default device. For reports and printout files, bitmap devices should be utilized. Furthermore, it can be said that the vector format is especially suitable for line drawings and plots with a low number of points. If you want to plot a large number of points, one of the bitmap formats should be taken.

In the following sections, we will check the best known and most widely used graphic packages of R in detail. We will also give a view on recent and interactive graphics packages.

The R graphics package—base

The inbuilt R graphics package, better known as the base plotting system, is the first address to start building a plot as it is the default method for plotting data. The `graphics` package, which provides the base plotting functions and the `grDevices` package, which includes the code to call the different system devices, are basically building the base plotting system.

The plot creation process can be divided into two phases.

1. The initialization of a new plot.
2. The extension of an existing plot.

The function, `plot()`, calls a graphic device and draws the data as a plot to the device. This plot function includes several basic graph types along with many arguments to annotate the plot. Furthermore, by using a very large number of different parameters, you can easily customize the created graph types.

Creating base plots

For the next plot, we are using the inbuilt, `library(datasets)`, and the `JohnsonJohnson` dataset, which represents the quarterly earnings per Johnson & Johnson shares from 1960 to 1980.

As our starting point, we only call the plot function to visualize the dataset:

```
plot(JohnsonJohnson)
```

This simple call results in the following line chart:

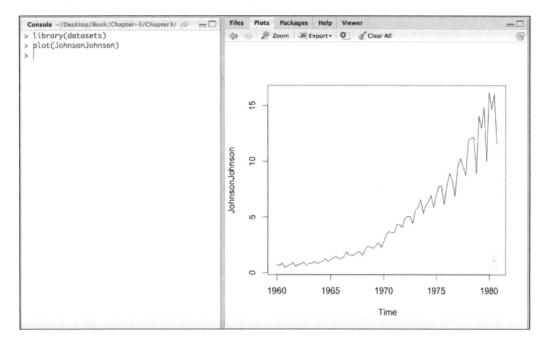

As you can see, RStudio directly renders the plot on screen in the **Plot** pane. The resulting chart is a line chart because the used dataset is a **Time-Series** object. When we use the `ChickWeight` dataset, which is a data frame with records of an experiment on the effect of a diet on the early growth of chicks, the output of the `plot()` function is quite different.

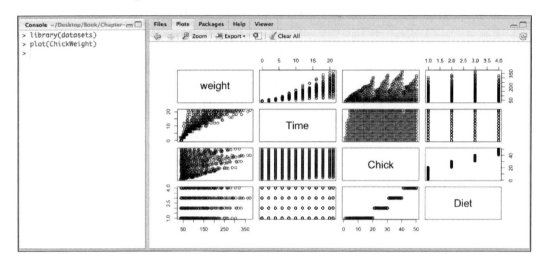

Instead of a simple line chart, we now see a jumble of boxes and points of the four variables of the dataset. This output is a simple scatterplot matrix, which gives a fast first view on a dataset.

Using the base graphics

Next to the `plot()` function, there are several different base plotting functions that create different types of graphics:

Plot Type	Function Call	Function Input
Histogram	`hist(x)`	*x* needs to be a numeric vector
Bar Chart	`barplot(height)`	Height needs to be a vector or matrix
Dot Plot	`dotchart(x, labels=)`	*x* needs to be a numeric vector, while `labels` is a vector of labels
Boxplot	`boxplot(x, data=)`	*x* is a formula, and `data` is the data frame
Scatterplot	`plot(x, y)`	*x* and *y* are the plotted variables of a numeric vector

Plot Type	Function Call	Function Input
Pie Chart	`pie(x, labels=)`	*x* is a numeric vector and needs to be positive, while `labels` is a vector of labels
Density Plot	`plot(density(x))`	*x* is a numeric vector
Matplot	`matplot(x,y)`	*x* and *y* are numeric vectors or matrices, where the number of rows should match

In the following diagram, we have plotted all the previously listed plot types. The used datasets are `mtcars` and `cars`.

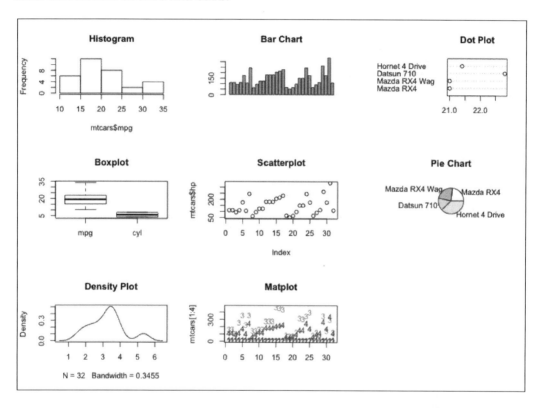

Base graphics parameters

The base graphics parameters are set by using the `par()` function, which acts as a global parameter for all plots in an R session. But these global parameters can be overridden by local, plot-specific parameters.

A simple `par()` function example is the last screenshot with the different plot types. Here, the parameter, `mfrow(c(nr, nc))` was used to print all seven plot types at once. `mfrow()` means the plots are drawn by rows, while `c(nr, nc)` is an *nr-by-nc* array.

The related R code looks like this:

```
par(mfrow=c(3,3))
hist(mtcars$mpg, main = "Histogram")
barplot(mtcars$hp, main = "Bar Chart")
dotchart(mtcars$mpg[1:4], labels=row.names(mtcars), main = "Dot Plot")
boxplot(mtcars[1:2], main = "Boxplot")
plot(mtcars$hp, main = "Scatterplot")
pie(mtcars$disp[1:4], labels=row.names(mtcars), main = "Pie Chart")
plot(density(mtcars$wt), main = "Density Plot")
matplot(mtcars[1:4], main = "Matplot")
```

As already stated, there are endless base graphic parameters, so we will just look at some of the most used. They are as follows:

- The `mfrow`, `mfcol` parameters denote the number of plots per row/column, drawn row, or column-wise
- The `mar` parameter is a numerical vector to set the margin size
- The `pch` parameter is an integer or single character to change the points of a plot
- The `las` parameter is a numeric value to change the orientation of the axis values
- The `lty` parameter is a numeric value to change the line type, for example, 3 stands for a dotted line
- The `bg` parameter adds a color to change the whole background of a plot
- The `col` parameter changes the color of the plot points
- The `col.lab` parameter changes the color for the *x* and *y* labels
- The `oma` parameter is a numerical vector to change the outer margin size
- You can find a complete list of available parameters in the *Appendix* section

In the following code script, we will use some of the learned parameters to change the look of a standard scatterplot:

```
## plain scatterplot
plot(mtcars$hp, main = "Standard Scatterplot")
## scatterplot with some adjusted parameters
```

```
par(bg = "grey", las = 2, mar = (c(10, 4, 4, 15) + 0.1), pch = 17,
col.lab = "blue", col.main = "red")
plot(mtcars$hp, main = "Scatterplot With Parameters")
```

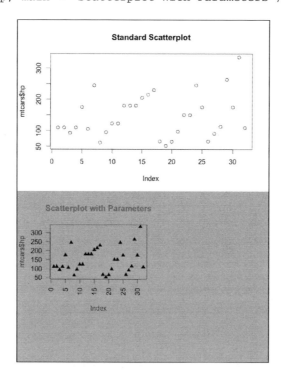

Annotating with base plotting functions

In addition to the already declared plot() function and equivalent commands to create different chart types, such as hist(), there are also a number of complementary base plotting functions. Here it is important to say that the following functions can only add information to an existing plot. Using them alone will not create a chart. But these functions can access the same parameters as the general plotting functions.

- lines: This connects the dots of an *x*, *y*-vector or a two-column matrix
- axis: This function adds an axis to the plot, with several of its own parameters, such as position, labels, ticks, side, and more
- points: This is used to draw points to an existing plot and can also specify coordinates
- text: By using text(), you can add strings to the *x*, *y* coordinates

- mtext: This is used to write strings to the inner or outer margins of the plot
- title: Use this function to add annotations to the title, subtitle, and more
- abline: This is used add one or more straight lines to a plot
- matlines, matpoints: Both these functions add a matplot() function to an existing plot, which plots the columns of one matrix against the columns of another

We added a bunch of base plotting parameters to a standard scatterplot, and with the help of the following code, we produced a clearly enhanced version of a simple scatterplot:

```
myData1 <- c(12, 45, 689, 87, 3, 45, 124, 356)
myData2 <- c(240, 36, 455, 33, 199, 10)
myData3 <- c(102, 155, 122, 77, 542, 652)
plot(myData1, main = "Scatterplot with Plotting Functions", lwd = 2)
lines(stats::lowess(myData1), lty = 6, lwd = 3)
points(myData2, pch = 5, col = "red", lwd =3)
abline(lsfit(1:6, myData2), lwd = 1.5)
title(sub = "Using the title function")
mtext("This is a mtext function", side = 4)
matpoints(myData3, col = "blue")
```

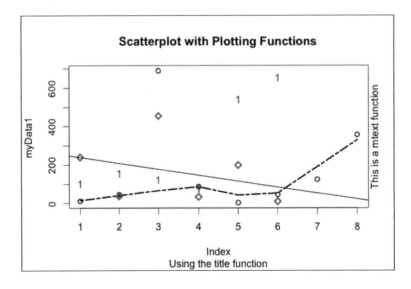

Basically, the base plotting system offers users a lot of customization options and a general control over the look of the output. Furthermore, we have learned that calling one or more plot functions creates a base plot.

Introducing the lattice package

In addition to the base plotting system, `lattice` is certainly one of the best known and most used packages for data visualization. The `lattice` package was written by Deepayan Sarkar and is not pre-installed in R. The implementation of the **lattice** plotting system is done by the package, `lattice`, which provides the code to build the Trellis graphics and grid, which supports an independent graphing system.

> *The lattice add-on package is an implementation of Trellis graphics for R. It is a powerful and elegant high-level data visualization system with an emphasis on multivariate data. It is designed to meet most typical graphics needs with minimal tuning, but can also be easily extended to handle most nonstandard requirements.*
>
> *Trellis Graphics, originally developed for S and S-PLUS at the Bell Labs, is a framework for data visualization developed by R. A. Becker, W. S. Cleveland, et al, extending ideas presented in Cleveland's 1993 book Visualizing Data. The Lattice API is based on the original design in S, but extends it in many ways.*
>
> - *Deepayan Sarkar* (http://lattice.r-forge.r-project.org/)

Creating lattice plots

In contrast to the base plotting system, a whole lattice plot, including any annotations, is produced with only a single function call. The basal format to provide a complete lattice plot looks as follows:

```
plotType(formula, data = )
```

The corresponding formula syntax occurs usually in the following manner: *variable – tilde – variable*, thus `y ~ x`. But, depending on the plot type, a variable can also be used alone in the formula notation, `~ x`. If a condition is used, one or more conditional variables follow the formula variables separated by a vertical bar. If there are two conditional variables, they are indicated by an asterisk. The attached argument to call the dataset is either a data frame, a list, or it can be left empty. In the last case, the parent data frame is used. So, the lattice format with example variables for the formula and conditions looks like this:

```
plotType(y ~ x | a * b, dataset)
```

It is important to know that only some of the plot parameters, as we know them from the base plotting system, also work for lattice plots. The following code creates a simple scatterplot by using lattice:

```
library(lattice)
library(datasets)
## Simple lattice scatterplot
xyplot(speed ~ dist, data = cars, main = "Lattice Scatterplot")
```

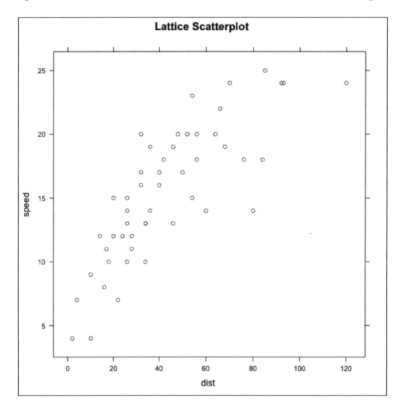

Getting to know the lattice plot types

Lattice also offers graph types of all stripes, for any purpose:

Plot Type	Function Call	Formula Syntax Example
Histogram	histogram()	~ x
Bar Chart	barchart()	x ~ y or y ~ x
Dotplot	dotplot()	~ x	a
Scatterplot	xyplot()	y ~ x	a

Boxplot (Box-and-Whisker)	`bwplot()`	`x ~ a or a ~ x`
Kernal Density Plot	`densityplot()`	`~ x	a * b`
Strip Plot	`stripplot()`	`a ~ x or x ~ a`
Theoretical Quantile Plot	`qqmath()`	`~ x	a`
Two-sample Quantile Plot	`qq()`	`y ~ x`
Scatterplot Matrix	`splom()`	`data frame`
Parallel Coordinates Plot	`parallel()`	`data frame`
3D Scatterplot	`cloud()`	`z ~ x * y	a`
3D Contour Plot	`contourplot()`	`z ~ x * y`
3D Level Plot	`levelplot()`	`z ~ x * y`
3D Wireframe Plot	`wireframe()`	`z ~ x * y`

Following we have plotted some lattice plot types as an example:

```
bwplot(count ~ spray, InsectSprays, main = "Boxplot")
```

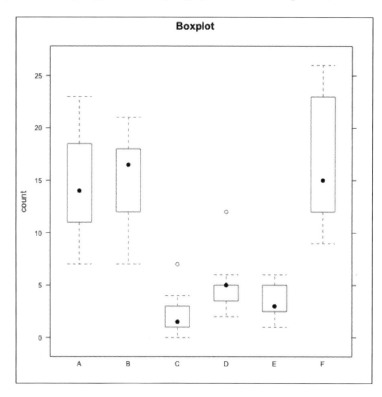

```
qqmath( ~ count | spray, InsectSprays, main = "Theoretical Quantile
Plot")
```

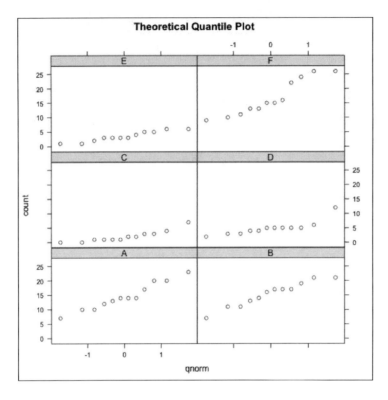

```
cloud(depth ~ lat * long, data = quakes,
      zlim = rev(range(quakes$depth)),
      screen = list(z = 105, x = -70), panel.aspect = 1,
      xlab = "Longitude", ylab = "Latitude", zlab = "Depth", main =
"3D Scatterplot")
```

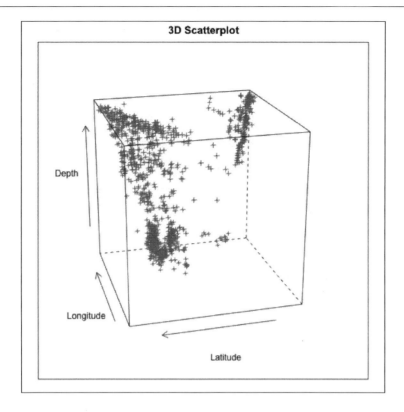

The lattice panel functions

The special features of the lattice system are certainly the panel functions.
These panel functions control the look of the called plot function and are comparable
with the base plot functions for plot annotating. Each lattice plot comes with a
default panel function that is customizable.

In the following code script, we customize the previously plotted *Theoretical Quantile Plot* to show only two panels, above each other, with the layout argument:

```
qqmath( ~ count | spray, InsectSprays, layout = c(2,1), main = "Two
Panels Look")
```

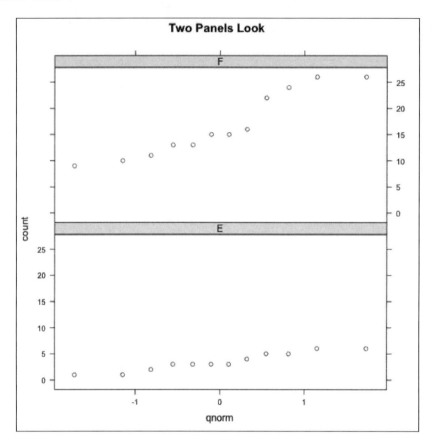

A more sophisticated example would look like this:

```
histogram( ~ count | spray, data = InsectSprays,
          ylab = "", main = "Using The Lattice Panel Functions",
          panel = function(x, ...) {
                  panel.histogram(x, ...)
                  panel.qqmathline(x, ..., col = "red", lty = 2, lwd
= 3)
                  panel.abline(h = median(x), col = "blue", lwd = 2)
          })
```

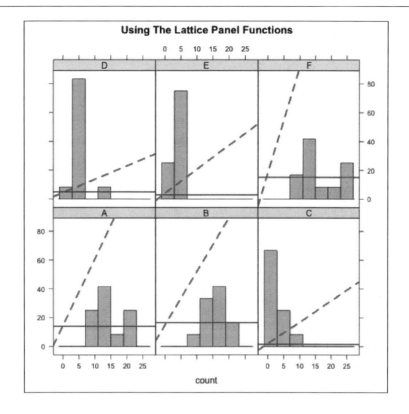

Lattice key points summary

As we have learned, there are some similarities between lattice and the base plotting system, but there are also some significant differences. Most obviously, while the base system directly plots to a graphic device, lattice returns a trellis class as an object. Because of that, the plotting is done by print methods or an object gets auto-printed. That also means, a whole lattice plot can be stored in a variable. Another important point is surely the fact that plotting and annotation are a single function call. The panel functions are certainly a unique feature.

All in all, it can be stated that lattice plots are most useful for conditioning plots, where you want to show the same variables under different conditions.

Introducing ggplot2

The `ggplot2` package is a data visualization package for R, which implements the so-called grammar of graphics, and makes it easy and accessible.

Looking at the history of ggplot2

Hadley Wickham mainly created the `ggplot2` package back in 2005. Since then, it has grown to be one of the most popular packages of the R language, and a huge community formed around it. Its main focus lies in making plotting in R very accessible, and so, it can be used as a replacement for the base graphics system.

The package, basically, is a successor of the famous `lattice` package and tries to take from it only the good parts and leave out the bad. So, it wants to make the creation of graphics easier.

On February 25, 2014, Hadley Wickham formally announced that `ggplot2` is shifting to maintenance mode. This means that features will no longer be added, but major bugs will still be fixed. This is not because they lost interest in the package, but because it is feature-complete, meaning that the package includes all the features needed to create powerful graphics and adapt them to your needs.

The Grammar of Graphics

The Grammar of Graphics is a book written by *Leland Wilkinson* in 2005. It is a framework that tries to sum up elements of designing, implementing, reading, and understanding graphics. Wilkinson divides the process of graphics creation into these steps: data transformation, scale, coordinates, elements, guides, and finally, display. The first part in this process, described as *data*, includes the actual statistical computations done on the given dataset that we want to visualize. Hadley Wickham tried to reflect these steps with the `ggplot2` package and managed it very successful.

Applying The Grammar of Graphics with ggplot2

The process and framework of *The Grammar of Graphics*, as explained by *Leland Wilkinson*, is very theoretical. So, in the next steps, we will apply this way of thinking to actual visualizations.

Using ggplot2

In the next few pages, you will see how to apply the principles of the *The Grammar of Graphics* with the `ggplot2` package. With this package, you are able to change a lot of details in your graphics and create your own individual style. We will give you examples of some of its main settings.

Installing the ggplot2 package

You can find the `ggplot2` package on CRAN, which makes it very easy to install it:

```
install.packages("ggplot2")
```

You are then able to simply load it with the following:

```
library(ggplot2)
```

Or, you can just check the box in front of the package name in the packages pane of RStudio:

☐	**ggmap**	A package for spatial visualization with Google Maps and OpenStreetMap	2.3	⊗
☑	**ggplot2**	An implementation of the Grammar of Graphics	1.0.0	⊗
☐	**gnm**	Generalized Nonlinear Models	1.0-7	⊗

Qplot() and ggplot()

The `ggplot2` package provides two functions to create graphic objects:

```
qplot()
```

```
ggplot()
```

`qplot` stands just for quick plot, and `ggplot` is an abbreviation of **grammar of graphics plot**, which shows its strong connection to the framework mentioned earlier.

`qplot` aims to be very similar to the basic plot function, and to be very simple to use. But it does not follow the full capacity of the framework and its elements.

For beginners, `ggplot` and its aspects are not easy to learn, but when you've made yourself familiar with the function, it is a very powerful way to create graphics.

Creating your first graph with ggplot2

`ggplot` always focuses on enabling the building of graphics using the three basic components:

- Data
- A set of geoms
- A coordinate system

But ggplot offers a lot of different options for these components.

For our first graph, we will use the preinstalled iris dataset. This data will be loaded automatically when you open R or RStudio. You can look at it using the following line:

```
head(iris)
```

We can then use the ggplot() function and add a data argument and an aesthetics element:

```
ggplot(iris,aes(Sepal.Length,Sepal.Width))
```

If you execute this line, you will get the following error message:

```
Error: No layers in plot
```

This is telling you that you have to add a geom object to the function call, which actually defines the type of the chart:

```
ggplot(iris, aes(Sepal.Length, Sepal.Width)) + geom_point()
```

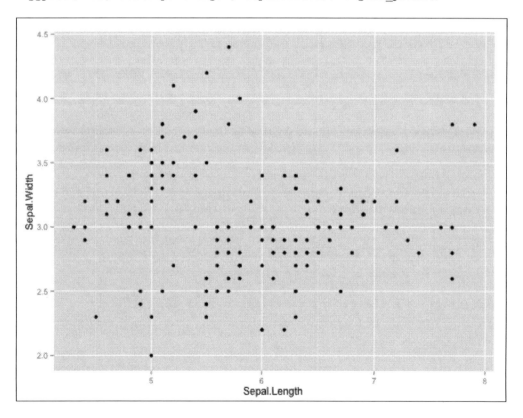

After adding some further options, you can see the power of ggplot2, and how easy it is with one line of code to create a complex data visualization:

```
ggplot(iris, aes(x=Sepal.Length, y=Sepal.Width, shape = Species, color
= Petal.Width)) + geom_point(size = 5)
```

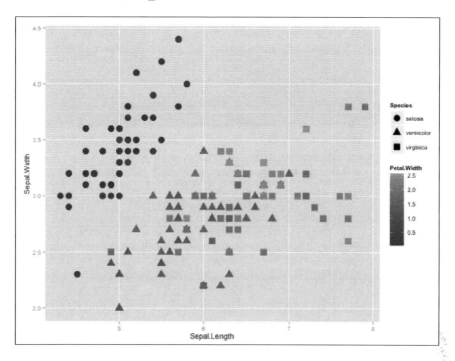

We will now take a closer look at the elements that we used to create this graph. But before we can do this, we have to look at the most significant difference from the base plotting system: the plus (+) operator.

Modifying ggplot objects with the plus operator

The + operator allows you to add objects to a ggplot object, or to overwrite them. You can add all the elements of the grammar of graphics that we described earlier.

Setting the aesthetics parameter

The aesthetics function helps you to define what data values should be added to the geom and how variables in the data are mapped to visual properties. You can define the *x* and *y* locations, as well as additional parameters such as the color or the size. This depends on the geom function that you use for your visualization. Different visualization forms understand different aesthetics inputs.

Adding layers using geoms

Basically, you have to decide on what geoms option to use, based on your dataset and what you want to visualize. Choosing a geom function is deciding how you want to represent data points and variables. The different geom functions return a layer that you can than add to your ggplot object with the + operator. So, to add a layer to our previous example, we could use the geom_point() option, which is often used if you want to visualize two variables and turn the output into a scatterplot:

```
ggplot(iris) + geom_point(aes(x = Sepal.Length, y = Sepal.Width)))
```

This will create the following output in the **Viewer** pane:

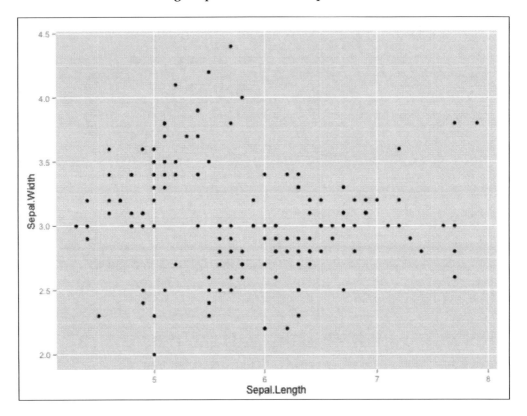

First, we created a ggplot object with the iris dataset. This will not display anything, as it does not include a layer. We add this to our object with the plus operator, and choose a geom_point() model in this case. For this layer object, we define the aesthetics to be Sepal.Length on the *x* axis, and Sepal.Width on the *y* axis.

Besides this, the `geom_point()` function understands seven different aesthetic inputs. They are:

- x
- y
- alpha
- color
- fill
- shape
- size

So, we can add another parameter to the aesthetics function of the `geom_point()` model. In this case, we define the color and shape of the data point to change according to the species it displays:

```
ggplot(iris ) + geom_point(aes(Sepal.Length, Sepal.Width,color =
Species, shape= Species))
```

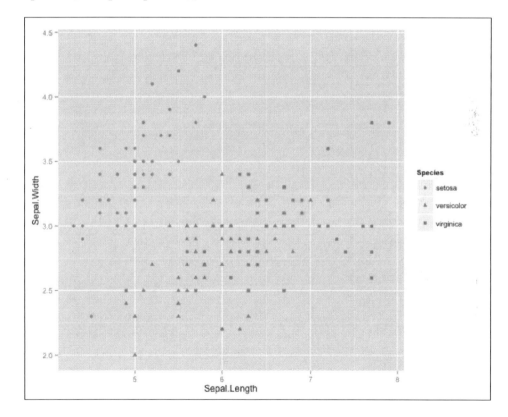

Choosing the right geom

Choosing the right geom is one of the most important tasks when you want to visualize your data. You need to have a vision of what you want to visualize, and what it should look like. And you also should know the variables that you want to display in your graphic.

ggplot2 offers a lot of different geoms, and you can choose one according to your needs. Basically, geoms are separated based on how many variables you want to visualize:

One Variable	Two Variables
Continuous Variable • geom_area • geom_density • geom_dotplot • geom_freqpoly • geom_histogram	Continuous X, Continuous Y variable • geom_blank • geom_jitter • geom_point • geom_point • geom_quantile • geom_rug • geom_smooth • geom_text
Discrete Variable • geom_bar	Discrete X, Continuous Y variable • geom_bar • beom_boxplot • geom_dotplot • geom_violin
Three Variables • geom_contour • geom_raster • geom_tile	Continuous Bivariate Distribution • geom_bin2d • geom_density2d • geom_hex

One Variable	Two Variables
Graphical Primitives	**Continuous Function**
• `geom_polygon`	• `geom_area`
• `geom_path`	• `geom_line`
• `geom_ribbon`	• `geom_step`
• `geom_segment`	• `Visualizing error`
• `geom_rect`	• `geom_crossbar`
	• `geom_errorbar`
	• `geom_linerange`
	• `geom_pointrange`

You can get more information about the `geom` types by searching through the `ggplot` package description for `geom`. In RStudio, you can do this by clicking on the **ggplot2** package in the **Package** browser. Then, the **Help** pane will open and you can search for **geom**.

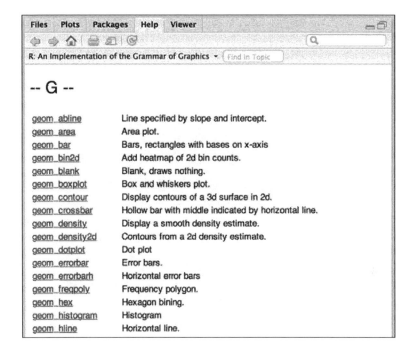

Modifying parameters

ggplot offers a lot of ways to modify your graphics. We will now take a look at three options:

- Color
- Shape
- Size

Changing the color of your plot

Often, different colors are needed for different groups in the dataset. As an example we will use the iris dataset again but this time we will use the geom_bar element to create a bar chart.

```
ggplot(iris, aes(Species, Sepal.Length)) + geom_bar(stat = "identity")
```

This code snippet will create the following chart:

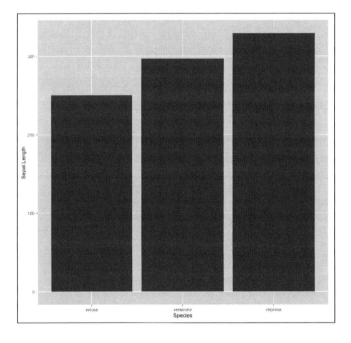

It is hard to differentiate the three categories at first glance. So, we use the fill option of the aesthetics function to make ggplot not just separate the data by Species, but also color the bars according to their species:

```
ggplot(iris, aes(Species, Sepal.Length, fill = Species)) + geom_
bar(stat = "identity")
```

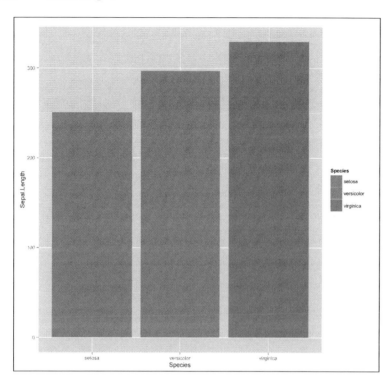

Changing the shape

Another way to include a third variable in the visualization is the use of the shape parameter. Similar to the previous example, we can set it to be a specific variable from the dataset. Now, the species are not differentiated by color but by the shape of the data points:

```
ggplot(iris, aes(Sepal.Length, Sepal.Width, shape = Species)) + geom_point()
```

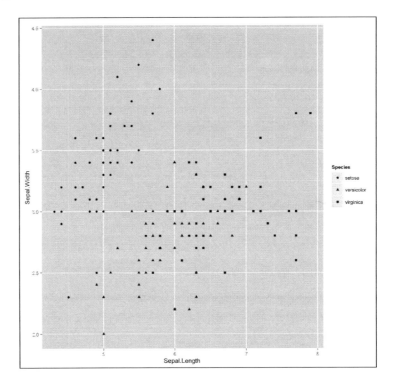

Changing the size

You can set the size of the data point shown with the help of the `size` parameter, and define it to be, for example, another variable to make the points in the scatterplot change their size according to this variable:

```
ggplot(iris, aes(Sepal.Length, Sepal.Width, color = Species, size = Petal.Width)) + geom_point()
```

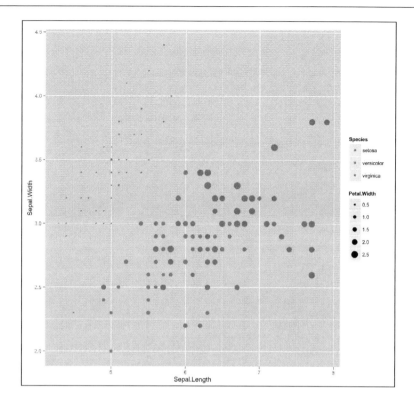

Saving ggplot objects in variables

You can also save your `ggplot` object in a variable. This makes it easier to add new elements and change something later. You can also use this principle to save different versions of a plot. The following lines of code are showing the mentioned methods:

```
d <- ggplot(iris)
```

```
bar_chart <- d + geom_bar(stat = "identity", aes(Species, Sepal.
Length, fill = Species))
```

```
point_chart <- d + geom_point(aes(Sepal.Length, Sepal.Width,color =
Species, shape= Species))
```

Using stats layers

Another way to add a layer is by using the `stats` element. These layers do not just display your data, but they also transform it. Some of the `geoms` elements already include `stat` objects. As do the `geom_area()` or `geom_bar()` functions. This one includes the `stat` argument to be `bin`, and the other one `identity`.

You can also include it on your own by adding a `stat` layer to your `ggplot` object:

```
d <- ggplot(iris, aes(Sepal.Length))
d + stat_bin()
```

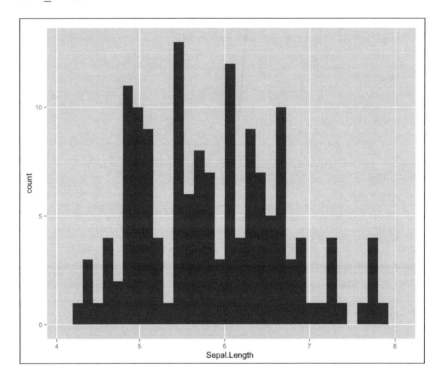

You can get a good overview of the `stats` options, as you could get for the `geom` options. This time, you search for `stats` in the `ggplot` package description:

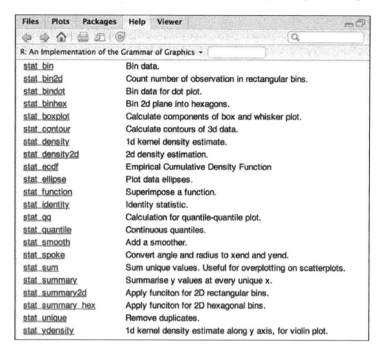

Saving ggplot graphs

Exporting graphics from R can sometimes be very hard when you are working with the base plotting system, but `ggplot2` offers you the `ggsave()` function. This function just needs a filename, including a file extension, to save your plot:

```
ggsave("Iris_graph.jpg")
```

The `ggsave` function currently recognizes the following extensions:

- `eps/ps`
- `tex` (PicTeX)
- `pdf`
- `jpeg`
- `tiff`
- `png`
- `bmp`
- `svg`
- `wmf` (Windows only)

Besides the file format, you can also set a scaling factor for the width, height, as well as the dpi to the user for raster graphics.

When called, `ggsave` saves the last displayed plot. But you can also specify a plot with the plot argument.

Customizing your charts

As mentioned before, one of the big advantages of `ggplot2` is that you can change nearly all elements according your individual needs. In the following section, we will show you some ways to customize your visualizations.

Subsetting your data

A very handy feature of `ggplot2` is the way you can subset data. Just add a subset function call to your graph to just visualize certain values. The subset you want to visualize can be set for all `geoms`:

```
ggplot(iris) %+% subset(iris,Species == "setosa") + geom_
point(aes(Sepal.Length, Sepal.Width))
```

Otherwise, you can set it for one geom in your graph:

```
ggplot(iris,aes(x = Sepal.Length,y = Sepal.Width,color = Species))   +
geom_point(data = subset(iris, Species %in% c("setosa","virginica")))
```

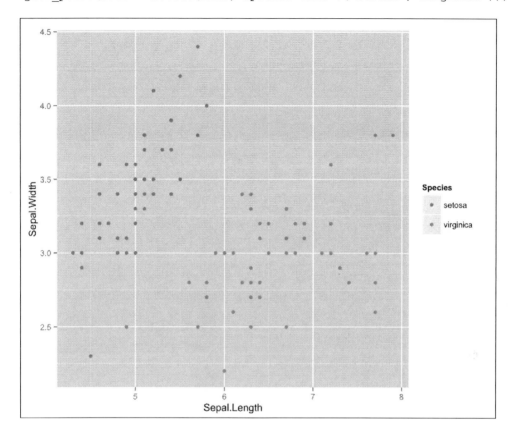

Setting titles

In `ggplot2` it is very easy to add titles to graphs. Therefore, it provides the `ggtitle` function. You can just add it to your graph with the plus (+) operator:

```
d <- ggplot(iris, aes(Species, Sepal.Length, fill = Species)) + geom_
bar(stat = "identity")
```

```
d + ggtitle("Iris data: Species vs Sepal Length")
```

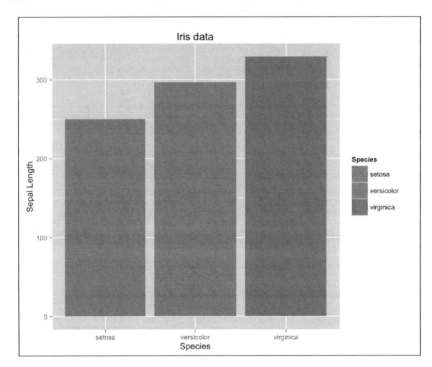

Changing the axis labels

Changing the axis labels is as easy as adding a title, because `ggplot` offers the `scale_x_continuous` and `scale_y_continuous` functions. These functions can be used to change all the settings related to the axis. You can, for example, change the title with the following:

```
d <- ggplot(iris ) + geom_point(aes(Sepal.Length, Sepal.Width,color =
Species, shape= Species))
  d +  scale_x_continuous("Sepal Length") +
  scale_y_continuous("Sepal Width")
```

Swapping the X and Y axes

ggplot2 also offers a great and very easy way to swap the *X* and *Y* axes of your graph. You just have to add the coord_flip() function to your graph:

```
d + coord_flip()
```

Improving the look of ggplot2 charts

ggplot2 offers, with its themes option, a great way to make your visualizations look much better and stand out against nearly every graph created with base plotting. In addition to this, there is a very interesting package by *Jeffrey B. Arnold* with the name, **ggthemes**. This package adds a whole bunch of extra options to the existing themes and scales of ggplot2. It includes, for example, a theme based on the design of the Economist, or one based on the Wall Street Journal's design.

Through the following code, we will show you how to make this graph look even better:

```
d <- ggplot(iris, aes(Sepal.Length, Sepal.Width, colour = Species)) +
geom_point()
```

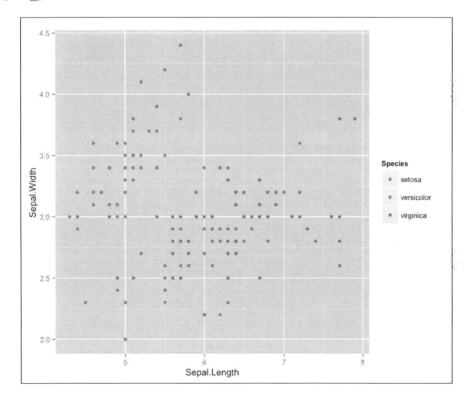

Creating graphs with the economist theme

Install and load the ggthemes package with the following lines:

```
install.packages("ggthemes")
library(ggthemes)
```

We can then add a new theme to our ggplot object, d. For this, we will use the theme_economist() and scale_color_economist() functions from the ggthemes package. The first adapts the graph background to the economist background, and the second one the scale:

```
d + theme_economist() + scale_color_economist() + ggtitle("Iris
Species: Sepal Length vs Sepal Width)
```

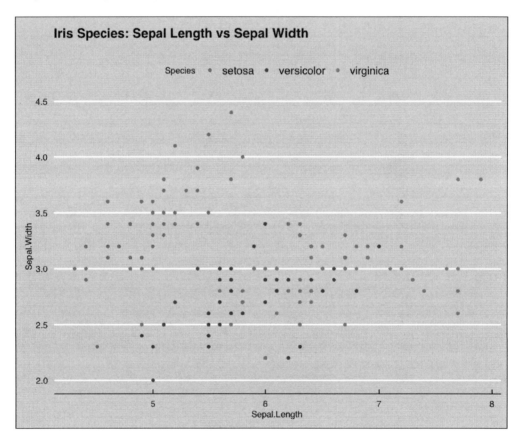

Creating graphs with the wall street journal theme

Similar to the use of the economist theme, we add the functions, theme_wsj() and scale_colour_wsj(), to our graph:

```
d + theme_wsj() + scale_colour_wsj("color6") + ggtitle("Iris Species:
Sepal Length vs Sepal Width")
```

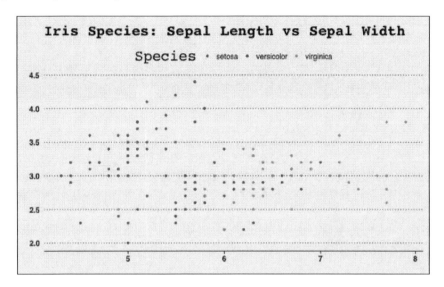

Interactive plotting systems

The base, lattice, or ggplot2 plotting systems make it possible to create all conceivable plot types, either quick and simple, or even utterly detailed and sophisticated. All these systems have their own features and peculiarities. But they also have one thing in common: the relevant plots are all purely static.

In particular, the ubiquitous use of the Internet and corresponding browsers make it possible to easily share interactive content. Interactivity, in turn, helps humans to better understand the contents by actively interacting with them. Interactive charts are, of course, a great improvement, since viewers can play with the displayed data, and thus discover possible coherences and differences among other things to get a better understanding of the shown plot.

Introducing ggvis

ggvis is practically the next evolutionary step forward from the successful data visualization package, ggplot2. *Hadley Wickham* (who is already the author of the ggplot2 package) and *Winston Chang* authored ggvis. The package description is as follows:

> *The goal is to combine the best of R (for example, every modeling function you can imagine) and the best of the web (everyone has a web browser). Data manipulation and transformation are done in R, and the graphics are rendered in a web browser using Vega. For RStudio users, ggvis graphics display in a viewer panel, which is possible because RStudio is a web browser.*
>
> *- Hadley Wickham, Winston Chang* (http://ggvis.rstudio.com)

So, the ggvis package uses the grammar of graphics theory, which is already known from ggplot2, and uses the rendering of the popular JavaScript package, vega. Furthermore, it takes advantage of a few R packages. The reactive programming model of Shiny, the pipe operator (%>%) of the magrittr package, and the data transformation grammar of the dplyr package are all integrated into ggvis. Thus, the package uses a variety of different technologies to achieve a modern and interactive plotting system.

Our first ggvis graphic

First of all, the ggvis package must be installed, of course. The mentioned packages, shiny, dplyr, and so on, will get imported through the ggvis installation, if they are not already installed. For our examples, we will use the swiss dataset, which is included in the preinstalled datasets package:

```
swiss %>% ggvis(~Fertility, ~Education, fill := "blue") %>% layer_
points()
```

This line of code produces the following chart:

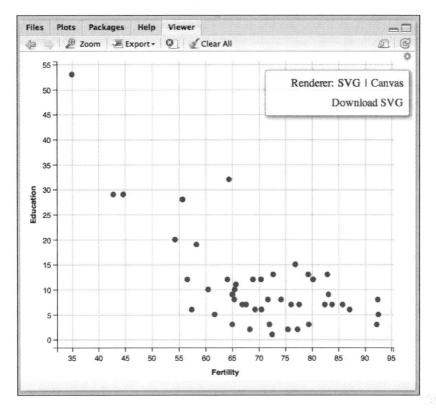

As you can see, we get a scatterplot that looks like a `ggplot2` graph. If we break down the previous code snippet, you can see the following structure for creating a `ggvis` graph:

```
Graph = Data + Coordinate System + Mark + Properties + ...
```

Furthermore, there are three types of syntaxes used. They are:

- `%>%`: This is the pipe operator from the `magrittr` package
- `~`: This is the tilde operator, which takes a column or a whole data frame
- `:=`: This is the setting operator, which sets properties such as color, size, and others

In the right corner of the **Viewer** pane of RStudio is a small gear icon. A click on this icon opens the controls, where you can render the graph in SVG or Canvas, and also additionally download the plot. This rendering is done by the mentioned `vega` library.

Interactive ggvis graphs

Since our first example is not interactive, in the following one we want to create an interactive `ggvis` plot:

```
## example partly taken from the ggvis interactivity vignette
swiss %>% ggvis(x = ~Fertility) %>%
        layer_densities(
                adjust = input_slider(0.1, 2, value = 1, step = .1,
label = "Bandwidth adjustment"),
                kernel = input_select(
                        c("Gaussian" = "gaussian",
                          "Epanechnikov" = "epanechnikov",
                          "Rectangular" = "rectangular",
                          "Triangular" = "triangular",
                          "Biweight" = "biweight",
                          "Cosine" = "cosine",
                          "Optcosine" = "optcosine"),
                        label = "Kernel")
        )
```

This code example provides interactivity by letting the viewer change the bandwidth and the kernel of the density plot. These input boxes are integrated through the Shiny package.

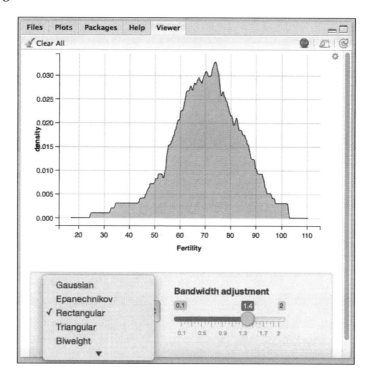

Although ggvis is still under intensive development, it can definitely be stated that this package represents the future of modern plotting systems in R.

A look at the rCharts package

rCharts is an R package to create, customize, and publish interactive JavaScript visualizations from R using a familiar lattice style plotting interface.

- Ramnath Vaidyanathan (http://rcharts.io/)

As indicated in this quote, the `rCharts` package can virtually be considered as an interactive successor to the lattice plotting system. Since `rCharts` is not on CRAN, you need to install this package with a package called `devtools` directly from the GitHub repository of the package creator, *Ramnath Vaidyanathan*:

```
library(devtools)
install_github("ramnathv/rCharts")
library(rCharts)
```

The following lines of code produce an interactive bar chart:

```
# interactive bar chart with d3js(NVD3)
# this code example was taken from http://ramnathv.github.io/rCharts/
hair_eye_male <- subset(as.data.frame(HairEyeColor), Sex == "Male")
n1 <- nPlot(Freq ~ Hair, group = "Eye", data = hair_eye_male, type =
"multiBarChart")
n1$print("chart3")
n1
```

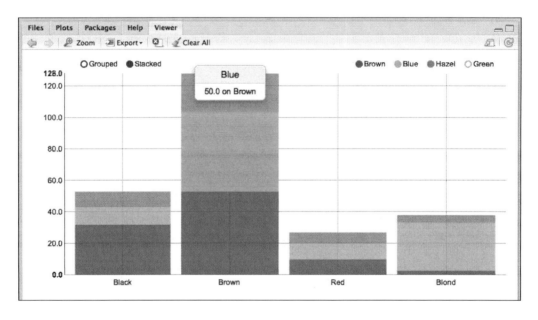

This bar chart is completely interactive. First, you can set the displayed bars as stacked or grouped. In the example, the stacked version is shown. Second, you can virtually switch on and off the eye colors. We switched the color green off; therefore it is not shown in the chart. Furthermore, you can hover over the bars to get the values of the plotted data.

Using googleVis

The googleVis package provides an interface between R and the Google Charts API. It allows users to create web pages with interactive charts based on R data frames. Charts are displayed locally via the R HTTP help server. A modern browser with Internet connection is required, and for some charts, a Flash player. The data remains local and is not uploaded to Google.

- Marcus Gesmann, Diego de Castillo
(https://github.com/mages/googleVis)

The googleVis package can be downloaded directly from CRAN. By using the Google Charts API, a variety of different types of charts in a familiar look and feel are available. One limitation, as compared other packages, is certainly the mandatory Internet connection needed to display the chart outputs.

The following code produces an interactive bar and line chart combination:

```
# interactive line line and bar with googleVis
# this code example was taken from the googleVis package vignette
CityPopularity$Mean=mean(CityPopularity$Popularity)
CC <- gvisComboChart(CityPopularity, xvar='City',
        yvar=c('Mean', 'Popularity'),
        options=list(seriesType='bars',
                    width=450, height=300,
                    title='City Popularity',
                    series='{0: {type:\"line\"}}'))
plot(CC)
```

The plot function call immediately opens a new browser window and displays the chart there:

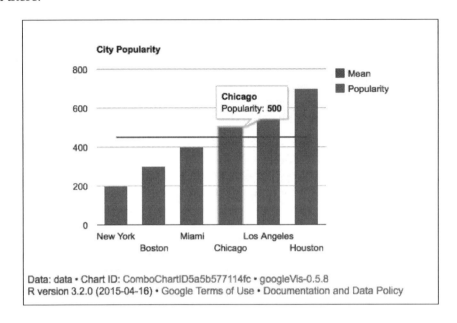

Here, interactivity is given by the fact that you can hover over the data, in this case the bars and the line, to know the exact values.

HTML widgets

The `htmlwidgets` package is a relatively new approach to provide R users with multiple ways to display data and related stories around data, mostly in an interactive manner. In its core, it provides a framework for creating R bindings to JavaScript libraries. That means there are different R packages that are based on the `htmlwidgets` package. One main advantage of this package, for our purposes, is that the interactive charts can seamlessly be embedded within R Markdown. You install it along with the included packages mostly directly from CRAN. Some packages must be installed from GitHub.

dygraphs

The dygraphs package is an R interface to the dygraphs JavaScript charting library. It provides rich facilities for charting time-series data in R.

- RStudio Inc. (`http://rstudio.github.io/dygraphs/`*)*

Plots created with the `dygraph` package are opened in the RStudio **Viewer** pane, and can also be easily integrated into Shiny applications and R Markdown files. Moreover, the syntax takes advantage of the `magrittr` package and the pipe operator. The following code produces an interactive `dygraph` with a predicted series:

```
## example taken from https://rstudio.github.io/dygraphs
hw <- HoltWinters(ldeaths)
p <- predict(hw, n.ahead = 36, prediction.interval = TRUE)
all <- cbind(ldeaths, p)
dygraph(all, "Deaths from Lung Disease (UK)") %>%
  dySeries("ldeaths", label = "Actual") %>%
  dySeries(c("p.lwr", "p.fit", "p.upr"), label = "Predicted")
```

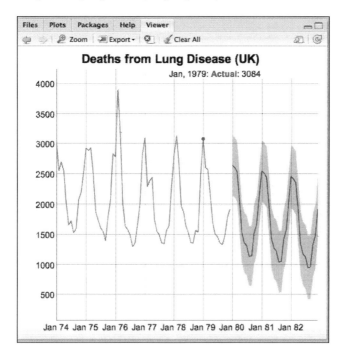

Leaflet

Leaflet is a popular JavaScript library for creating interactive maps. This website describes an R package that makes it easy to integrate and control Leaflet maps from directly within R.

- RStudio Inc. (`http://rstudio.github.io/leaflet`)

The `leaflet` package needs to be downloaded from GitHub in the usual manner:

```
library(devtools)
install_github("rstudio/leaflet")
library(leaflet)
```

With the `leaflet` package, you can easily create maps and customize them by adding different types of layers, such as UI, Raster, Vector, and others.

The following code produces an interactive map, as we know them from our daily use of maps and navigation systems. Even inside the **Viewer** pane, you can zoom in and out, or stumble around:

```
leaflet() %>% addTiles() %>%
    addMarkers(174.7690922, -36.8523071, icon = icons(
        iconUrl = 'http://cran.rstudio.com/Rlogo.jpg',
        iconWidth = 40, iconHeight = 40
)) %>%
    addPopups(174.7690922, -36.8523071, 'R was born here!')
```

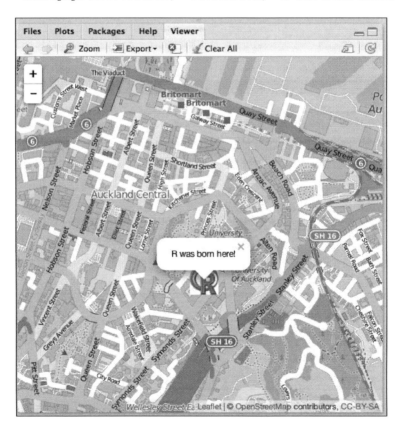

rbokeh

A relatively new package, in this context, is `rbokeh`. This package is an interface to *Bokeh*.

> *Bokeh is a visualization library that provides a flexible and powerful declarative framework for creating web-based plots. Bokeh renders plots using HTML canvas and provides many mechanisms for interactivity. Bokeh has interfaces in Python, Scala, Julia, and now R.*
>
> *- Ryan Hafen (*`http://hafen.github.io/rbokeh`*)*

Download it from a GitHub repository, again, to install this package:

```
library(devtools)
install_github("bokeh/rbokeh")
library(rbokeh)
```

`rbokeh` adapts known principles from the `ggplot2` geoms and `ggvis` layers, but also has traces of the base plotting system. The code and the output of an `rbokeh` scatterplot with an annotation line look like this:

```
p <- figure() %>%
  ly_points(cars$speed, cars$dist) %>%
  ly_abline(-17.6, 3.9)
p
```

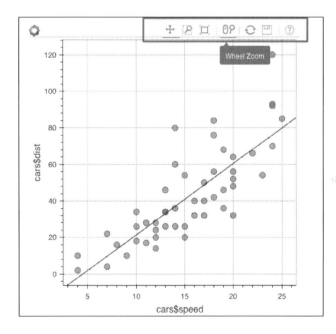

As shown, each `rbokeh` graph has a setting bar, which in turn provides various tools to interact with the displayed chart. These settings are powerful features for viewers. Since `rbokeh` is still in its infancy, we can certainly expect a lot more from this plotting system in the future.

Summary

In this chapter, we gave you an overview of the landscape of plotting packages in R. We got an introduction to graphic devices and the fundamental `graphic` package base. This includes the base graphic parameters, and how to annotate with base plotting functions. The basic process of plot creation with this package is first, the initialization of a new plot, and second, the extension of an existing plot.

This was followed by a short overview of the famous `Lattice` package, which makes it possible to create a plot including any annotations with only a single function call.

After that, we gave you an introduction into the world of `ggplot2`. *Hadley Wickham* created this graphics package, and it is based on *The Grammar of Graphics* book, written by *Leland Wilkinson*. You can use this package to create powerful graphics and adapt them completely to your needs. Graphics created with the `ggplot2` package consist of three elements: data, a set of `geoms`, and a coordinate system.

At the end of this chapter, we showed you some packages for creating interactive graphics. These included the packages, `ggvis`, `rCharts`, and `googleVis`. We also gave a glimpse into the future with the introduction of the `htmlwidgets` package, which in turn provides the basis for a number of interactive packages for various topics. For this purpose, we have looked at examples of `dygraphs`, `leaflet`, and `rbokeh`. Interactivity is a great improvement to charts that gives viewers more ways to discover connections and differences, which will result in a better understanding of the displayed plot.

The next chapter will give you an introduction to Shiny, a web-app framework for R. We will learn how to create our first Shiny app, and to create a dynamic user interface.

4
Shiny – a Web-app Framework for R

This chapter covers the following topics:

- An introduction to the Shiny app framework
- Creating your first Shiny app
- The connection between the server file and the user interface
- The concept of reactive programming
- Different types of interface layouts, widgets, and Shiny tags
- How to create a dynamic user interface
- Ways to share your Shiny applications with others
- How to deploy Shiny apps to the web

Introducing Shiny – the app framework

The `Shiny` package delivers a powerful framework to build fully featured interactive Web applications just with R and RStudio. Basic Shiny applications typically consist of two components:

```
~/shinyapp
|-- ui.R
|-- server.R
```

While the `ui.R` function represents the appearance of the user interface, the `server.R` function contains all the code for the execution of the app. The look of the user interface is based on the famous Twitter bootstrap framework, which makes the look and layout highly customizable and fully responsive. In fact, you only need to know R and how to use the `shiny` package to build a pretty web application. Also, a little knowledge of HTML, CSS, and JavaScript may help.

If you want to check the general possibilities and what is possible with the `Shiny` package, it is advisable to take a look at the inbuilt examples. Just load the library and enter the example name:

```
library(shiny)
runExample("01_hello")
```

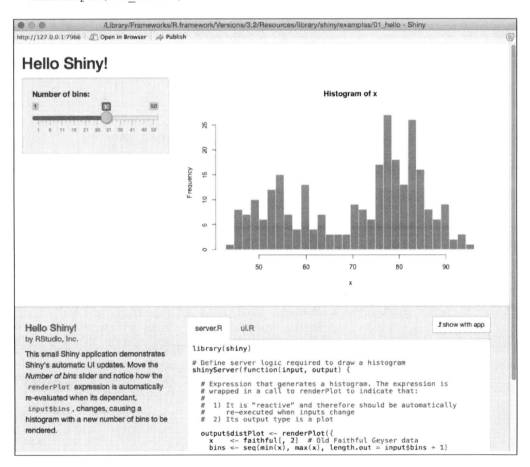

As you can see, running the first example opens the Shiny app in a new window. This app creates a simple histogram plot where you can interactively change the number of bins. Further, this example allows you to inspect the corresponding `ui.R` and `server.R` code files.

There are currently eleven inbuilt example apps:

- 01_hello
- 02_text
- 03_reactivity
- 04_mpg
- 05_sliders
- 06_tabsets
- 07_widgets
- 08_html
- 09_upload
- 10_download
- 11_timer

These examples focus mainly on the user interface possibilities and elements that you can create with Shiny.

Creating a new Shiny web app with RStudio

RStudio offers a fast and easy way to create the basis of every new Shiny app. Just click on **New Project** and select the **New Directory** option in the newly opened window:

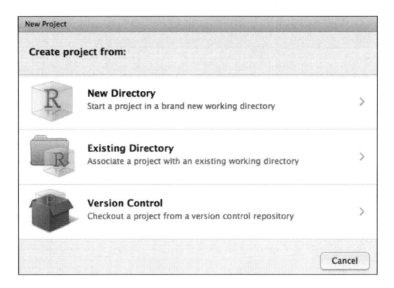

After that, click on the **Shiny Web Application** field:

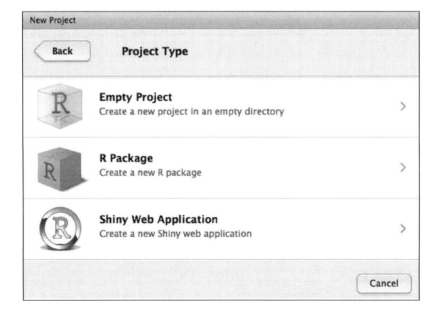

Give your new app a name in the next step, and click on **Create Project:**

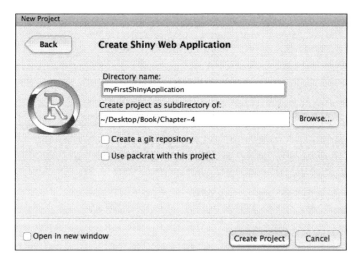

RStudio will then open a ready-to-use Shiny app by opening a prefilled `ui.R` and `server.R` file:

```
1
2  # This is the user-interface definition of a Shiny web application.
3  # You can find out more about building applications with Shiny here:
4  #
5  # http://shiny.rstudio.com
6  #
7
8  library(shiny)
9
10 shinyUI(fluidPage(
11
12   # Application title
13   titlePanel("Old Faithful Geyser Data"),
14
15   # Sidebar with a slider input for number of bins
16   sidebarLayout(
17     sidebarPanel(
18       sliderInput("bins",
19                   "Number of bins:",
20                   min = 1,
21                   max = 50,
22                   value = 30)
23     ),
24
25     # Show a plot of the generated distribution
26     mainPanel(
```

You can click on the now visible **Run App** button in the right corner of the file pane to display the prefilled example application.

Creating your first Shiny application

In your effort to create your first Shiny application, you should first create or consider rough sketches for your app. Questions that you might ask in this context are, What do I want to show? How do I want it to show?, and so on.

Let's say we want to create an application that allows users to explore some of the variables of the mtcars dataset.

> *The data was extracted from the 1974 Motor Trend US magazine, and comprises fuel consumption and 10 aspects of automobile design and performance for 32 automobiles (1973–74 models).*

Sketching the final app

We want the user of the app to be able to select one out of the three variables of the dataset that gets displayed in a histogram. Furthermore, we want users to get a summary of the dataset under the main plot. So, the following figure could be a rough project sketch:

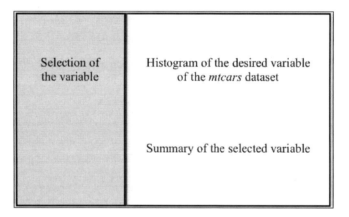

Constructing the user interface for your app

We will reuse the already opened ui.R file from the RStudio example, and adapt it to our needs. The layout of the ui.R file for your first app is controlled by nested Shiny functions and looks like the following lines:

```
library(shiny)

shinyUI(pageWithSidebar(
```

```
        headerPanel("My First Shiny App"),

        sidebarPanel(
                selectInput(inputId = "variable",
                            label = "Variable:",
                            choices = c("Horsepower" = "hp",
                                        "Miles per Gallon" = "mpg",
                                        "Number of Carburetors" =
"carb"),
                            selected = "hp")

        ),

        mainPanel(
                plotOutput("carsPlot"),
                verbatimTextOutput("carsSummary")
        )
))
```

Creating the server file

The server file holds all the code for the execution of the application:

```
library(shiny)
library(datasets)

shinyServer(function(input, output) {

        output$carsPlot <- renderPlot({

                hist(mtcars[,input$variable],
                     main = "Histogram of mtcars variables",
                     xlab = input$variable)
        })

        output$carsSummary <- renderPrint({

                summary(mtcars[,input$variable])
        })
})
```

The final application

After changing the `ui.R` and the `server.R` files according to our needs, just hit the
Run App button and the final app opens in a new window:

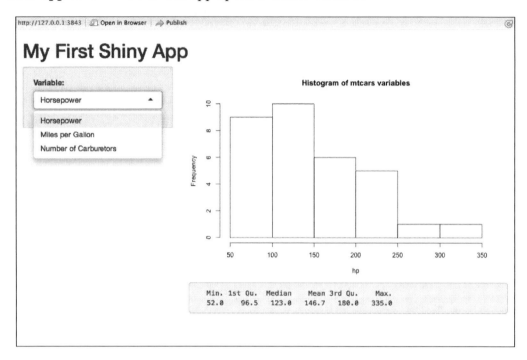

As planned in the app sketch, the app offers the user a drop-down menu to choose
the desired variable on the left side, and shows a histogram and data summary of the
selected variable on the right side.

Deconstructing the final app into its components

For a better understanding of the Shiny application logic and the interplay of the
two main files, `ui.R` and `server.R`, we will disassemble your first app again into its
individual parts.

The components of the user interface

We have divided the user interface into three parts:

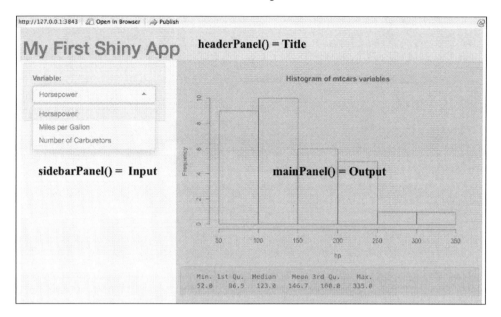

After loading the `Shiny` library, the complete look of the app gets defined by the `shinyUI()` function. In our app sketch, we chose a sidebar look; therefore, the `shinyUI` function holds the argument, `pageWithSidebar()`:

```
library(shiny)

shinyUI(pageWithSidebar(
...
```

The `headerPanel()` argument is certainly the simplest component, since usually only the title of the app will be stored in it. In our `ui.R` file, it is just a single line of code:

```
library(shiny)

shinyUI(pageWithSidebar(

        titlePanel("My First Shiny App"),
...
```

The `sidebarPanel()` function defines the look of the sidebar, and most importantly, handles the input of the variables of the chosen `mtcars` dataset:

```
library(shiny)

shinyUI(pageWithSidebar(

        titlePanel("My First Shiny App"),

        sidebarPanel(
                selectInput(inputId = "variable",
                            label = "Variable:",
                            choices = c("Horsepower" = "hp",
                                        "Miles per Gallon" = "mpg",
                                        "Number of Carburetors" =
"carb"),
                            selected = "hp")
        ),
...
```

Finally, the `mainPanel()` function ensures that the output is displayed. In our case, this is the histogram and the data summary for the selected variables:

```
library(shiny)

shinyUI(pageWithSidebar(

        titlePanel("My First Shiny App"),

        sidebarPanel(
                selectInput(inputId = "variable",
                            label = "Variable:",
                            choices = c("Horsepower" = "hp",
                                        "Miles per Gallon" = "mpg",
                                        "Number of Carburetors" =
"carb"),
                            selected = "hp")
        ),

        mainPanel(
                plotOutput("carsPlot"),
                verbatimTextOutput("carsSummary")
        )
))
```

The server file in detail

While the `ui.R` file defines the look of the app, the `server.R` file holds instructions for the execution of the R code. Again, we use our first app to deconstruct the related `server.R` file into its main important parts. After loading the needed libraries, datasets, and further scripts, the function, `shinyServer(function(input, output) {} )`, defines the server logic:

```
library(shiny)
library(datasets)

shinyServer(function(input, output) {
  ...
```

The marked lines of code that follow translate the inputs of the `ui.R` file into matching outputs. In our case, the server side `output$` object is assigned to `carsPlot`, which in turn was called in the `mainPanel()` function of the `ui.R` file as `plotOutput()`. Moreover, the `render*` function, in our example it is `renderPlot()`, reflects the type of output. Of course, here it is the histogram plot. Within the `renderPlot()` function, you can recognize the `input$` object assigned to the variables that were defined in the user interface file:

```
library(shiny)
library(datasets)

shinyServer(function(input, output) {

        output$carsPlot <- renderPlot({

                hist(mtcars[,input$variable],
                    main = "Histogram of mtcars variables",
                    xlab = input$variable)
        })
  ...
```

In the following lines, you will see another type of the render function, `renderPrint()`, and within the curly braces, the actual R function, `summary()`, with the defined input variable:

```
library(shiny)
library(datasets)

shinyServer(function(input, output) {

        output$carsPlot <- renderPlot({
```

```
            hist(mtcars[,input$variable],
                  main = "Histogram of mtcars variables",
                  xlab = input$variable)
      })

      output$carsSummary <- renderPrint({

            summary(mtcars[,input$variable])
      })

})
```

There are plenty of different render functions. The most used are as follows:

- `renderPlot`: This creates normal plots
- `renderPrin`: This gives printed output types
- `renderUI`: This gives HTML or Shiny tag objects
- `renderTable`: This gives tables, data frames, and matrices
- `renderText`: This creates character strings

> Every code outside the `shinyServer()` function runs only once on the first launch of the app, while all the code in between the brackets and before the output functions runs as often as a user visits or refreshes the application. The code within the output functions runs every time a user changes the widget that belongs to the corresponding output.

The connection between the server and the ui file

As already inspected in our decomposed Shiny app, the input functions of the `ui.R` file are linked with the output functions of the `server` file. The following figure illustrates this again:

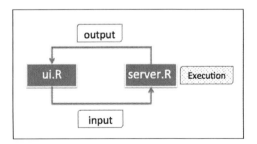

The concept of reactivity

Shiny uses a reactive programming model, and this is a big deal. By applying reactive programming, the framework is able to be fast, efficient, and robust. Briefly, changing the input in the user interface, Shiny rebuilds the related output. Shiny uses three reactive objects:

- Reactive source
- Reactive conductor
- Reactive endpoint

For simplicity, we use the formal signs of the RStudio documentation:

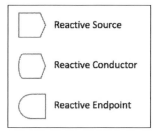

The implementation of a reactive source is the reactive value; that of a reactive conductor is a reactive expression; and the reactive endpoint is also called the observer.

The source and endpoint structure

As taught in the previous section, the defined input of the ui.R links is the output of the server.R file. For simplicity, we use the code from our first Shiny app again, along with the introduced formal signs:

```
    . . .
            output$carsPlot <- renderPlot({

                    hist(mtcars[,input$variable],
                        main = "Histogram of mtcars variables",
```

```
                              xlab = input$variable)
        })
  . . .
```

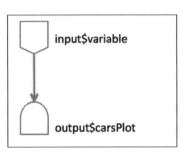

The input variable, in our app these are the *Horsepower; Miles per Gallon,* and *Number of Carburetors choices*, represents the reactive source. The histogram called `carsPlot` stands for the reactive endpoint. In fact, it is possible to link the reactive source to numerous reactive endpoints, and also conversely. In our Shiny app, we also connected the input variable to our first and second output—`carsSummary`:

```
  . . .
        output$carsPlot <- renderPlot({

                hist(mtcars[,input$variable],
                      main = "Histogram of mtcars variables",
                      xlab = input$variable)
        })

        output$carsSummary <- renderPrint({

                summary(mtcars[, input$variable])
        })
  . . .
```

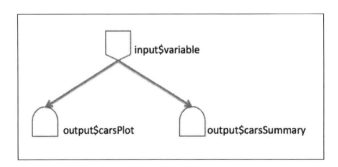

To sum it up, this structure ensures that every time a user changes the input, the output refreshes automatically and accordingly.

The purpose of the reactive conductor

The reactive conductor differs from the reactive source and the endpoint is so far that this reactive type can be dependent and can have dependents. Therefore, it can be placed between the source, which can only have dependents and the endpoint, which in turn can only be dependent. The primary function of a reactive conductor is the encapsulation of heavy and difficult computations. In fact, reactive expressions are caching the results of these computations. The following graph displays a possible connection of the three reactive types:

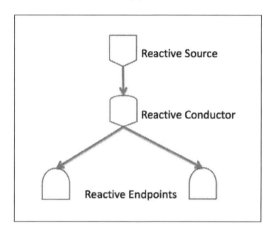

In general, reactivity raises the impression of a logically working directional system; after input, the output occurs. You get the feeling that an input pushes information to an output. But this isn't the case. In reality, it works vice versa. The output pulls the information from the input. And this all works due to sophisticated server logic. The input sends a callback to the server, which in turn informs the output that pulls the needed value from the input and shows the result to the user. But of course, for a user, this all feels like an instant updating of any input changes, and overall, like a responsive app's behavior. Of course, we have just touched upon the main aspects of reactivity, but now you know what's really going on under the hood of Shiny.

Discovering the scope of the Shiny user interface

After you know how to build a simple Shiny application, as well as how reactivity works, let us take a look at the next step: the various resources to create a custom user interface. Furthermore, there are nearly endless possibilities to shape the look and feel of the layout. As already mentioned, the entire HTML, CSS, and JavaScript logic and functions of the layout options are based on the highly flexible bootstrap framework. And, of course, everything is responsive by default, which makes it possible for the final application layout to adapt to the screen of any device.

Exploring the Shiny interface layouts

Currently, there are four common `shinyUI()` page layouts:

- `pageWithSidebar()`
- `fluidPage()`
- `navbarPage()`
- `fixedPage()`

These page layouts can be, in turn, structured with different functions for a custom inner arrangement structure of the page layout. In the following sections, we are introducing the most useful inner layout functions. As an example, we will use our first Shiny application again.

The sidebar layout

The sidebar layout, where the `sidebarPanel()` function is used as the input area, and the `mainPanel()` function as the output, just like in our first Shiny app. The sidebar layout uses the `pageWithSidebar()` function:

```
library(shiny)

shinyUI(pageWithSidebar(

        headerPanel("The Sidebar Layout"),

        sidebarPanel(
                selectInput(inputId = "variable",
                        label = "This is the sidebarPanel",
                        choices = c("Horsepower" = "hp",
                                "Miles per Gallon" = "mpg",
```

```
                                     "Number of Carburetors" =
       "carb"),
                              selected = "hp")
          ),

          mainPanel(
                  tags$h2("This is the mainPanel"),
                  plotOutput("carsPlot"),
                  verbatimTextOutput("carsSummary")
          )
))
```

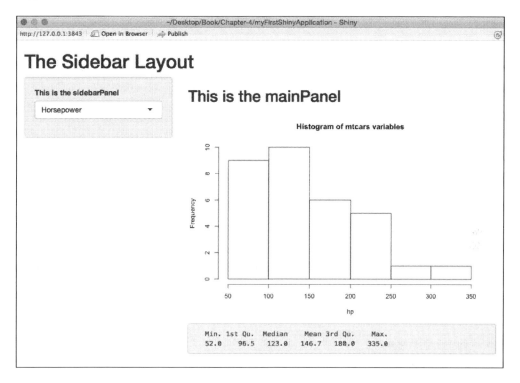

When you only change the first three functions, you can create exactly the same look as the application with the `fluidPage()` layout. This is the sidebar layout with the `fluidPage()` function:

```
library(shiny)

shinyUI(fluidPage(

        titlePanel("The Sidebar Layout"),
```

```
    sidebarLayout(

            sidebarPanel(
                    selectInput(inputId = "variable",
                                 label = "This is the
sidebarPanel",
                                 choices = c("Horsepower" = "hp",
                                             "Miles per Gallon" =
"mpg",
                                             "Number of
Carburetors" = "carb"),
                                 selected = "hp")
            ),

            mainPanel(
                    tags$h2("This is the mainPanel"),
                    plotOutput("carsPlot"),
                    verbatimTextOutput("carsSummary")
            )
        )
))
```

The grid layout

The grid layout is where rows are created with the `fluidRow()` function. The input and output are made within free customizable columns. Naturally, a maximum of 12 columns from the bootstrap grid system must be respected. This is the grid layout with the `fluidPage()` function and a 4-8 grid:

```
library(shiny)

shinyUI(fluidPage(

        titlePanel("The Grid Layout"),

        fluidRow(

            column(4,
                    selectInput(inputId = "variable",
                                 label = "Four-column input area",
                                 choices = c("Horsepower" = "hp",
                                             "Miles per Gallon" =
"mpg",
```

```
                                                    "Number of
Carburetors" = "carb"),
                                      selected = "hp")
                    ),

                column(8,
                        tags$h3("Eight-column output area"),
                        plotOutput("carsPlot"),
                        verbatimTextOutput("carsSummary")
                )
        )
))
```

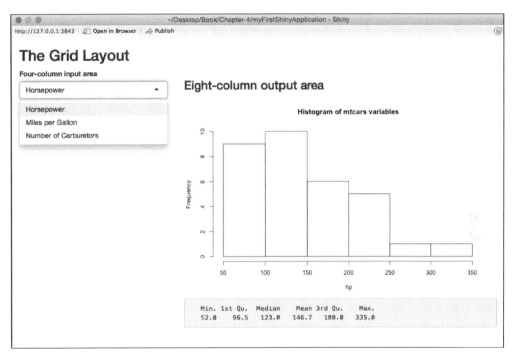

As you can see from inspecting the previous ui.R file, the width of the columns is defined within the fluidRow() function, and the sum of these two columns adds up to 12. Since the allocation of the columns is completely flexible, you can also create something like the grid layout with the fluidPage() function and a 4-4-4 grid:

```
library(shiny)

shinyUI(fluidPage(

        titlePanel("The Grid Layout"),

        fluidRow(

                column(4,
                        selectInput(inputId = "variable",
                                    label = "Four-column input area",
                                    choices = c("Horsepower" = "hp",
                                                "Miles per Gallon" =
"mpg",
                                                "Number of Carburetors"
= "carb"),
                                    selected = "hp")
                ),

                column(4,
                        tags$h5("Four-column output area"),
                        plotOutput("carsPlot")
                ),
                column(4,
                        tags$h5("Another four-column output area"),
                        verbatimTextOutput("carsSummary")
                )
        )
))
```

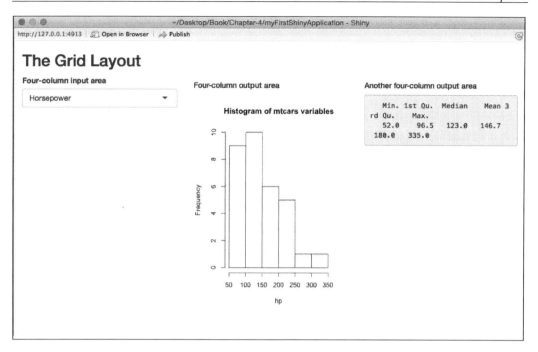

The tabset panel layout

The `tabsetPanel()` function can be built into the `mainPanel()` function of the aforementioned sidebar layout page. By applying this function, you can integrate several tabbed outputs into one view. This is the tabset layout with the `fluidPage()` function and three tab panels:

```
library(shiny)

shinyUI(fluidPage(

    titlePanel("The Tabset Layout"),

    sidebarLayout(

        sidebarPanel(
            selectInput(inputId = "variable",
                        label = "Select a variable",
                        choices = c("Horsepower" = "hp",
                                    "Miles per Gallon" = "mpg",
                                    "Number of Carburetors" = "carb"),
                        selected = "hp")
        ),
```

```
       mainPanel(
       tabsetPanel(
        tabPanel("Plot", plotOutput("carsPlot")),
        tabPanel("Summary", verbatimTextOutput("carsSummary")),
        tabPanel("Raw Data", dataTableOutput("tableData"))
                      )
                  )
            )
   ))
```

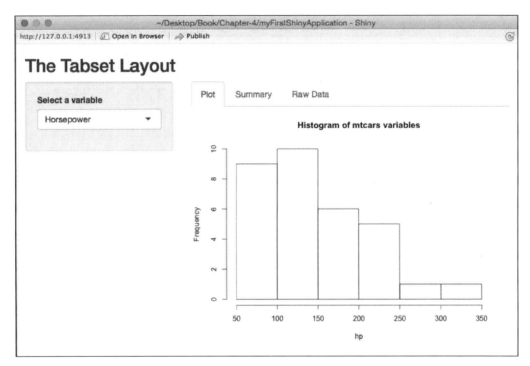

After changing the code to include the `tabsetPanel()` function, the three tabs with the `tabPanel()` function display the respective output. With the help of this layout, you are no longer dependent on representing several outputs among themselves. Instead, you can display each output in its own tab, while the sidebar does not change. The position of the tabs is flexible and can be assigned to be above, below, right, and left. For example, in the following code file detail, the position of the `tabsetPanel()` function was assigned as follows:

```
...
mainPanel(
        tabsetPanel(position = "below",
            tabPanel("Plot", plotOutput("carsPlot")),
            tabPanel("Summary", verbatimTextOutput("carsSummary")),
            tabPanel("Raw Data", tableOutput("tableData"))
                    )
        )
...
```

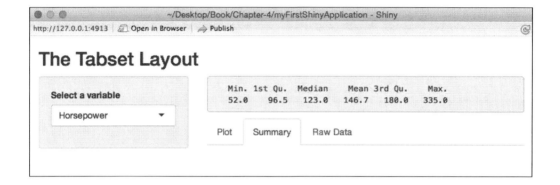

The navlist panel layout

The navlistPanel() function is similar to the tabsetPanel() function, and can be seen as an alternative if you need to integrate a large number of tabs. The navlistPanel() function also uses the tabPanel() function to include outputs:

```
library(shiny)

shinyUI(fluidPage(

        titlePanel("The Navlist Layout"),

        navlistPanel(
            "Discovering The Dataset",
            tabPanel("Plot", plotOutput("carsPlot")),
            tabPanel("Summary", verbatimTextOutput("carsSummary")),
            tabPanel("Another Plot", plotOutput("barPlot")),
            tabPanel("Even A Third Plot", plotOutput("thirdPlot"),
            "More Information",
```

```
        tabPanel("Raw Data", tableOutput("tableData")),
        tabPanel("More Datatables", tableOutput("moreData"))
    )

))
```

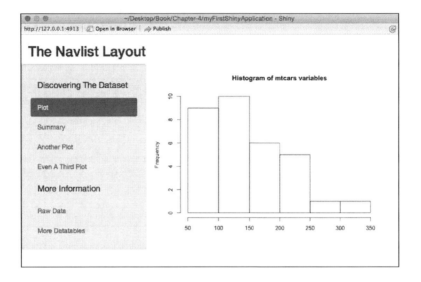

The navbar page as the page layout

In the previous examples, we have used the page layouts, `fluidPage()` and
`pageWithSidebar()`, in the first line. But, especially when you want to create an
application with a variety of tabs, sidebars, and various input and output areas, it is
recommended that you use the `navbarPage()` layout. This function makes use of the
standard top navigation of the bootstrap framework:

```
library(shiny)

shinyUI(navbarPage("The Navbar Page Layout",

    tabPanel("Data Analysis",

        sidebarPanel(
            selectInput(inputId = "variable",
            label = "Select a variable",
            choices = c("Horsepower" = "hp",
                        "Miles per Gallon" = "mpg",
                        "Number of Carburetors" = "carb"),
            selected = "hp")
            ),
```

```
                    mainPanel(
                        plotOutput("carsPlot"),
                        verbatimTextOutput("carsSummary")
                    )
                ),
            tabPanel("Calculations"

        ...

            ),
            tabPanel("Some Notes"

            ...

            )

    ))
```

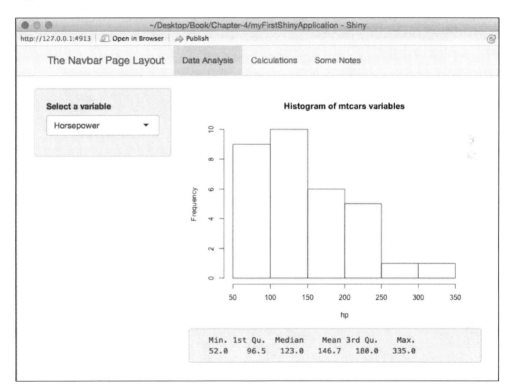

Adding widgets to your application

After inspecting the most important page layouts in detail, we now look at the different interface input and output elements. By adding these widgets, panels, and other interface elements to an application, we can further customize each page layout.

Shiny input elements

Already, in our first Shiny application, we got to know a typical Shiny input element: the selection box widget. But, of course, there are a lot more widgets with different types of uses. All widgets can have several arguments; the minimum setup is to assign an `inputId`, which instructs the input slot to communicate with the server file, and a label to communicate with a widget. Each widget can also have its own specific arguments.

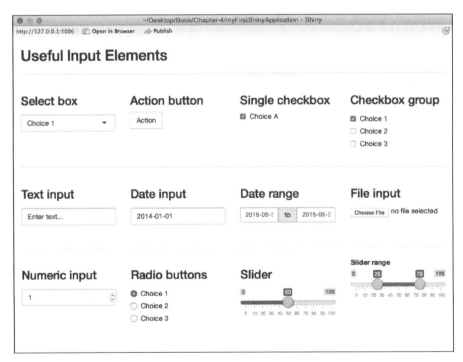

As an example, we are looking at the code of a slider widget. In the previous screenshot are two versions of a slider; we took the slider range for inspection:

```
sliderInput(inputId = "sliderExample",
            label = "Slider range",
            min = 0,
```

```
max = 100,
value = c(25, 75))
```

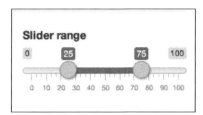

Besides the mandatory arguments, `inputId` and `label`, three more values have been added to the slider widget. The `min` and `max` arguments specify the minimum and maximum values that can be selected. In our example, these are 0 and 100. A numeric vector was assigned to the value argument, and this creates a double-ended range slider. This vector must logically be within the set minimum and maximum values.

Currently, there are more than twenty different input widgets, which in turn are all individually configurable by assigning to them their own set of arguments.

A brief overview of the output elements

As we have seen, the output elements in the `ui.R` file are connected to the rendering functions in the server file. The mainly used output elements are:

* `htmlOutput`
* `imageOutput`
* `plotOutput`
* `tableOutput`
* `textOutput`
* `verbatimTextOutput`
* `downloadButton`

Due to their unambiguous naming, the purpose of these elements should be clear.

Individualizing your app even further with Shiny tags

Although you don't need to know HTML to create stunning Shiny applications, you have the option to create highly customized apps with the usage of raw HTML or so-called Shiny tags. To add raw HTML, you can use the HTML() function. We will focus on Shiny tags in the following list. Currently, there are over a 100 different Shiny tag objects, which can be used to add text styling, colors, different headers, visual and audio, lists, and many more things. You can use these tags by writing tags$tagname. Following is a brief list of useful tags:

- tags$h1: This is first level header; of course you can also use the known h1-h6
- tags$hr: This makes a horizontal line, also known as a thematic break
- tags$br: This makes a line break, a popular way to add some space
- tags$strong = This makes the text bold
- tags$div: This makes a division of text with a uniform style
- tags$a: This links to a webpage
- tags$iframe: This makes an inline frame for embedding possibilities

The following ui.R file and corresponding screenshot show the usage of Shiny tags by an example:

```
library(shiny)

shinyUI(fluidPage(

        fluidRow(
                column(6,
                        tags$h3("Customize your app with Shiny tags!"),
                        tags$hr(),
                        tags$a(href = "http://www.rstudio.com", "Click
me"),
                        tags$hr()

                ),
                column(6,
                        tags$br(),
                        tags$em("Look - the R project logo"),
                        tags$br(),
                        tags$img(src = "http://www.r-project.org/Rlogo.
png")
                )
```

```
                ),
          fluidRow(
                column(6,
                      tags$strong("We can even add a video"),
                      tags$video(src = "video.mp4", type = "video/
  mp4", autoplay = NA, controls = NA)
                ),
                column(6,
                      tags$br(),
                      tags$ol(
                            tags$li("One"),
                            tags$li("Two"),
                            tags$li("Three"))
                )
          )
  ))
```

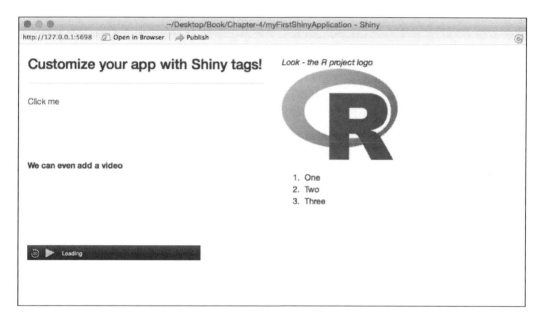

Creating dynamic user interface elements

We know how to build completely custom user interfaces with all the bells and whistles. But all the introduced types of interface elements are fixed and static. However, if you need to create dynamic interface elements, Shiny offers three ways to achieve it:

- The `conditinalPanel()` function:
- The `renderUI()` function
- The use of directly injected JavaScript code

In the following section, we only show how to use the first two ways, because firstly, they are built into the `shiny` package, and secondly, the JavaScript method is indicated as experimental.

Using conditionalPanel

The `condtionalPanel()` functions allow you to show or hide interface elements dynamically, and is set in the `ui.R` file. The dynamic of this function is achieved by JavaScript expressions, but as usual in the `shiny` package, all you need to know is R programming.

The following example application shows how this function works for the `ui.R` file:

```
library(shiny)

shinyUI(fluidPage(

    titlePanel("Dynamic Interface With Conditional Panels"),

    column(4, wellPanel(
            sliderInput(inputId = "n",
                    label= "Number of points:",
                    min = 10, max = 200, value = 50, step = 10)
        )),

    column(5,
            "The plot below will be not displayed when the slider
    value",
            "is less than 50.",
            conditionalPanel("input.n >= 50",
                    plotOutput("scatterPlot", height = 300)
                        )
            )
))
```

The following example application shows how this function works for the Related
`server.R` file:

```
library(shiny)

shinyServer(function(input, output) {

    output$scatterPlot <- renderPlot({
        x <- rnorm(input$n)
        y <- rnorm(input$n)
        plot(x, y)
    })

})
```

 The code for this example application was taken from the
Shiny gallery of RStudio (http://shiny.rstudio.com/
gallery/conditionalpanel-demo.html).

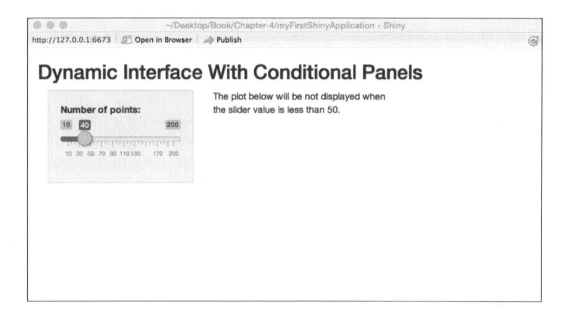

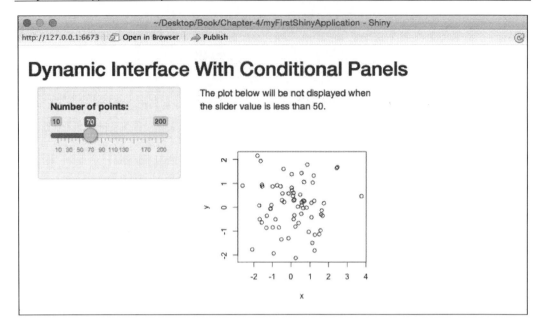

As readable in both code files, the defined function, `input.n`, is the linchpin for the dynamic behavior of the example app. In the `conditionalPanel()` function, it is defined that `inputId="n"` must have a value of 50 or higher, while the input and output of the plot will work as already defined.

Taking advantage of the renderUI function

The `renderUI()` function is hooked, contrary to the previous model, to the server file to create a dynamic user interface. We have already introduced different render output functions in this chapter.

The following example code shows the basic functionality using the `ui.R` file:

```
# Partial example taken from the Shiny documentation
numericInput("lat", "Latitude"),
numericInput("long", "Longitude"),
uiOutput("cityControls")
```

The following example code shows the basic functionality of the Related `sever.R` file:

```
# Partial example
output$cityControls <- renderUI({
  cities <- getNearestCities(input$lat, input$long)
  checkboxGroupInput("cities", "Choose Cities", cities)
})
```

As described, the dynamic of this method gets defined in the `renderUI()` process as an output, which then gets displayed through the `uiOutput()` function in the `ui.R` file.

Sharing your Shiny application with others

Typically, you create a Shiny application not only for yourself, but also for other users. There are a two main ways to distribute your app; either you let users download your application, or you deploy it on the web.

Offering a download of your Shiny app

By offering the option to download your final Shiny application, other users can run your app locally. Actually, there are four ways to deliver your app this way. No matter which way you choose, it is important that the user has installed R and the `Shiny` package on his/her computer.

Gist

Gist is a public code sharing pasteboard from GitHub. To share your app this way, it is important that both the ui.R file and the server.R file are in the same Gist and have been named correctly. Take a look at the following screenshot:

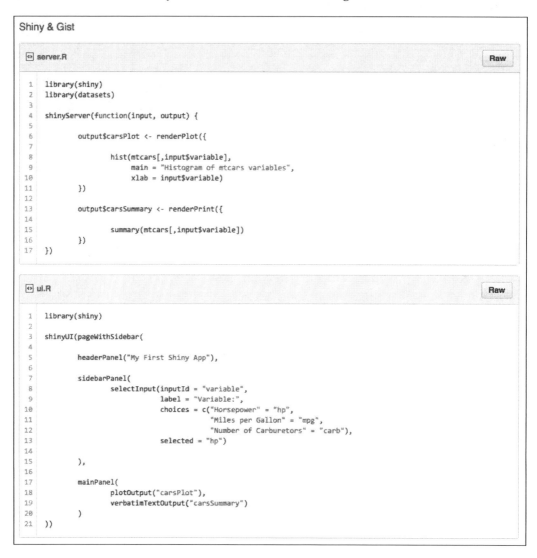

There are two options to run apps via Gist. First, just enter runGist("Gist_URL") in the console of RStudio; or second, just use the Gist ID and place it in the shiny::runGist("Gist_ID") function.

```
> runGist("https://gist.github.com/mhnierhoff/1568a36e757e56da6131")
Downloading https://gist.github.com/mhnierhoff/1568a36e757e56da6131/download

Listening on http://127.0.0.1:6673

> shiny::runGist("1568a36e757e56da6131")
Downloading https://gist.github.com/1568a36e757e56da6131/download

Listening on http://127.0.0.1:6673
```

Gist is a very easy way to share your application, but you need to keep in mind that your code is published on a third-party server.

GitHub

The next way to enable users to download your app is through a GitHub repository:

To run an application from GitHub, you need to enter the command, shiny::runGitHub("Repository_Name", "GitHub_Account_Name"), in the console:

```
> shiny::runGitHub("Shiny-GitHub", "mhnierhoff")
Downloading https://github.com/mhnierhoff/Shiny-GitHub/archive/master.tar.gz

Listening on http://127.0.0.1:6673
```

Zip file

There are two ways to share a Shiny application by zip file. You can either let the user download the zip file over the web, or you can share it via email, USB stick, memory card, or any other such device. To download a zip file via the Web, you need to type `runUrl("Zip_File_URL")` in the console.

```
> runUrl("https://github.com/mhnierhoff/Shiny-GitHub/blob/master/Zip_File/Shiny-Github.zip")
Downloading https://github.com/mhnierhoff/Shiny-GitHub/blob/master/Zip_File/Shiny-Github.zip
```

Package

Certainly, a much more labor-intensive but also publically effective way is to create a complete R package for your Shiny application. This especially makes sense if you have built an extensive application that may help many other users. Another advantage is the fact that you can also publish your application on CRAN. Later in the book, we will show you how to create an R package.

Deploying your app to the web

After showing you the ways users can download your app and run it on their local machines, we will now check the options to deploy Shiny apps to the web.

Shinyapps.io

`http://www.shinyapps.io/` is a Shiny app-hosting service by RStudio. There is a free-to-use account package, but it is limited to a maximum of five applications, 25 so-called active hours, and the apps are branded with the RStudio logo. Nevertheless, this service is a great way to publish one's own applications quickly and easily to the web.

To use `http://www.shinyapps.io/` with RStudio, a few R packages and some additional operating system software needs to be installed:

- `RTools` (If you use Windows)
- `GCC` (If you use Linux)
- `XCode` Command Line Tools (If you use Mac OS X)
- The `devtools` R package
- The `shinyapps` package

Since the `shinyapps` package is not on CRAN, you need to install it via GitHub by using the `devtools` package:

```
if (!require("devtools"))
        install.packages("devtools")
devtools::install_github("rstudio/shinyapps")
library(shinyapps)
```

When everything that is needed is installed ,you are ready to publish your Shiny apps directly from the RStudio IDE. Just click on the **Publish** icon, and in the new window you will need to log in to your `http://www.shinyapps.io/` account once, if you are using it for the first time. All other times, you can directly create a new Shiny app or update an existing app.

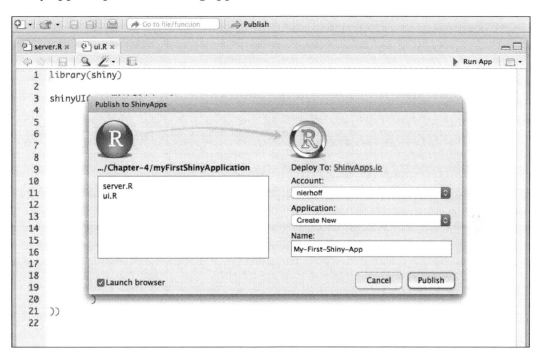

After clicking on **Publish**, a new tab called **Deploy** opens in the console pane, showing you the progress of the deployment process. If there is something set incorrectly, you can use the deployment log to find the error.

```
Console   Deploy ×
.../Chapter-4/myFirstShinyApplication
Preparing to deploy application...DONE
Uploading application bundle...DONE
Deploying application: 44838...
Waiting for task: 38430729
  building: Fetching packages
  building: Installing packages
  building: Installing files
  building: Pushing image: 191949
  deploying: Starting instances
  terminating: Stopping old instances
Application successfully deployed to https://nierhoff.shinyapps.io/My-First-Shiny-App
ShinyApps deployment completed: https://nierhoff.shinyapps.io/My-First-Shiny-App
```

When the deployment is successful, your app will be publically reachable with its own web address on `http://www.shinyapps.io/`.

Setting up a self-hosted Shiny server

There are two editions of the Shiny Server software: an open source edition and the professional edition. The open source edition can be downloaded for free and you can use it on your own server. The Professional edition offers a lot more features and support by RStudio, but is also priced accordingly. In *Chapter 9, R for your Organization – Managing the RStudio Server* we will show you how to set up a self-hosted Shiny server with the open source version of the software.

Diving into the Shiny ecosystem

Since the Shiny framework is such an awesome and powerful tool, a lot of people, and of course, the creators of RStudio and Shiny have built several packages around it that are enormously extending the existing functionalities of Shiny. These almost infinite possibilities of technical and visual individualization, which are possible by deeply checking the Shiny ecosystem, would certainly go beyond the scope of this chapter. Therefore, we are presenting only a few important directions to give a first impression.

Creating apps with more files

In this chapter, you have learned how to build a Shiny app consisting of two files: the server.R and the ui.R. To include every aspect, we first want to point out that it is also possible to create a single file Shiny app. To do so, create a file called app.R. In this file, you can include both the server.R and the ui.R file. Furthermore, you can include global variables, data, and more. If you build larger Shiny apps with multiple functions, datasets, options, and more, it could be very confusing if you do all of it in just one file. Therefore, single-file Shiny apps are a good idea for simple and small exhibition apps with a minimal setup.

Especially for large Shiny apps, it is recommended that you outsource extensive custom functions, datasets, images, and more into your own files, but put them into the same directory as the app. An example file setup could look like this:

```
~/shinyapp
|-- ui.R
|-- server.R
|-- helper.R
|-- data
|-- www
|-- js
|-- etc
```

To access the helper file, you just need to add `source("helpers.R")` into the code of your `server.R` file. The same logic applies to any other R files. If you want to read in some data from your data folder, you store it in a variable that is also in the head of your `server.R` file, like this:

```
myData <- readRDS("data/myDataset.rds")
```

Expanding the Shiny package

As said earlier, you can expand the functionalities of Shiny with several add-on packages. There are currently ten packages available on CRAN with different inbuilt functions to add some extra magic to your Shiny app.

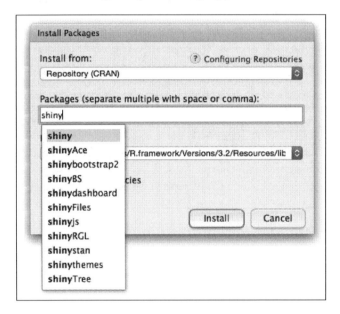

- `shinyAce`: This package makes available Ace editor bindings to enable a rich text-editing environment within Shiny.
- `shinybootstrap2`: The latest Shiny package uses bootstrap 3; so, if you built your app with bootstrap 2 features, you need to use this package.
- `shinyBS`: This package adds the additional features of the original Twitter `Bootstraptheme`, such as tooltips, modals, and others, to Shiny.

- `shinydashboard`: This packages comes from the folks at RStudio and enables the user to create stunning and multifunctional dashboards on top of Shiny.

- `shinyFiles`: This provides functionality for client-side navigation of the server side file system in Shiny apps.

- `shinyjs`: By using this package, you can perform common JavaScript operations in Shiny applications without having to know any JavaScript.

- `shinyRGL`: This package provides Shiny wrappers for the RGL package. This package exposes RGL's ability to export WebGL visualization in a shiny-friendly format.

- `shinystan`: This package is, in fact, not a real add-on. `Shinystan` is a fantastic full-blown Shiny application to give users a graphical interface for Markov chain Monte Carlo simulations.

- `shinythemes`: This packages gives you the option of changing the whole look and feel of your application by using different inbuilt bootstrap themes.

- `shinyTree`: This exposes bindings to `jsTree`—a JavaScript library that supports interactive trees—to enable rich, editable trees in Shiny.

Of course, you can find a bunch of other packages with similar or even more functionalities, extensions, and also comprehensive Shiny apps on GitHub.

Summary

In this chapter, you learned what you need to create stunning web applications with the famous Shiny framework. This includes the whole process of planning, creating, and sharing a Shiny application. Next, we explained the link between the `ui.R` file and the `server.R` file. Then, we dedicated ourselves to the concept of reactive programming, which requires a more in-depth explanation and is used to make the Shiny framework fast, robust, and efficient. Furthermore, you got an in-depth introduction to the many possibilities for building a compelling user interface by taking advantage of highly flexible page layouts, widgets, and so-called Shiny tags. Moreover, we have shown several different ways to share your Shiny applications with others. In the next chapter, we will explore the opportunities when creating interactive documents with R Markdown.

5
Interactive Documents with R Markdown

This chapter covers:

- The two main ways to create interactive R Markdown documents
- Creating R Markdown and Shiny documents and presentations
- Using the `ggvis` package with R Markdown
- Embedding different types of interactive charts in documents
- Deploying interactive R Markdown documents

Creating interactive documents with R Markdown

In *Chapter 2, Communicating Your Work with R Markdown*, we learned how to structure and create R Markdown documents and presentations in RStudio. But all previous R Markdown formats were purely static. In this chapter, we want to focus on the opportunities to create interactive documents with R Markdown and RStudio. This is, of course, particularly interesting for the readers of a document, since it enables them to interact with the document by changing chart types, parameters, values, or other similar aspects. In principle, there are two ways to make an R Markdown document interactive. Firstly, you can use the Shiny web application framework of RStudio, or secondly, there is the possibility of incorporating various interactive chart types by using corresponding packages.

Using R Markdown and Shiny

In the previous chapter, we presented the Shiny framework of RStudio in detail. Besides building complete web applications, there is also the possibility of integrating entire Shiny applications into R Markdown documents and presentations. Since we have already learned all the basic functions of R Markdown, and the use and logic of Shiny, we will focus on the following lines of integrating a simple Shiny app into an R Markdown file.

In order for Shiny and R Markdown to work together, the argument, `runtime:` `shiny` must be added to the YAML header of the file. Of course, the RStudio IDE offers a quick way to create a new Shiny document presentation. Click on the new file, choose `R Markdown`, and in the popup window select **Shiny** from the left-hand side menu. In the **Shiny** menu, you can decide whether you want to start with a **Shiny Document** option or a **Shiny Presentation** option:

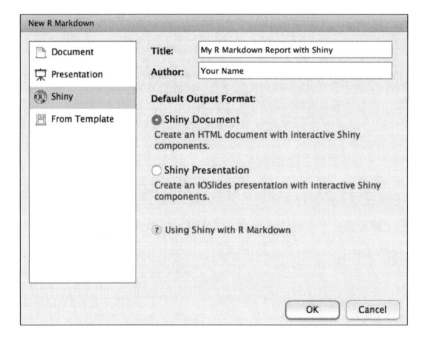

Shiny Document

After choosing the **Shiny Document** option, a prefilled .Rmd file opens. It is different from the known R Markdown interface in that there is the **Run Document** button instead of the knit button and icon.

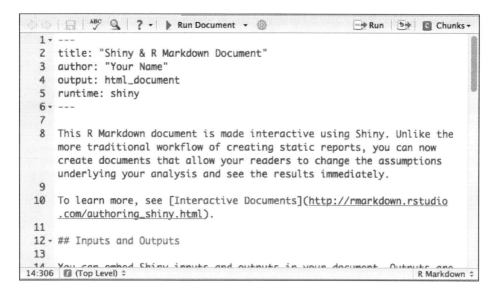

The prefilled .Rmd file produces an R Markdown document with a working and interactive Shiny application. You can change the number of bins in the plot and also adjust the bandwidth. All these changes get rendered in real time, directly in your document.

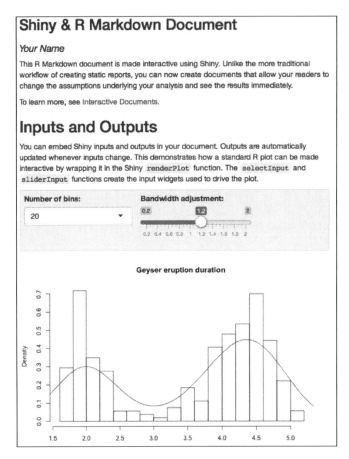

Shiny Presentation

Also, when you click on **Shiny Presentation** in the selection menu, a prefilled .Rmd file opens. Because it is a presentation, the output format is changed to ioslides_presentation in the YAML header. The button in the code pane is now called **Run Presentation**:

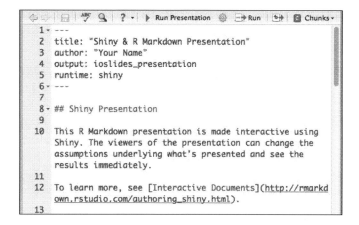

Otherwise, **Shiny Presentation** looks just like normal R Markdown presentations. The Shiny app gets embedded in a slide and you can again interact with the underlying data of the application:

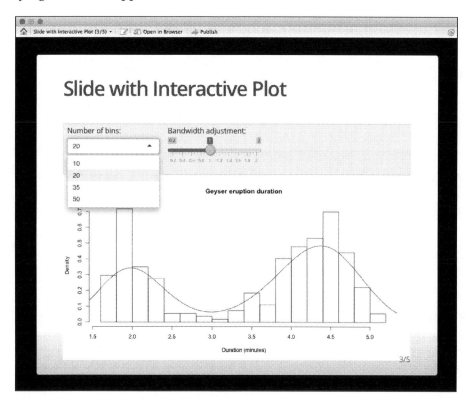

Disassembling a Shiny R Markdown document

Of course, the question arises that how is it possible to embed a whole Shiny application onto an R Markdown document without the two usual basic files, `ui.R` and `server.R`? In fact, the `rmarkdown` package creates an invisible `server.R` file by extracting the R code from the code chunks. Reactive elements get placed into the `index.html` file of the HTML output, while the whole R Markdown document acts as the `ui.R` file.

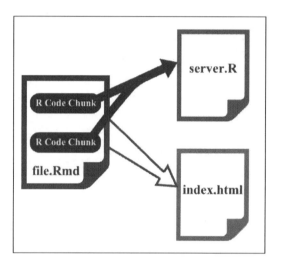

Embedding interactive charts into R Markdown

The next way is to embed interactive chart types into R Markdown documents by using various R packages that enable us to create interactive charts. Some of these package, we have already been introduced to in *Chapter 3, R Lesson I – Graphics System*. They are as follows:

- `ggvis`
- `rCharts`
- `googleVis`
- `dygraphs`

Therefore, we will not introduce them again, but will introduce some more packages that enable us to build interactive charts. They are:

- `threejs`
- `networkD3`
- `metricsgraphics`
- `plotly`

Please keep in mind that the interactivity logically only works with the HTML output of R Markdown.

Using ggvis for interactive R Markdown documents

We already know the `ggvis` package from *Chapter 3, R Lesson I: Graphics System*. Broadly speaking, `ggvis` is the successor to the well-known graphic package, `ggplot2`. The interactivity options of `ggvis`, which are based on the reactive programming model of the Shiny framework, are also useful for creating interactive R Markdown documents.

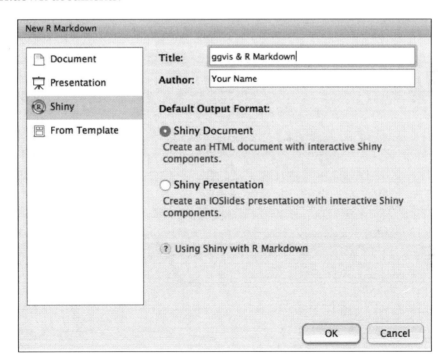

If you want to include an interactive `ggvis` plot within a normal R Markdown file, make sure to include the `runtime: shiny` argument in the YAML header. To create an interactive R markdown document with `ggvis`, you need to click on the new file, then on **R Markdown...**, choose **Shiny** in the left menu of the new window, and finally, click on **OK** to create the document. As told before, since `ggvis` uses the reactive model of Shiny, we need to create an R Markdown document with `ggvis` this way.

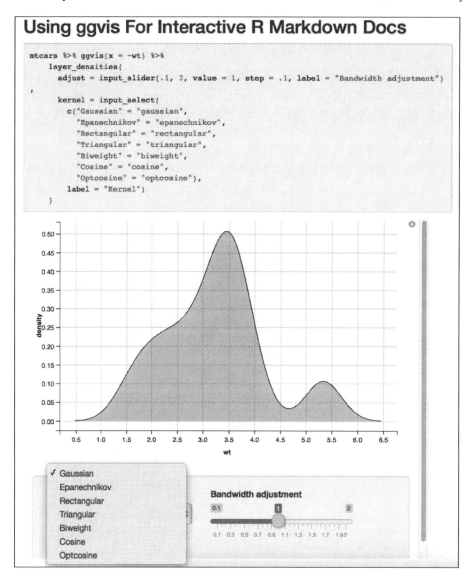

As shown, readers of this R Markdown document can easily adjust the bandwidth, and also, the kernel model. The interactive controls are created with `input_`. In our example, we used the controls, `input_slider()` and `input_select()`. For example, some of the other controls are `input_checkbox()`, `input_numeric()`, and so on. These controls have different arguments depending on the type of input. For both controls in our example, we used the `label` argument, which is just a text label shown next to the controls. Other arguments are `ID` (a unique identifier for the assigned control) and `map` (a function that remaps the output).

rCharts

Since the `rCharts` package creates JavaScript visualizations, the corresponding R code just needs to be embedded in the normal code chunks. The following code produces an interactive line chart:

```
---
title: "My Interactive Report"
author: "Your Name"
output: html_document
---


## Interactive documents with rCharts

```{r}
library(rCharts)
```


```{r results = 'asis', message=FALSE}
# interactive line chart with MorrisJS
# this code example was taken from http://ramnathv.github.io/rCharts/
data(economics, package = 'ggplot2')
econ <- transform(economics, date = as.character(date))
m1 <- mPlot(x = 'date', y = c('psavert', 'uempmed'), type = 'Line',
  data = econ)
m1$set(pointSize = 0, lineWidth = 1)
m1$print('chart2', include_assets = TRUE)


...
```
```

It is important to include the argument, `results = 'asis'`, in the plot rendering chunk. Furthermore, you need to add the argument, `include_assets = TRUE`, to the printing function:

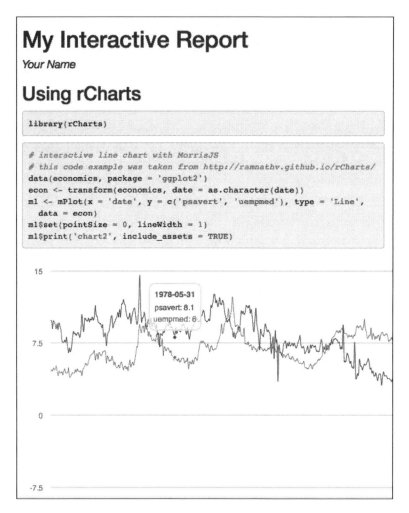

googleVis

The `googleVis` package uses the Google Charts API, and therefore, its charts can also be easily executed within the code chunks. The following code produces an interactive bar and line chart combination:

```
---
title: "My Interactive Report"
author: "Your Name"
output: html_document
---


## Using googleVis

   {r, message=FALSE}
library(googleVis)
op <- options(gvis.plot.tag="chart")
...


   {r results = 'asis', message=FALSE}
# interactive line line and bar with googleVis
# this code example was taken from the googleVis package vignette
CityPopularity$Mean=mean(CityPopularity$Popularity)
CC <- gvisComboChart(CityPopularity, xvar='City',
        yvar=c('Mean', 'Popularity'),
        options=list(seriesType='bars',
                    width=450, height=300,
                    title='City Popularity',
                    series='{0: {type:\"line\"}}'))
plot(CC)
...
```

Again, it is important to include the argument, `results = 'asis'`, in the chunk that creates the chart.

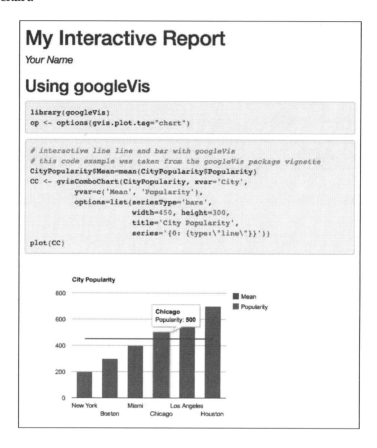

HTML widgets

We already introduced the `htmlwidgets` package that enables R users to create interactive web visualizations. Of course, you can also embed HTMNL widgets in R Markdown documents to make them interactive.

dygraphs

As already known from `rCharts` and `googleVis`, the `dygraphs` package, which was created directly by RStudio, only works with the HTML output of R Markdown.

The following code produces an interactive `dygraph` with a range selector:

```
---
title: "My Interactive Report"
author: "Your Name"
output: html_document
---

## Using htmlwidgets & dygraphs

    {r, message=FALSE}
library(htmlwidgets)
library(dygraphs)


```{r, fig.width=6, fig.height=2.5}
# example was taken from http://rstudio.github.io/dygraphs/r-markdown.
html
dygraph(nhtemp, main = "New Haven Temperatures") %>%
  dyRangeSelector(dateWindow = c("1920-01-01", "1960-01-01"))
...
```

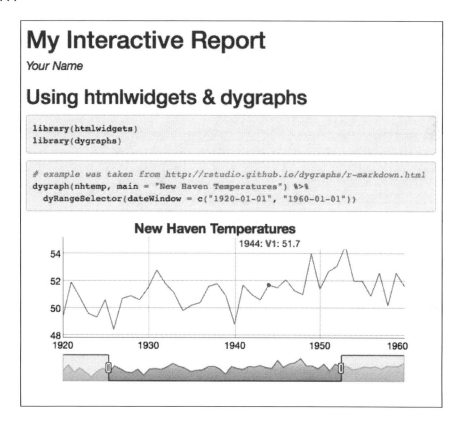
```

Three.js and R

The threejs package defines an interactive 3-d scatterplot and globe plot using three.js and the htmlwidgets package for R. These examples render like normal R plots in RStudio. They also work in R Markdown documents, shiny, and from the R command line.

B.W. Lewis (http://bwlewis.github.io/rthreejs/)

Since `threejs` is not on CRAN and must be installed via GitHub in the usual manner, we use the following code snippet:

```
library(devtools)
install_github("bwlewis/rthreejs")
library(threejs)
```

The following code example produces an interactive 3D scatterplot, on which axes can virtually move freely back and forth:

```
---
title: "My Interactive Report"
author: "Your Name"
output: html_document
---

## Using htmlwidgets & threejs

    {r, message=FALSE}
library(htmlwidgets)
library(threejs)

    {r}
# example was taken from http://bwlewis.github.io/rthreejs/
N <- 100
i <- sample(3, N, replace=TRUE)
x <- matrix(rnorm(N*3),ncol=3)
lab <- c("small", "bigger", "biggest")
scatterplot3js(x, color=rainbow(N), labels=lab[i], size=i,
renderer="canvas")
```

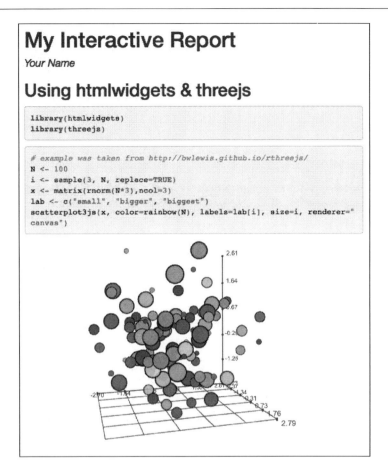

networkD3

The `networkD3` package is based on the `d3Network` package and also uses the capabilities of the `htmlwidgets` package to create D3 JavaScript network graphs with R. The package can be downloaded from CRAN and was created by Cristopher Gandrud and JJ Allaire. The `networkD3` package supports different types of interactive network graphs. In the following example, we use the `forceNetwork` graph type. Interactivity is given by the options to hover over all the nodes and read the inputs, and further, you can move the whole network back and forth:

```
---
title: "My Interactive Report"
author: "Your Name"
output: html_document
---
```

```
## Using htmlwidgets & networkD3

```{r}
library(htmlwidgets)
library(networkD3)
```


forceNetwork

```{r}
# example was taken from http://christophergandrud.github.io/
networkD3/#force
data(MisLinks)
data(MisNodes)
forceNetwork(Links = MisLinks, Nodes = MisNodes, Source = "source",
             Target = "target", Value = "value", NodeID = "name",
             Group = "group", opacity = 0.4)
```
```

metricsgraphics

metricsgraphics is an htmlwidget interface to the MetricsGraphics.js JavaScript/ D3 chart library. [...] Building metricsgraphics charts follows the "piping" idiom made popular through the magrittr, ggvis, and dplyr packages. This makes it possible to avoid one giant function with a ton of parameters and facilitates, breaking out the chart building into logical steps. While MetricsGraphics.js charts may not have the flexibility of ggplot2, you can build functional, interactive [multi-]line, scatterplot bar charts & histograms, and + even link charts together.

Bob Rudis (http://hrbrmstr.github.io/metricsgraphics/)

After installing the required htmltools package via CRAN, you need to install the metricsgraphics package from GitHub:

```
library(devtools)
install_github("hrbrmstr/metricsgraphics")
library(metricsgraphics)
```

The following code produces a D3 scatterplot of the mtcars dataset variables, wt and mpg, and adds a least square regression line within an R Markdown document. The interactivity is given by the fact that you can hover over the dots to get the exact values:

```
---
title: "My Interactive Report"
author: "Your Name"
output: html_document
---


## Using htmlwidgets & metricsgraphics

```{r}
library(htmlwidgets)
library(htmltools)
library(metricsgraphics)
```
```

```{r}
# example was taken from http://rpubs.com/hrbrmstr/53741
mtcars %>%
  mjs_plot(x=wt, y=mpg, width=400, height=300) %>%
  mjs_point(least_squares=TRUE) %>%
  mjs_labs(x="Weight of Car", y="Miles per Gallon")
```

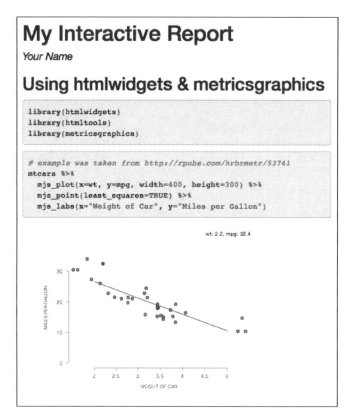

Publishing interactive R Markdown documents

There are several ways to publish your interactive R Markdown documents. But, based on how the interactivity was created in the respective document, the final product can be published. So, if we remember the introduction of this chapter, there are two ways to create interactivity: first, using the Shiny framework; second, integrating interactive chart packages.

All R Markdown documents that are based on the Shiny framework can easily be deployed by typing `shinyapps::deployApp()` into the console of the `http://www.shinyapps.io/` service (introduced in *Chapter 4, Shiny – a Web-app Framework for R*), and of course, into our own Shiny servers. This applies not only to Shiny documents and presentations, but also to documents with interactive `ggvis` elements, since `ggvis` uses the Shiny framework.

In contrast, R Markdown documents that are created with interactive chart packages, such as `rCharts`, `googleVis`, `dygraphs`, and so on, can also be published on `http://rpubs.com/`, `http://www.shinyapps.io/`, and our own Shiny servers:

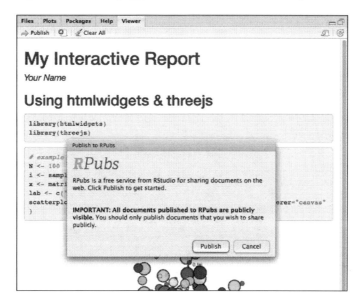

Summary

In this chapter, we have learned the two main ways to create interactive R Markdown documents. On the one hand, there is the versatile, usable Shiny framework. This includes the inbuilt Shiny documents and presentations options in RStudio, and also the `ggvis` package, which takes the advantages of the Shiny framework to build its interactivity. On the other hand, we introduced several already known, and also some new, R packages that make it possible to create several different types of interactive charts. Most of them achieve this by binding R to Existing JavaScript libraries. In the next chapter, you will learn how to write robust R functions.

6

Creating Professional Dashboards with R and Shiny

This chapter covers the following topics:

- The concept of using dashboards to display data
- Getting to know the `shinydashboards` package
- Explaining the structure and elements of `shinydashboards`
- Building your own sophisticated KPI dashboard with RStudio
- Accessing different types of data sources to fuel your dashboard

Explaining the concept of dashboards

In today's business world, dashboards are a central concept in aggregating and displaying all kinds of information. More and more data becomes available every day, and so, the need to understand this endlessly growing data is urgent. People have to get insights on these large amounts of data and use them for their business decisions. In a nutshell, a dashboard can be summed up with the following quote:

> *"An easy to read, often single page, real-time user interface, showing a graphical presentation of the current status (snapshot) and historical trends of an organization's key performance indicators (KPIs) to enable instantaneous and informed decisions to be made at a glance." (Source: Peter McFadden CEO of ExcelDashboardWidgets)*

The concept of data dashboards exists from as far back as the 1980s, and since then, they've gained a lot of importance for companies and are now a key concept for every company that wants to work in a data-driven fashion.

Introducing the shinydashboard package

We have already gotten to know the Shiny framework, and learned how to create interactive web applications. This concept would perfectly apply to the concept of dashboards, as they also have to be available to the whole company. Therefore, the creators of the Shiny framework went one step further and developed an add-on to the Shiny library called `shinydashboard`. This package gives you the perfect structure to build your own dashboard powered by R.

Installing shinydashboard

Before you can install `shinydashboard`, you have to be sure that you have installed the Shiny package, as we learned in *Chapter 4, Shiny – a Web-app Framework for R.*

Installing the `shinydashboard` package is easy, as it is available on CRAN. So, we can install it by typing:

```
install.packages("shinydashboard")
```

Explaining the structure of shinydashboard

Dashboards built with `shinydashboard` have the same underlying structure as other applications built with the Shiny framework. Their basic structure is separated in a `server.R` and `ui.R` file.

A dashboard, and so a dashboard built with `shinydashboard`, consists of three main elements:

- The dashboard header
- The dashboard sidebar
- The dashboard body

For each of these elements, `shinydashboard` provides a function. By adding arguments to the function call, we can add elements the specific part of the dashboard. To build this structure for a dashboard, we use the following code structure in the `ui.R` file:

```
library(shinydashboard)

dashboardPage(
  dashboardHeader(),
  dashboardSidebar(),

dashboardBody(),
)
```

If we then run the app, we will see our dashboard structure:

This is the basic structure that we will use to add elements and visualize information.

Showing the elements of shinydashboard

The shinydashboard package provides dashboard-specific elements that we can add to our dashboard:

> In the following sections, we will show you the most important elements and their basic functionality of having enough space to show you how to build a real hands-on dashboard with R and shinydashboard. If you want to find out more about the elements and functions of the shinydashboard package, please visit the official page at https://rstudio.github.io/ shinydashboard/.

Header elements

The header of our dashboard includes, among others, the title of the dashboard, but it can also have drop-down menus. These menus can be:

- A message menu

- A notification menu

- A task menu

Setting the title argument can change the dashboard title. We can also set the size of the title box of the header. Another thing we can set to our needs is the color of the header. Shinydashboard provides several color themes. The default is set to blue, but we can also change it to purple, green, yellow, red, or black. Therefore, we have to set the skin argument to the name of the color we want the header to be in:

```
dashboardHeader(
title = "Mastering RStudio - KPI Dashboard",
titleWidth = 350,
skin = "yellow"

)
```

Sidebar elements

The sidebar, in nearly any dashboard, is used for fast navigation through different screens or pages. So, it also gives an overview of the available screens. It behaves like the tabs from the **tabPanel** we know from Shiny. But we can also add input elements from Shiny:

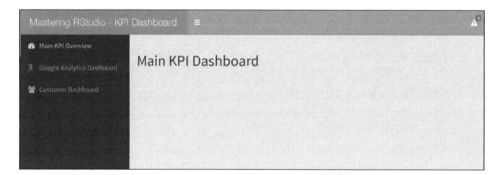

We add these elements by adding menu items to our sidebar in the `ui.R` file, and then defining the content of these tab pages in the `dashboardBody()` function. Therefore, we have to make sure that the name we give `menuItem` in the `dashboardBody` function is exactly the same as that which we give `tabItem` in the `dashboardBody` function:

```
dashboardSidebar(

  sidebarMenu(

    menuItem("Main KPI Overview",
             tabName = "mainDashboard",
             icon = icon("dashboard")),

    menuItem("Google Analytics Dashboard",
             tabName = "googleAnalytics",
             icon = icon("google")),

    menuItem("Customer Dashboard",
             tabName = "customerDashboard",
             icon = icon("users"))

  )
)

dashboardBody(

  tabItems(

    tabItem(tabName = "mainDashboard",

      h2("Main KPI Dashboard")

    ),

    tabItem(tabName = "googleAnalytics",

      h2("Google Analytics Dashboard")

    ),

    tabItem(tabName = "customerDashboard",

      h2("Customer Dashboard")
```

```
        )

      )

  )
```

Another handy feature of `shinydashboard` is the way it handles icons. As you can see, we used the `icon()` function in the Sidebar menu. We set the icons to dashboard, Google, and users. These icons are provided by `shinydashboard` as it uses Font Awesome, and so, it provides access to nearly 600 different icons. We can find all the icons at `http://fontawesome.io/icons/`.

Body elements

As `shinydashboard` is based on Shiny, we can use regular Shiny elements in the body. But `shinydashboard` adds some of its own elements to make the dashboard look more structured, and to make it easier to read and understand. Therefore, it provides boxes and fluid rows.

Boxes

When we build a dashboard with `shinydashboard`, boxes are one of the most important elements. They provide the structure we need for a dashboard to display different information from different sources on one page.

We add a box to `dashboardBody` with the `box()` function:

```
tabItem(tabName = "mainDashboard",

        h2("Main KPI Dashboard"),


        box(
          "Box 1 content",
          br(),
          "More Box content"
        ),

        box(
          "Box 2 content",
          br(),
          "Even More Box content"
        ),
```

```
box(
  "Box 3 content",
  br(),
  "Even More Box content"
),

box(
  "Box 4 content",
  br(),
  "Even More Box content"
)

)
```

In this example, we added four boxes to our dashboard. Shinydashboard arranges them in a structured way:

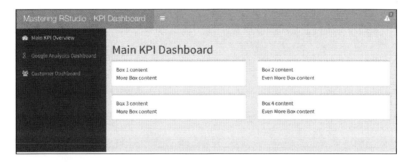

This design also adapts to the screen size as it is responsive. So, we can also view our dashboards on mobile devices, for example:

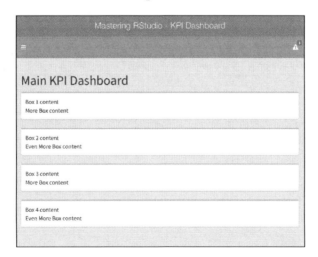

FluidRows

An additional way to structure our dashboard is by using **fluidRows**. They provide you with the possibility of organizing boxes in a row-based or column-based layout.

To order our boxes this way, we have to use the `fluidRow()` function. If we take the row-based layout as an example, this function lets you define which boxes should be displayed in a row. In the following example, we define that Box 1 should be alone in the first row, and the other three boxes should be structured in the following rows:

```
tabItem(tabName = "mainDashboard",

    h2("Main KPI Dashboard"),

    fluidRow(
    box(
      "Box 1 content",
      br(),
      "More Box content"
    )
    ),

    fluidRow(
      box(
        "Box 2 content",
        br(),
        "Even More Box content"
      ),

      box(
        "Box 3 content",
        br(),
        "More Box content"
      ),

      box(
        "Box 4 content",
        br(),
        "Even More Box content"
      )
      )
    )
```

The output of the code looks like the following screenshot:

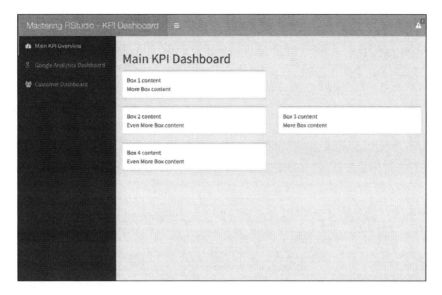

InfoBox and valueBox

As the main purpose of a dashboard is to aggregate data, we often have just one single number that summarizes several insights. For this, shinydashboard provides two elements: infoBox and valueBox. These two special boxes are used for displaying simple numeric or text values with an icon. They both are differentiated only by their design:

```
fluidRow(


infoBox("New Customers", 10 * 2,
icon = icon("users")),

infoBox("New Orders", 10 * 3,
        icon = icon("truck"),
        color="black"),

    infoBox("Views", 10 * 23,
        icon = icon("eye"),
        color="yellow")
    ),

fluidRow(
```

```
        valueBox(10 * 12, "New Customers",
               icon = icon("users")),

        valueBox(10 * 4, "New Orders",
               icon = icon("truck"),
               color="maroon"),

        valueBox(10 * 29, "Views",
               icon = icon("eye"),
               color="yellow")

)
```

The default color for these boxes is blue. So, if we do not set the color argument, the box will be blue:

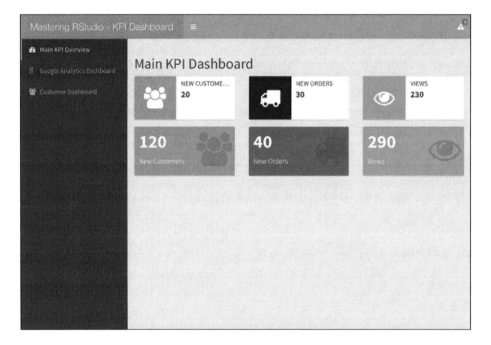

Building your own KPI dashboard

Let's imagine we are working for a company called *FantasticFutureTec*. This company manufactures and sells products such as Hoverboards, Lightsabers, Neuralizers, and all the cool stuff from the future, which we would like to have right now. FantasticFutureTec is a pure online business, which means people can buy their products on the company website only.

We get a job to build a central company dashboard with all the relevant key performance indicators. Of course, we create this dashboard with R, RStudio, the Shiny framework, and the `shinydashboard` package.

Creating our data architecture

First of all, we need to bring the expressed requirements and their feasibility under one roof. FantasticFutureTec uses Google Analytics as a website analytics tool, and furthermore, writes all customer details automatically from the website into a MySQL database. The current product inventory gets manually written into a Google Sheets file. The company is also very active on Twitter. Therefore, it is important to access Twitter data.

Since the MySQL database with the customer data is our own, we will directly access it from our Shiny app. Twitter, Google Analytics, and Sheets are not our own tools, therefore it is desired that we import the data from these services into the company's business Dropbox. This Dropbox acts as a data storage system, and also as a backup service for our datasets. In the case of the Twitter data, the Dropbox solution also helps to build a data history, since you are not able to extract historical data from Twitter. So, for our specific setup, we have five different data sources that we need to access.

The whole process should work like this:

- We need to extract the desired data form our given data sources
- Then, we need to transform the datasets into our desired format and space
- We need to at least be able to load the right data in the right format

This described process is called **Extract, Transform, Load**; which is abbreviated to **ETL**. ETL is nowadays a very important process with regard to data movement, database management, and data warehousing. In fact, we will build a simple (and very small) data warehouse to power our planned dashboard.

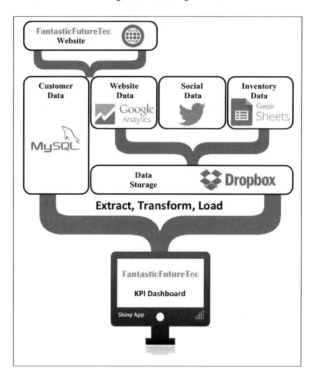

The data sources and storage layout plan might look complex at first glance, but with your knowledge of R, Shiny, and RStudio, you are already equipped to make this work. Of course, this data and app setup is only one of many, many possibilities. If there is an R package or API, you can connect every database, service, and tool, which is generating data with your Shiny dashboard app.

Sketching the look of our dashboard

In the first part of this chapter, we have learned how to build dashboards with R by taking advantage of the `shinydashboard` package. Now, it is time to sketch the desired dashboard of our company. Creating such a visualization will help us get a better view of possible bottlenecks and important cornerstones. On the other hand, we can discuss the first draft with our stakeholders, and again, catch some useful feedback.

The following figure is the draft for the main KPI dashboard:

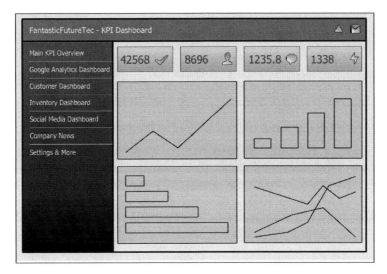

In this sketch, we can see the desired dashboard structure, each planned dashboard, and the structure of the **Main KPI Overview** dashboard with value and chart boxes. These boxes should display the most important metrics of each of the single-service dashboards.

Transferring our plan into R code

Now that we've put in a lot of thought and made a reasonable plan for the data architecture and appearance of the entire dashboard application, it is time to transfer the whole plan into R code. So, let's get back to RStudio. We will create a new Shiny application, using what you have learned in the Shiny chapter.

Considering a file and folder structure

An extensive code project, such as our planned company dashboard, can quickly lead to thousands of lines of code. In order to not lose track of such a project, it makes sense to prepare a reasonable file and folder structure beforehand. Therefore, let's brainstorm to find a great file and folder structure.

Basically, we already have the `ui.R` and `server.R` files. Thinking back to the diagram with the planned data structure, it also makes sense to outsource the extraction of all the data from the given sources into a new file. We will call this file `import.R`, But there is a bottleneck. Before we can extract, transform, and load any data from the sources, we need to authenticate ourselves with the related services to obtain the permission needed to access all the data from R.

Since we need to build simple applications to get the so-called tokens and secrets needed to communicate with the API of a service, we will also create a file called `auth.R`. This file will store all the sensible authentication information such as passwords, tokens, and more. Furthermore, it will store all obtained tokens and authentication information in a folder called `auth`. All imported data will be stored in a local data folder to make the app faster. As explained earlier, we will also store the data from Twitter, Google Analytics, and Sheets in the company's Dropbox. But loading the data directly from Dropbox into our Shiny app depends on the file size, and a general delay of the Dropbox downloading makes the process a little bit slow.

Overall, we need to load a lot of different R packages, each with diverse purposes. Therefore, we create a file called `libs.R`, which will then be sourced within each one of our files. When you are in the development process, you often need to try a lot of things, and maybe you need to test several libraries for the same purpose, for example, to find the best package, or to check if a package still works.

By using the approach of a central file for all needed R packages, you only need to maintain one place and not several files. But, in general, this is of course a matter of taste.

The logic of our data architecture and therefore the first step, the data extraction process, is now grossly transferred into R files. Next, we need to transfer the look of our dashboard app. As stated, the basic files, `ui.R` and `server.R`, are already present. In principle, these two files must handle the complete transformation and loading process of our data architecture logic along with their general tasks. Therefore, we will outsource each transformation and the loading process of each specific dashboard into our own R file. All these dashboard files are placed logically in the folder named dashboards.

In summary, after consideration our final files and folder structure will look like this:

Accessing our data sources

After all our planning and preparation, we should now get down to business.
In the following sections, you will learn how to access our data sources with R.

MySQL – the customer data

First of all, we want to access our customer data, which is stored in our database.
This MySQL database is remotely running as an instance on **Amazon Web Services**
(**AWS**).

For this task, we will use the RMySQL package that can be downloaded from CRAN.
This package acts as a database interface and a MySQL driver for R. There are a few
options to connect with the MySQL driver; one way is demonstrated as follows:

```
mySQLcon <- dbConnect(RMySQL::MySQL(),
        dbname = "customerdata",
        host = "customerdata.aaa.eu-central-1.rds.amazonaws.com",
        user = "xxxxxx", password = "xxxxxx")

mySQLtable <- "customerData"
```

```
mySQLquery <- sprintf("SELECT * FROM %s", mySQLtable)
mySQLdata <- dbGetQuery(mySQLcon, mySQLquery)
write.csv(mySQLdata, file = "data/customerDF.csv")
dbDisconnect(mySQLcon)
```

After storing the needed connection information, which is the database name, the host address, the username, and the password, we are able to open a direct connection with our database. With the function, `dbListTable()`, and the stored connection access, `mySQLcon`, we can easily read the existing tables. In our case, there is only one table, which is called **customerData**:

```
> dbListTables(mySQLcon)
[1] "customerData"
```

After assigning the table name to the variable, `mySQLtable`, we use a function to get all the data from the table into a new variable called `mySQLquery`. This can be done with the `sprintf` function and the SQL command for selecting everything, `SELECT * FROM %S`.

Next, we combine the MySQL connection variable and the query variable to download all the data into R. The data then gets written into a `.csv` file and stored in the data folder. Don't forget to close the MySQL connection at the end. With `head(mySQLdata)`, you can directly check the dataset:

```
> head(mySQLdata)
  id first_name last_name              email   company street_name street_number           city
1  1     Gloria  Marshall  gmarshall0@furl.net   Wikibox      Shopko            80      Jiangchuan
2  2       Jose      Cruz     jcruz1@usgs.gov   Flipbug       Barby           585  Nueva Vida Sur
3  3      Maria    Martin mmartin2@unicef.org Realbridge     Del Sol             1          Sufang
4  4      Helen    Little hlittle3@eventbrite.com Photobug   Ludington             4         Hongqi
5  5    Charles     Henry   chenry4@youku.com   Zoomdog     Mayfield         89501           Jetak
6  6      Carol     Ellis  cellis5@wikia.com   Centizu    Arrowood            41          Yamaga
```

Dropbox – our data storage system

Since we want to store all the accessed data of Twitter, Google Analytics, and Sheets into our company's Dropbox, we need to connect with this storage service from R. To do this, we take advantage of the `rdrop2` package, which provides programmatic access to Dropbox from R. This package is also on CRAN and can be installed in the usual way.

First of all, we need to authenticate with Dropbox. In fact, it is a very easy process; the following code is quite sufficient:

```
dropboxToken <- drop_auth() # opens a browser window
saveRDS(dropboxToken, "auth/dropboxToken.rds")
```

Please be careful, since you and everyone with this token can access your whole Dropbox account:

Now you can easily upload and download data from Dropbox using the functions, `drop_get()` and `drop_upload()`. There is also a function called `drop_read_csv()`, which makes it possible to read data into R on-the-fly (which means without storing it). It is recommended that you pass the Dropbox token to each function of the `rdrop2` package in order for it to work within the Shiny framework. This can be applied with the following code:

```
dropboxToken <- readRDS("auth/dropboxToken.rds ")
drop_acc(dtoken = dropboxToken)
```

Google Analytics – the website data

The website of FantasticFutureTec uses Google Analytics, which is clearly the world's most used website analytics tool. Therefore, there are several R packages that promise to enable a connection with this tool. We will use a package called `ganalytics`, since this library delivers easy and fast authentication. Furthermore, it enables you to query the Google Analytics core reporting, real-time, multi-channel funnel, and management APIs, as well as the Google Tag Manager API.

The `ganalytics` package is not on CRAN; therefore, you need to install it via GitHub and with the help of the `devtools` package:

```
install.packages("devtools")
devtools::install_github("jdeboer/ganalytics")
```

Now you need to create a Google API application to obtain your Client ID and Client Secret to connect and authenticate R with your desired Google APIs. Go to `https://console.developers.google.com/project` and create a new project. Click on your created project and navigate to **APIs & auth**. Then click on **APIs** and then on **Analytics API**, which can be found under the headline **Advertising APIs**. Hit the blue **Enable API** button and the first step is done. Now, head over to the **Credentials** page, click on the **Add credentials** button, and choose **OAuth 2.0 client ID**:

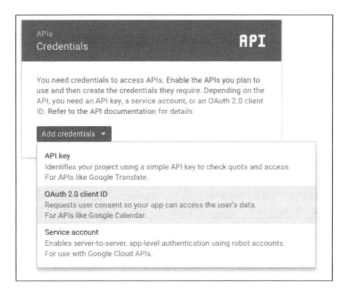

Next, you need to choose **Other** as the **Application** type, but before you can do this, you need to create an **OAuth consent** screen. Here you just need to enter a name for you app as a minimal setup. Copy the Client ID and the Secret, and you are down. In our code, the authentication looks like this:

```
gaToken <- GoogleApiCreds(
             userName = "your@email.com",
             list(
               client_id = "your client ID",
               client_secret = "your client secret")
             )

save(gaToken, file = "auth/gaToken")
```

In order to complete the authentication process, you need to get the Google Analytics `View ID` of your website. Then, enter the following R code:

```
myQuery <- GaQuery(your_view_id, gaToken)
GetGaData(myQuery)
```

A browser window opens and you need to allow access:

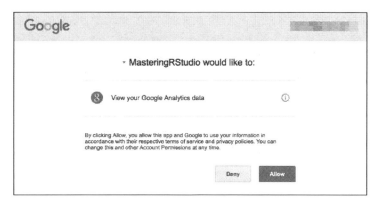

You have finished the authentication and you can now extract all the data you would like from Google Analytics into R. A possible data extraction could look like this:

```
load("auth/gaToken") # loading the Google Analytics token

query <- GaQuery(view = "XXXXXX", gaToken)

# Get the number of daily sessions
DateRange(query) <- c("2015-03-01", "2015-05-31")
Metrics(query) <- c("sessions","pageviews","sessionDuration")
Dimensions(query) <- c("date", "dayOfWeek", "hour", "isMobile")
query_result <- GetGaData(query)

write.csv(query_result, file = "data/gaDF.csv") # store a local copy

drop_upload("data/gaDF.csv", dest = "Dashboard_Data") # Dropbox upload
```

Twitter – the social data

Our company, FantasticFutureTec, uses Twitter intensively; on the one hand, for marketing campaigns, and on the other hand, to maintain direct contact with our customers. Thus, it is very important to show Twitter metrics in our dashboard. Since Twitter does not make it possible to extract historical data, we take advantage of our storing solution, Dropbox, to start saving historical data.

To connect with Twitter, we will use the `twitteR` package, which can be downloaded from CRAN. In order to let R communicate with Twitter, and to access the data you need again, create a simple application. Head over to `https://apps.twitter.com`, log in with your Twitter account, and click on the **Create New App** button:

After the fast and easy setup, you will be able to get the *Consumer Key* (*API Key*), the *Consumer Secret* (*API Secret*), the *Access Token*, and finally, the *Access Token Secret*.

We will do the whole `OAuth` authentication handshake again in our `auth.R` file:

```
tw_oauth <- setup_twitter_oauth(
        # API Key
        "zvMjVAv8kGlcfh1eDGtN2TUlh",
        # API Secret
        "a6eFOQVgcMx1FD4jX5QPmDpjaAKPiYoIc3KN5pGvKhJlTig77b",
        # Access token
        "140772912-N6rcE4cYeq0AFiGNhjBykkOU3KuDIkdhemZaGOCL",
        # Access secret
        "QlGKa8Z4lyMHEjdTbwtvisOYKZSbHaHhp8kgXsYLJl14g")


tw_oauth <- get("oauth_token", twitteR:::oauth_cache)

save(tw_oauth, file = "auth/tw_oauth")
```

The process directly leads `OAuth` authentication into your RStudio console, instead of opening a browser window and so on. Choose your authentication type and you are ready to get your Twitter data.

As stated, we need to build a data history; therefore, we will create a simple procedure in our `import.R` file to download the latest tweets and add the new ones to an existing file with the tweets that we extracted before:

```
load("auth/tw_oauth")

# return the last 1000 tweets
tweets_new <- userTimeline("Twitter_Username", n = 1000)

tweetsDF_new <- twListToDF(tweets_new)
# now we have the latest tweets including text, favorited,
favoriteCount,
# replyToSN (user name), created (Date/Time), truncated, replyToSID
(ID),
# id (of the tweet), replyToUID, statusSource, screenName,
retweetCount,
# isRetweet, retweeted, long, lat

# get the old tweets stored in dropbox
tweets_old <- drop_get("Dashboard_Data/tweetsDF.csv")
# just a temporary fix till drop_get works!
tweets_old <- drop_read_csv("Dashboard_Data/tweetsDF.csv")
# delete X column
tweets_old <- tweets_old[,!(names(tweets_old) %in% "X")]

# add the new tweets to the old tweets
new_tweets <- rbind(tweets_old, tweetsDF_new)

# filter the duplicated tweet
tweetsDF <- new_tweets[!duplicated(new_tweets[,c('id')]),]

# save the lastest version in the local data folder
write.csv(tweetsDF_new, file = "data/tweetsDF.csv")

# upload the latest version to dropbox
drop_upload("data/tweetsDF.csv", dest = "Dashboard_Data")
```

As a result, you now have a growing data frame with a lot of Twitter information.

Google Sheets – the inventory data

Last but not least, we want to connect R with Google Sheets, since the current inventory information gets manually stored in such a sheet. To make this possible, we use the package, `googlesheets`, which can be installed from CRAN.

The authentication process is dead simple. We authorize by using OAuth2:

```
# Give googlesheets the permission to access your google drive
gs_auth()
```

This will open the well-known browser window, where you need to allow access.

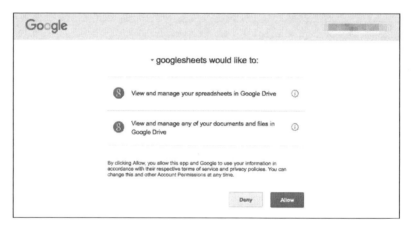

Now, you can access every existing sheet in your account. Furthermore, you can create new files, delete them, and make use of many more functions. In fact, the `googlesheets` package makes it possible to manage nearly all sheets options directly from R.

In your case, we just want to read the current inventory of FantasticFutureTec into our dashboard. To do so, the following R code in our `import.R` catches the data from the Google Sheet, stores it locally, and of course, uploads the file to our Dropbox:

```
inventoryData <- gs_title("InventoryData") %>%
        gs_download(ws = "current_stock", # access the worksheet
                    overwrite = TRUE, # overwrite the outdated file
                    to = "data/inventoryDF.csv")

# upload the latest version to dropbox
drop_upload("data/inventoryDF.csv", dest = "Dashboard_Data")
```

That's all. You can now retrieve your current product stock whenever you want to.

Putting it all together

We have now fully implemented our planned data architecture with R. Specifically, we had started with slightly differing authentication procedures for our desired data sources, and then we moved ahead with the mentioned process of extracting, transforming, and loading the right data into R. The next step is to display the data in the dashboard as we have sketched it.

In the first part of this chapter, you already learned how to set up a dashboard with R and the `shinydashboard` package. This includes the general structure elements of a dashboard, as well as how to create the different types of boxes needed to display the data.

As mentioned in the files and folder section, we want to create an individual R file for each of the dashboards. This plan leads to the fact that we have a better overview and code structure, otherwise, we have to implement code in three files: `mainDashboard.R`, `ui.R`, and `server.R`. Of course, you can also skip the `mainDashboard.R` file and add all your code to the `ui.R` and `server.R` files, but as mentioned, if you write a lot of code lines, you can quickly lose the overview.

Of course, we cannot display how we write the code for all the planned dashboards and their data boxes. Therefore, we show in the following section, by example, the dashboard for the main KPI overview, and specifically, how to create a box that displays the retweets and favorites of our Twitter account per day, in an interactive manner.

Creating the Twitter engagement box

The final Twitter box will look like the following screenshot. As we discussed it is an interplay of the three files: `mainDashboard.R`, `ui.R`, and `server.R`:

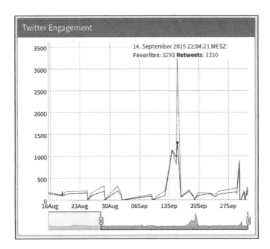

The relevant code for our `mainDashboard.R` file is the following lines:

```
############################ Loading The Libraries
source("libs.R")

############################ Loading The Datasets
loadTwitterData <- function() {
        twitterDF <- read.csv(file = "data/tweetsDF.csv",
                              header = TRUE,
                              sep = ",")
        return(twitterDF)
}

############################ Twitter Engagement Box
twitterEngagement <- function(){

        twitterDF <- loadTwitterData()

        # Tweet aggregation
        tweetData <- ddply(
                twitterDF,
                ~created,
                summarise,
                favorites = sum(favoriteCount),
                retweets = sum(retweetCount)
        )

        tweetData$created <- as.POSIXct( tweetData$created)

        # dygraph needs a time-series, zoo makes it easier
        ts_data <- zoo(tweetData[,c("favorites","retweets")],
                      order.by = tweetData[,'created'])

        start <- Sys.Date() - 450
        end <- Sys.Date() - 1

        dygraph(ts_data, main=str_to_title(paste(""))) %>%
                dyRangeSelector(dateWindow = c(start, end)) %>%
                dySeries("favorites", label = str_to_
title("favorites")) %>%
                dySeries("retweets", label = str_to_title("retweets"))
}
```

So, the `mainDashboard.R` function first loads `libs.R`, which is the central library file. Then, we load the locally stored Twitter data into a function called `loadTwitterData`. Next, we create the box content by using our previously created data loading function to aggregate the needed Retweet and Favorite data. Then, we take advantage of the `dygraphs` package to create an interactive line chart. The whole process gets stored in a new function called `twitterEngagement`. This function now gets called in the `ui.R` and the `server.R` functions in the `shinydashboard` structure:

```
ui.R
############################ Loading Helper Files
source("libs.R")
source("dashboards/mainDashboard.R")
# [...]
                box(
                        title = "Twitter Engagement",
                        status = "primary",
                        solidHeader = TRUE,
                        collapsible = FALSE,
                        dygraphOutput("twitterEngagement")


                )
```

As you can see, after sourcing our files, `libs.R` and `mainDashboard.R`, we build a box around the function `twitterEngagement`, which holds the retweet and favorite data:

```
server.R
############################ Loading Helper Files

source("libs.R")
source("dashboards/mainDashboard.R")

shinyServer(function(input, output) {

# [...]
############################## Main Dashboard

        output$twitterEngagement <- renderDygraph({

                twitterEngagement()
        })
```

As seen in `ui.r`, we are sourcing the needed helper files and then creating the server output function for the `dygraph` object that displays our Twitter engagement numbers.

And, that's it. A finished **Main KPI Overview** dashboard could look like this one:

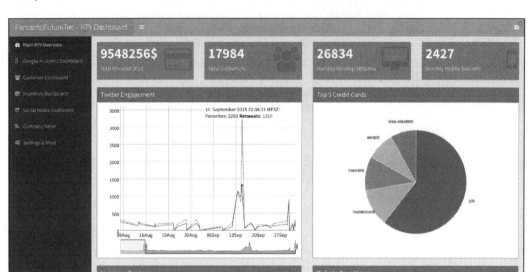

Summary

In this chapter, you have learned how to take advantage of the useful `shinydashboard` packages, which extensively enhance the Shiny app framework to build professional dashboards. In the beginning, we dedicated ourselves fully to the general layout structure of a Shiny dashboard. You have learned how to set up the header, sidebars, and body. Furthermore, you learned how to create different data boxes and options to customize the whole appearance of a dashboard application.

In the second part of this chapter, we imagined that we work for a fictional company called FantasticFutureTec. It was our task to build a useful KPI dashboard for our company by using all of our current knowledge about R, RStudio, and the Shiny framework. We started this by thinking about the right data architecture and ETL processes to obtain the data from our sources. Next, we drew up a fast dashboard sketch to visualize our final ideas and the planned look and feel. Thereafter, it was hands-on work and we showed you how to fulfill an authentication process with specific R packages in order to download your data from a MySQL database, Twitter, Google Analytics, and Sheets, as well as how to upload data to Dropbox. As an example, we built a data box with Twitter engagement data. Finally, we showed you our version of a main KPI overview dashboard, with data from all the sources we have connected to R.

In the next chapter, we will show you how to create R packages with RStudio. The chapter will explain, step-by-step, how to start from a minimal package setup, and get to a fully working R package with all the details and files needed to get published on CRAN.

7
Package Development in RStudio

This chapter covers:

- Understanding the structure of R packages
- Creating package projects with RStudio
- Documenting your functions with R documentations files and **roxygen2**
- Building and testing your package

Understanding R packages

Packages are the most important aspect of the R language to create reproducible code and analysis. They are collections of R functions, data, and compiled code in a very standardized way. This makes it very easy to share them across R users and add new elements from others to already installed packages to take your R analysis to the next level. These packages can help to solve many tasks with R without having to write every single line of code on your own. If you take machine-learning algorithms for example, you can use implementations of these algorithms without the need to implement them line-by-line. Packages are mostly developed in R, but can also contain elements written in other languages such as Java or C++.

R already comes with some preinstalled packages like the `base` package, which consists of the basic functions to make R a real language. There are many package resources on the Internet. The most important of these libraries for R is **Comprehensive R Archive Network (CRAN)**. It currently has nearly 7,000 packages in its repository. These packages can be sorted by *Task Views* such as **Econometrics** or **Graphics**. This gives you the possibility of filtering the packages based on your current needs.

Developing packages became very easy with RStudio. It offers many functions that make the creation of a package possible with just a few clicks. But, nevertheless, there are some things we have to pay attention to when developing our own package.

Understanding the package structure

Packages have a very well defined structure. This structure can make them look a little bit confusing at first, but after understanding the basics of package development, this structure can make programming with R much more efficient.

Basically, an R package consists of seven parts and the package itself can be stored as source, bundle, or binary on disk:

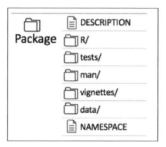

Following list describes all the seven parts of the R package:

- **Description**: Basic information of the package.
- **R:** This is the folder for all your R code. In here you can place all scripts and functions that should be made available with this package.
- **Test**: Test scripts are placed here, which can help you to validate the results and the functionality of your implemented functions in the package.
- **Man**: A subdirectory for documentation files.
- **Vignettes**: A more detailed and more scenario-oriented version of the documentation.

- **Data**: This folder can contain datasets that are needed for the execution of the package.
- **Namespace**: This is the definition of which functions from the package are made available to the user when the package is loaded.

Installing devtools

Devtools is a package written Hadley Wickham and Winston Chang, who are both part of the team developing RStudio. The package calls itself a *collection of package development tools* and aims to make package development in R much easier.

You can install it via CRAN with:

```
install.packages("devtools")
```

The tools included in devtools can help you during the whole process of package development and with sharing your package after development. It can also help you to install packages that are not on CRAN but on GitHub, for example.

Devtools focus on building the package by using the existing conventions to deliver a standardized way of package development. This also makes it easy to distribute your package. The functions included in the devtools package will be used often during this chapter.

Building packages with RStudio

RStudio combines the power of devtools with its GUI, which makes the development of your own packages very easy and manageable with just a few clicks.

Creating a new package project with RStudio

To create a new package with RStudio, just click on **File** | **New Project...** and select **New Directory**.

Then you can select **R Package** from the upcoming menu:

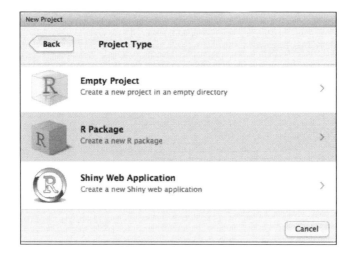

Now you have to set the necessary parameters for your R package. These include the type of the package, the package name, the option to create a package based on source files, and to create the package project as a subdirectory of another directory.

Furthermore, you can check the options for creating a Git repository or for using **Packrat** with your project.

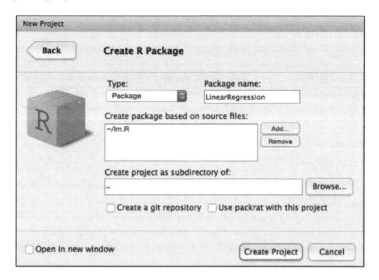

If you want to create a package just containing R code, you should select the type to be **Package**. However, if you want to create a package that also uses C++ code, you should choose **Package w/ Rcpp** as it automatically sets up all necessary dependencies for using the Rcpp package that helps you to access or extend R objects at the deep C++ level.

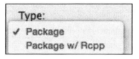

Looking at the created files

After we save our project, RStudio automatically creates the necessary files and the file structures. This includes the folders and the DESCRIPTION and NAMESPACE file.

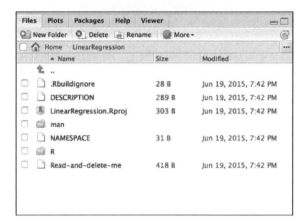

When the package is created, a new file with the name hello.R will be opened in the source pane. This file includes a basic hello world example in R and some useful shortcuts for RStudio when you create a package.

```
 1  # Hello, world!
 2  #
 3  # This is an example function named 'hello'
 4  # which prints 'Hello, world!'.
 5  #
 6  # You can learn more about package authoring with RStudio at:
 7  #
 8  #     http://r-pkgs.had.co.nz/
 9  #
10  # Some useful keyboard shortcuts for package authoring:
11  #
12  #     Build and Reload Package:  'Cmd + Shift + B'
13  #     Check Package:             'Cmd + Shift + E'
14  #     Test Package:              'Cmd + Shift + T'
15
16  hello <- function() {
17    print("Hello, world!")
18  }
19
```

The shortcuts for package authoring are:

- Build and reload package (*Cmd* + *Shift* + *B*)
- Check package (*Cmd* + *Shift* + *E*)
- Test package (*Cmd* + *Shift* + *T*)

Using Packrat with a project

During the creation of our package, we saw the option to use Packrat with this project. Packrat is a very important tool when you make your package as reproducible as possible. It basically stores all the packages needed and so creates a private package library. When you load this package, R will automatically restore the needed packages from this private library.

We can set up our project to use Packrat right when you create it. In the dialogue box we just have to check the **Use packrat with this project** checkbox. RStudio will then set up our private library and fill it with the packages.

When we look at the package pane, we can see the content of our packrat library. This private library has an extra column showing the version included in the private library and the source of this library.

Name	Description	Version	Packrat	Sou...
Packrat Library				
digest	Create cryptographic hash digests of R objects	0.6.4	0.6.4	CRAN
evaluate	Parsing and evaluation tools that provide more details than the default.	0.5.5	0.5.5	CRAN
formatR	Format R Code Automatically	0.10	0.10	CRAN
highr	Syntax highlighting for R	0.3	0.3	CRAN
knitr	A general-purpose package for dynamic report generation in R	1.6	1.6	CRAN
markdown	Markdown rendering for R	0.7	0.7	CRAN
mime	Map filenames to MIME types	0.1.1	0.1.1	CRAN
packrat	A Dependency Management System for Projects and their R Package Dependencies	0.4.4	0.4.4	CRAN
stringr	Make it easier to work with strings.	0.6.2	0.6.2	CRAN
testthat	Testthat code. Tools to make testing fun :)	0.8.1	0.8.1	CRAN

In the screenshot, there are also packages included in the private library because Packrat was turned on in an existing project. You can do this in the project options by checking the box **Use packrat with this project**.

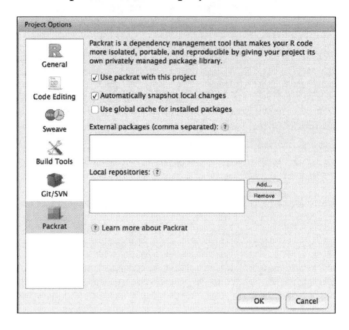

When we install new packages in the current project, Packrat will automatically add these to our private library. On the other hand, if we uninstall packages, Packrat will not delete them instantly because of safety reasons. It will ask for our permission to remove them from the library.

We can find other handy functions in the Packrat menu in the packages pane. Here we can, for example, find the **Clean Unused Packages...** function that automatically removes packages from our private library that are no longer used.

Writing the documentation for a package

As mentioned, the man folder contains all the necessary documentation files. It consists of R documentation files, which can be recognized by their file extension Rd.

Documenting our R code as well as possible is very important. It gives other people the chance to understand our functions and how to actually implement them into their workflow.

After creating the project, this folder contains a basic documentation file for the project in general. The R documentation files are written in the so-called Rd-format, which is closely related to LaTeX and can be processed into various output formats including HTML or plain text.

Creating Rd documentation files

We have two ways to create an Rd file:

- We can call the prompt() function in the R console and send as an argument the function we want to create a documentation file for. So the function call prompt(lm) would create the lm.Rd file in our current working directory. We can then move this file to the man folder.

- We can simply navigate to **File | New | R Documentation**.

This will create an Rd file with some dummy content in it.

We can then choose a name for the file and a preset template for the files layout. There we can choose between function and dataset. So we can also create documentation files for attached datasets.

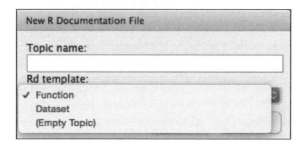

Looking at an example documentation file

The following is a slightly modified excerpt from the load function of the base R package:

```
\File src/library/base/man/load.Rd
% Part of the R package, http://www.R-project.org
% Copyright 1995-2014 R Core Team
% Distributed under GPL 2 or later

\name{load}
\alias{load}
\title{Reload Saved Datasets}
\description{
    Reload datasets written with the function \code{save}.
  }
\usage{
  load(file, envir = parent.frame(), verbose = FALSE)
  }
\arguments{
    \item{file}{a (readable binary-mode) \link{connection} or a
character string
                    giving the name of the file to load (when \
link{tilde expansion}
                                                           is
done).}
    \item{envir}{the environment where the data should be loaded.}
    \item{verbose}{should item names be printed during loading?}
  }
\details{
```

```
    \code{load} can load \R objects saved in the current or any
earlier
    format.  It can read a compressed file (see \code{\link{save}})
    directly from a file or from a suitable connection (including a
call
                                                        to \code{\
link{url}}).

  }

\value{
    A character vector of the names of objects created, invisibly.
  }
\section{Warning}{
    Saved \R objects are binary files, even those saved with
    \code{ascii = TRUE}, so ensure that they are transferred without
    conversion of end of line markers.  \code{load} tries to detect
such a
    conversion and gives an informative error message.

 }
\examples{
  ## save all data
  xx <- pi # to ensure there is some data
  save(list = ls(all = TRUE), file= "all.RData")
  rm(xx)

  ## restore the saved values to the current environment
  local({
       load("all.RData")
       ls()
    })

  \dontrun{
    con <- url("http://some.where.net/R/data/example.rda")
    ## print the value to see what objects were created.
    print(load(con))
    close(con) # url() always opens the connection
    }}
\keyword{file}
```

We can use it to get a first idea of the structure of such an R documentation file. The file starts with a header giving information about the file name and basic copyright information. After a short description of the function, there is information about how to use the function we are documenting and what arguments it expects. Then there is the **details** section providing more context to the function calls.

The file ends with an examples section showing small code snippets showing how to apply this function in a workflow.

If we click on the **Preview** button above the text editor pane in RStudio, the file will be converted to HTML:

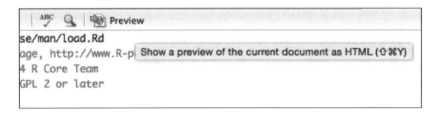

The output then looks like the standard documentation file we are used to when working with R.

> **Guidelines for Rd files**
>
> When we write R documentation files, we should stick to some suggested guidelines. These can increase the readability of our documents and make our package easier to use. We can find more information about these guidelines here: http://developer.r-project.org/Rds.html.

Adding examples

The best way to understand functions is to read through some example code. So most, if not all, packages contain some lines of example code that show a certain function call, mostly with dummy data.

When we add an examples section to our documentation file, this section has to include executable R code. This code can also have the function of test code, which can be executed in the process of testing the package. Further, this code will be run, if the `example()` function for a package is called.

We can add example code by simply adding an example section to our documentation file and placing the R code between the brackets.

```
\examples{

data(cats, package="MASS")

linearModel <- lm(Hwt~Hwt*Sex, data=cats)

summary(linearModel)

}
```

The examples section can have two special markup commands: `dontrun` and `dontshow`.

dontrun

This version makes the code inside brackets not be executed by the tests or the `example()` function. This can be applied, for example, `for` functions, which need access to the Internet or user interaction while they are being executed.

dontshow

The code in here will be executed by the tests, but it will not be shown to the user opening the documentation file. This way we can add additional tests, which are not valuable for the documentation of the package.

Editing the DESCRIPTION file

The purpose of the DESCRIPTION file is to store metadata and information that our package needs to be installed and to be used. It is one of the most, if not the most, central files of our package. For example, RStudio or devtools use this file to recognize a directory as a package. Further, CRAN and R use it to handle packages metadata and versioning.

When we create a project with RStudio, the DESCRIPTION file will automatically contain a general structure and give us a small overview of the information that should be included in this file.

```
Package: LinearRegression
Type: Package
Title: What the package does (short line)
Version: 1.0
Date: 2015-06-19
Author: Who wrote it
Maintainer: Who to complain to <yourfault@somewhere.net>
Description: More about what it does (maybe more than one line)
License: What license is it under?
```

The DESCRIPTION file uses the **Debian Control Format** with the simple structure that each line contains a field name and a corresponding value. If we have to use sentences that are longer than one line, for example for the description, we have to use a space or tab in the new line.

General information

The general fields that should be included in the file explain themselves. Enter a good title for your package and a good description.

The DESCRIPTION file also contains an **Author** and a **Maintainer** field. These fields should be filled with plain text. But we can also add an Author@R field, which combines these fields in a machine-readable format. We have to create an object of the class person. This object can be created with the help of c(). In this object we can define several roles such as:

- aut: For authors
- cre: For package maintainers
- ctb: For contributors
- cph: For copyright holders

An example would look like this:

```
Authors@R: c(
  person( "Julian", "Hillebrand",email = "julian@mastering-rstudio.
com", role = "cre"),

  person( "Maximilian", "Nierhoff", email = "max@mastering-rstudio.
com", role "aut"))
```

Dependencies

We should add the packages to the DESCRIPTION file that our package needs to be used. When people call our package in R, these packages will automatically load into the environment. We can also add a minimum version number to the package names. Basically, we have two different options: **Imports** and **Suggests**. The packages we define with **Imports** are necessary to use the package and the package does not work without them, whereas the packages defined with **Suggests** are optional. So the package also runs without them, but it can take advantage of them when they are loaded.

An example would look like:

```
Imports:
  plyr(>= 1.7),
  MASS

Suggests:
  gtable(>= 0.1)
  reshape2
```

License

Defining the license we want to distribute our package which is as easy as adding the other parts. But here the hard part is to choose the right license, as it is very important to include license information as R is based on the *free or open source software* concept and if we do not include a license, others might not be allowed to share or even use our package.

We can define the license in the DESCRIPTION file by adding an abbreviation of a standard open source license or we can add a pointer to a LICENSE file.

We can get a good overview of the different available licenses at http://www.r-project.org/Licenses/.

Understanding the namespaces of a package

Another important file is the NAMESPACE file. The content of this file, and the context of namespaces in R packages itself, is a more advanced topic. It does not matter that much when we develop packages for our own use. But we should pay attention to it when we want to distribute our packages to a broader audience.

There are many packages available for R and these packages include even more functions. So it is surely possible that some packages include functions with the same name. And if we have loaded both packages, R does not know which of these packages we mean with this function function call and will take the one from the package that was loaded last.

When we create our empty package project with RStudio, the NAMEPSACES file will contain the following line:

```
exportPattern("^[[:alpha:]]+")
```

This makes every function in the package available in the global environment, when the package is loaded, that does not start with a single period. This can be fine if we have a smaller package just for ourselves, but if we want to share our code with others, we should make sure that just the most important functions are exported and the others stay just for the internal use in the package.

> **Getting a closer look at NAMESPACES**
>
> If we want to dive deeper into the topic of namespaces, we should look in the namespaces section of the **r-project.org** manual: http://cran.r-project.org/doc/manuals/r-release/R-exts.html#Package-namespaces.

Building and checking a package

As we have seen before, RStudio makes many steps very easy when we want to build our own R package. RStudio also helps us with the finalizing steps of our package. These include building and testing our package and we can find the necessary options to perform these tasks in the build menu of RStudio.

These do not just help us as the final steps, but we also have to build and load our package a lot during the development process. This is the only way we can test all the functions of our package. To test our package, we should stick to the following steps:

1. Tweak our code and perform changes to our packages code base.
2. Build our package.
3. Install the package.
4. Unload the package.
5. Reload the package.

RStudio actually performs all these steps with the command **Build and Reload**.

We can see the output in the **Build** pane.

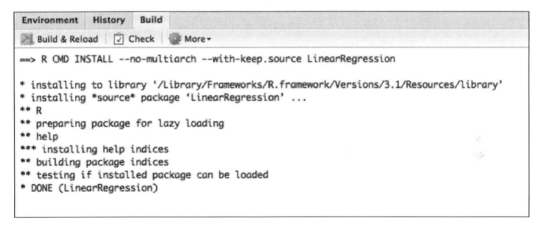

Checking a package

The Check Package function in the **Build** menu will check all dependencies of our package. This is very useful as it shows us exactly where errors in our package occurred during the testing procedure, which makes it easier to fix these errors.

```
* using session charset: UTF-8
* using option '--no-build-vignettes'
* checking for file 'LinearRegression/DESCRIPTION' ... OK
* checking extension type ... Package
* this is package 'LinearRegression' version '1.0'
* checking package namespace information ... OK
* checking package dependencies ... OK
* checking if this is a source package ... OK
* checking if there is a namespace ... OK
* checking for executable files ... OK
* checking for hidden files and directories ... OK
* checking for portable file names ... OK
* checking for sufficient/correct file permissions ... OK
* checking whether package 'LinearRegression' can be installed ... OK
* checking installed package size ... OK
* checking package directory ... OK
* checking DESCRIPTION meta-information ... OK
* checking top-level files ... OK
* checking for left-over files ... OK
* checking index information ... OK
* checking package subdirectories ... OK
* checking R files for non-ASCII characters ... OK
* checking R files for syntax errors ... OK
* checking whether the package can be loaded ... OK
* checking whether the package can be loaded with stated dependencies ... OK
```

Customizing the package build options

More advanced users can also customize the build and check functions in RStudio. There we can go to the project option under **Tools | Project Options** and select **Build Tools**. To get an overview of the the different options, for example for the check function, you can execute the following command in a terminal window: R CMD check -help.

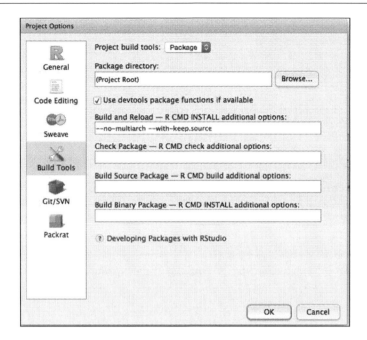

Using roxygen2 for package documentation

As seen before, the documentation of our package is very important but can also get very complex when our package reaches a certain size and number of different functions.

But an alternative to creating and editing all the documentation files on our own is using the roxygen2 package. It was developed by Hadley Wickham, Peter Danenberg, and Manuel Eugster.

The basic idea of roxygen2 is it to make it possible to describe functions directly in comments next to their definition in the code file. The roxygen2 package will then go through the code files and create the corresponding Rd files in the man folder.

Installing the roxygen2 package

The roxygen2 package is available on CRAN and can be installed in the R console with the following command:

```
install.packages("roxygen2")
```

If we want to have the latest development version from GitHub, we can install it with the devtools package:

```
devtools::install_github("klutometis/roxygen")
```

Generating Rd Files

The basic process for creating our package documentation with roxygen2 is:

1. Add our describing comments to our code files.
2. Call the function roxygenise() function from the roxygen2 package that converts our comments to Rd files.
3. The Rd files will then be converted to human readable files.

We can add our information for the roxygen2 package like we would add comments to our code. But to distinguish them from normal comments, roxygen comments start with #'. After adding this combination to one line, RStudio will automatically add these to the new line when we hit the enter button. This makes it very easy to add even longer roxygen comment sections.

As an example, we will take a simple function that transforms the input to a percentage value. As input, it accepts the number we want to transform as *x* and the number of digits *y* we want this number to have.

```
#' Transform values to percentage values
#'
#'@param x A number
#'@param y A number
#'@return The percentage value of \code{x} with \code{y} digits.
#'@examples
#'percent(0.56733, 2)
#'percent(0.04757213, 4)

 percent <- function(x,y) {

   percent <- round(x * 100 , digits = y)
   result <- paste(percent, "%", sep = "")
   return(result)

 }
```

Normally, we write down what the function does in the first line; just a short summary of what this function is good for. Then we can add the parameters this function accepts as an input with the **@param** option.

After we added our function description, we can use the document function of the `devtools` package with:

```
devtools::document()
```

Or by hitting the key combination: *Ctrl/Cmd + Shift + D.*

The console will then output something like:

```
Updating LinearRegression documentation
Loading LinearRegression
First time using roxygen2 4.0. Upgrading automatically...
Writing percent.Rd
```

And create the file `percent.Rd`. This file contains the processed documentation information in the typical `.Rd` format. Roxygen also adds the information in which file this function was defined and so where we can find the raw documentation information.

```
% Generated by roxygen2 (4.1.0): do not edit by hand
% Please edit documentation in R/lm.R
\name{percent}
\alias{percent}
\title{Transform values to percentage values}
\usage{
percent(x, y)
}
\arguments{
\item{x}{A number}

\item{y}{A number}
}
\value{
The percentage value of \code{x} with \code{y} digits.
}
\description{
Transform values to percentage values
}
\examples{
percent(0.56733, 2)
percent(0.04757213, 4)
}
```

The output of this .Rd file then looks like the typical R documentation file. We can see how the information we added as a comment is now transformed into a headline and content of the file.

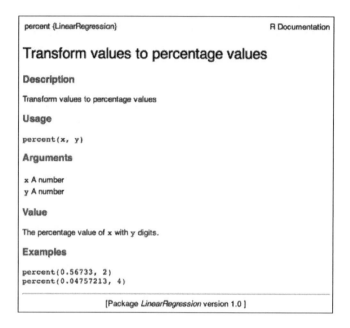

Testing a package

When we build a package, it is very important to test it. Packages can get very complex structures and this creates a high potential for bugs. The most basic way to test your package is to build and load it again and again and test all its functions simply by using them. But this only works up to a certain package size. If our package gets too big, we cannot test every single function after every change we made to the package.

The better way to test our packages when they reach a certain size is the testthat package, created by Hadley Wickham, who also created the devtools package. This package is available on CRAN, so we can simply install it with the install.packages() function.

Using testthat in a package

Before we can use `testthat` in your project, we have to call the `use_testthat()` function from the `devtools` package once. This function will set up all folders and dependencies and create the `tests` folder.

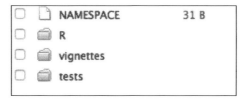

This folder includes a `testthat.R` file and the `testthat` folder, which will contain our test scripts.

We will now take a look at a sample `testthat` file:

```
library(stringr)
context("String length")

test_that("str_length is number of characters", {
  expect_equal(str_length("a"), 1)
  expect_equal(str_length("ab"), 2)
  expect_equal(str_length("abc"), 3)
})

test_that("str_length of factor is length of level", {
  expect_equal(str_length(factor("a")), 1)
  expect_equal(str_length(factor("ab")), 2)
  expect_equal(str_length(factor("abc")), 3)
})

test_that("str_length of missing is missing", {
  expect_equal(str_length(NA), NA_integer_)
  expect_equal(str_length(c(NA, 1)), c(NA, 1))
  expect_equal(str_length("NA"), 2)
})
```

As we can see in the sample test file from the `stringr` package, the test file starts with loading the package we want to test and adding a testing context. This is a description of what the following tests are about.

Then the tests follow. The `test_that()` function is called and the first argument is a string describing what will be tested in the following line. What then follows are the tests. The `test_that()` function can handle different test criteria.

- `expect_that(x, is_true() )`
- `expect_that(x, is_false() )`
- `expect_that(x, is_a(y) )`
- `expect_that(x, equals(y) )`
- `expect_that(x, is_equivalent_to(y) )`
- `expect_that(x, is_identical_to(y) )`
- `expect_that(x, matches(y) )`
- `expect_that(x, prints_text(y) )`
- `expect_that(x, shows_message(y) )`
- `expect_that(x, gives_warning(y) )`
- `expect_thatx, throws_error(y) )`

If you want to get more information about how to use the `testthat` package and how to write tests with it, you should visit Hadley Wickham's R packages website: `http://r-pkgs.had.co.nz/tests.html`.

Adding a dataset to a package

Packages are also used to deliver research and research results to people and make them reproducible. Therefore, it is often necessary to include a dataset in our R package. Many packages also use this possibility to include this data into their demo code, to give users the possibilities to execute a demo version of the package's functions instantly without the need to import your own data.

To include this data, R provides several options. The choice of the option depends on what kind of data we want to attach to the package and what this data will be used for.

The most common way is to include it in the `data` subdirectory. This way is often used when our dataset is used for the example code. Another way to include it is an `.rda` file in the `sysdata.rda` file. We can use this function if we do not want the package's users to have full access to these datasets.

The data files we can include in the package can be in three formats:

- R code
- Tables (.txt or .csv* files)
- Save() images (.RData or .rda files)

> ***CSV files**
>
> Please note, that the csv files in this context are not *normal* csv files. They have to be in a special format to be included this way. We can find more information about this format at: http://tools.ietf.org/html/rfc4180.

Creating .rda files

To create .rda files we can create them in R or load them into R and then call the save() function. This function will then save this data to an .rda file.

The following code shows how to create such a data file:

```
df = data.frame(matrix(rnorm(10), nrow = 5))
save(df, file = "dataFile.Rda")
```

This code will create the file dataFile.Rda, which can then be found in the home directory of our project.

These .Rda files can be loaded into the working environment simply by clicking on them. This will open a pop up where we can confirm that this RData file should be loaded.

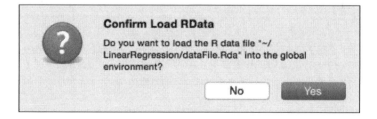

After loading the file into the environment, we can find it in the **Environment** panel. Then we can work with them like we are used to.

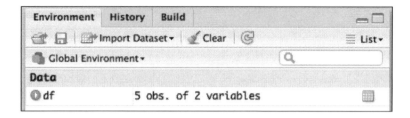

The compression with the `save()` function is also the best way when we want to ship very large datasets with our package.

Using LazyData with a package

As R has to load every dataset into the memory before it can be used, it is important, especially when we have bigger datasets, to use `LazyData` in our package. We can activate it by adding the following line to the `DESCRIPTION` file:

```
LazyData: true
```

Then, our datasets are not loaded into the memory until we really use them. This often saves a lot of memory and you should use `LazyData` in all packages that include data files.

Writing a package vignette with R markdown

When we develop our R package, we can also add documents in other formats than the `.Rd` format we talked about earlier. Normally we save them in the `inst/doc` folder in our package directory.

These documents are called **vignettes** and can be described as long-form documentation. These documents usually do not explain the package based on the functions, but on use cases or workflows we normally would use this package for. We can say that a vignette describes our package on a higher level and with more context than the classical documentation file. A definition accepted by many R users is: vignettes are optional supplemental documentation.

That is, they are in addition to the required boilerplate documentation for R functions and dataset. Vignettes are written in the spirit of sharing knowledge, and assisting new users in learning the purpose and use of a package.

Vignettes are included in many packages. We can take a look at the vignettes of our installed packages with:

```
browseVignettes()
```

This will open a web browser showing us a list of available vignettes.

```
                                              Vignettes found by "browseVignettes()"

Vignettes in package BradleyTerry2

    • Bradley-Terry models in R - PDF source R code

Vignettes in package car

    • Using car functions inside user functions - PDF source R code

Vignettes in package caret

    • A Short Introduction to the caret Package - PDF source R code

Vignettes in package colorspace

    • HCL-Based Color Palettes in R - PDF source R code

Vignettes in package data.table

    • Frequently asked questions - PDF source R code
    • Quick introduction - PDF source R code

Vignettes in package doMC

    • Getting Started with doMC and foreach - PDF source R code

Vignettes in package dplyr

    • Adding new database support to dplyr - HTML source R code
    • Databases - HTML source R code
    • Hybrid Evaluation - HTML source R code
    • Introduction to dplyr - HTML source R code
    • Memory usage - HTML source R code
    • Window functions - HTML source R code
```

For example, the package `data.table`, providing the data structure with the same name, has a vignette with the name *Introduction to the data.table package in R*. This is basically a tutorial showing us how to use the package and explaining all the elements step by step.

Introduction to the **data.table** package in R

Revised: October 2, 2014
(A later revision may be available on the homepage)

Introduction

This vignette is aimed at those who are already familiar with creating and subsetting `data.frame` in R. We aim for this quick introduction to be readable in **10 minutes**, briefly covering a few features: 1. Keys; 2. Fast Grouping; and 3. Fast *ordered* join.

Creation

Recall that we create a `data.frame` using the function `data.frame()`:

```
> DF = data.frame(x=c("b","b","b","a","a"),v=rnorm(5))
> DF

  x        v
1 b  0.1913554
2 b  1.2556559
3 b -0.3871878
4 a  0.7918896
5 a -0.8527794
```

A `data.table` is created in exactly the same way:

```
> DT = data.table(x=c("b","b","b","a","a"),v=rnorm(5))
> DT
```

Every vignette contains three elements:

- The original source file
- An HTML version of the vignette
- The corresponding R code

Before R version 3.0.0, we could just write these package vignette files in Sweave. Sweave is similar to LaTeX and sometimes pretty hard to understand. But now vignettes can also be written in other languages with the help of so-called *vignette engines*.

For example, the `knitr` package provides such an engine, which makes it possible to write vignette files in R markdown and then transform them to HTML files.

Creating vignette files

When we want to create our own vignette files, the best way to do it is using the `devtools` package. Load the package and call the `use_vignette()` function.

```
require(devtools)
use_vignettes("LinearRegressionHowTo")
```

The console output looks like:

```
> devtools::use_vignette("LinearRegressionHowTo")
Draft vignette created in /Users/julian/LinearRegression/vignettes/LinearRegressionHowTo.Rmd
```

This function will create the folder `vignettes` in our package `home` folder. In this folder we will find the `LinearRegressionHowTo.Rmd` file.

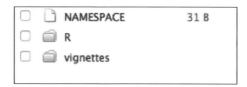

The function will also take care of all dependencies that have to be adjusted to replace the Sweave engine with the **knitr** engine for building vignettes.

This file will then contain dummy code. But this code gives us a good overview of how we can design our own vignette.

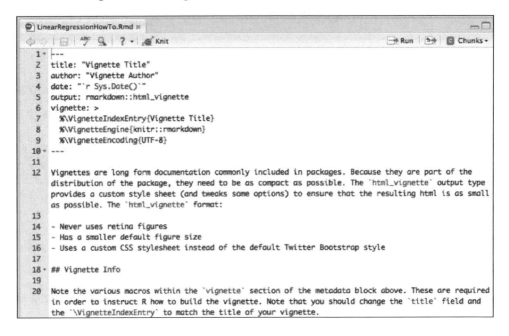

```
LinearRegressionHowTo.Rmd ×                                                    Run    Chunks ▾
                          ABC   Q   ? ▾   Knit
  1  ---
  2  title: "Vignette Title"
  3  author: "Vignette Author"
  4  date: "`r Sys.Date()`"
  5  output: rmarkdown::html_vignette
  6  vignette: >
  7    %\VignetteIndexEntry{Vignette Title}
  8    %\VignetteEngine{knitr::rmarkdown}
  9    %\VignetteEncoding{UTF-8}
 10  ---
 11
 12  Vignettes are long form documentation commonly included in packages. Because they are part of the
     distribution of the package, they need to be as compact as possible. The `html_vignette` output type
     provides a custom style sheet (and tweaks some options) to ensure that the resulting html is as small
     as possible. The `html_vignette` format:
 13
 14  - Never uses retina figures
 15  - Has a smaller default figure size
 16  - Uses a custom CSS stylesheet instead of the default Twitter Bootstrap style
 17
 18  ## Vignette Info
 19
 20  Note the various macros within the `vignette` section of the metadata block above. These are required
     in order to instruct R how to build the vignette. Note that you should change the `title` field and
     the `\VignetteIndexEntry` to match the title of your vignette.
```

The vignette documents written with R markdown contain three elements: the META information at the beginning of the document, the text formatted with markdown and the code examples formatted for `knitr`.

References for further information

Package development with R is a very complex topic, although it got much easier with the help of RStudio and packages such as devtools. If we want to go deeper in the package development, we can take a look at the following links:

- **Devtools Google Group**: `https://groups.google.com/forum/#!forum/rdevtools`

- **GitHub repository of devtools**: `https://github.com/hadley/devtools`

One of the most essential guides to package development is surely the manual on the r-project page: `http://cran.r-project.org/doc/manuals/r-release/R-exts.html`.

It explains nearly every aspect of the package development process in great detail.

If you made yourself familiar with package development in R and created a great package, you should think about sharing it with the whole R community by submitting it to CRAN. You can do it via an online form at `https://cran.r-project.org/submit.html`.

```
                        Submit package to CRAN

            Step 1                    Step 2                    Step 3
           (Upload)                (Submission)             (Confirmation)


Your name*:        [                    ]
Your email*:       [                    ]
Package*:          [ Choose File ] No file chosen
                   (*.tar.gz files only, max 100 MB size)

Optional comment:  [                              ]
                   [                              ]
                   [                              ]
                   [                              ]


*: Required Fields

Before uploading please ensure the following:
 • The package contains a DESCRIPTION file
 • DESCRIPTION file contains valid maintainer field "NAME <EMAIL>"
 • You are familiar with the CRAN policies
              [ Upload package ]

In case of problems, contact the CRAN sysadmin team
```

But before you upload your package, you should read the CRAN repository policy carefully and check that your package applies to it. You can find the policy at: `https://cran.r-project.org/submit.html`.

Summary

In this chapter, we learned how to create packages with RStudio and got an overview of the development process of our own package. We learned that RStudio combines great tools, which make package development much easier. Tools such as `roxygen2` give you the possibility of building great documentations for your packages to make them easier to understand for other users.

In the next chapter, we will learn how to collaborate with Git. We will understand the fundamentals, how to install it, and we will see the powerful integration of RStudio with Git.

8

Collaborating with Git and GitHub

The following topics will be covered in this chapter:

- Understanding the fundamentals of Git and GitHub
- Installing Git and setting up RStudio for using it
- Working with RStudio and GitHub

Introducing version control

Data analytics projects with R can sometimes get very complex, especially when we have to work on our analysis over a longer period of time. To keep track of our changes and our progress in the project, it is important to use a version control system that can support us on these tasks. The best known of these version control approaches is Git. It helps us annotate every change we make to our code. This is also very helpful when we collaborate with other people, or when other people have to read and understand our code later on, and also when they need to understand the steps of its development. Git describes itself as a free and open source distributed version control system designed to handle everything from small to very large projects with speed and efficiency. You can read about it at `https://git-scm.com/`.

Gits can be created on servers, or on our local machine. Their distributed nature lets you sync commits with other machines. An alternative to creating your own, is using a hosted version control system. To do this, we can create an account on platforms such as GitHub, Bitbucker, or GitLab. Most of them offer free accounts, and if we take the example of GitHub, everybody can create repositories with an unlimited number of collaborators and public projects. This means that everybody can see our code on the website and use it. If we want to have private repositories, we have to buy a plan.

Installing Git

First of all, we should create an account on GitHub at https://github.com/join. After that, we can install the Git client from the official website, http://git-scm.com/.

Installing Git on Windows

For Windows, there is an .exe file available. So, you just have to download the installer file from git-scm.com/download/win, and execute it.

Installing Git on Linux

Installation on Linux is also very easy, as there is a binary installer available. So, we can install it with apt-get:

```
sudo apt-get install git
```

Installing Git on other Linux distributions

If you do not use a Debian-based Linux distribution, you can find an overview of how to install it for your distribution at http://git-scm.com/download/linux.

Configuring Git

After the successful installation and creation of our GitHub user account, we can go on and configure our Git client.

Open a new shell/console window and type in git. This will show you all the possible options. If you use windows, you can use the Git bash emulation, which behaves just like the git command in Linux.

We now have to set our username and email address. We do this with the following:

```
git config --global user.name 'Your Username'
git config --global user.email 'Your Email Adress'
```

Explaining the basic terminology

The Git system comes with some terminology. We do not have to know everything, but we should take a look at the fundamental elements of this version control system.

Repository

We begin with *Repository*, as the most basic element. You can think of it as a folder where your project is saved. This folder will also save the history when we change something, along with what exactly was changed. It will also keep track of who changed something.

Commit

Commit is actually the process of adding a change to the repository. This change will normally have a unique identifier and message, where we explain why we changed something.

Diff

Diff stands for the difference in changes between two commits. It shows us what was added or deleted in the repository and in every single affected file.

Branch

A *branch* is a parallel version of a repository. It is located in our repository but does not affect the master branch. It is often used to experiment with new functionalities.

Merge

Merging is the process of taking changes from one branch and applying them to another, normally in the same repository.

Fetch

Fetching refers to the process of getting the latest changes from a remote repository (such as `https://github.com/`) without merging them with your local repository.

Pull

Pull is the combination of fetching changes and merging them. This is connected to *Pull Request*, which are requests to merge a certain change into the repository. This is often used when several users are working on a repository.

Push

Pushing is the process of sending your local changes of a repository to a remote repository, such as `https://github.com/`.

Using Git via shell

The traditional way to use Git is via the shell. Normally, we begin with creating a new local repository with the following:

```
git init
```

We can then create files in this repo and add them to the version control structure with the `add` command:

```
git add lm.R
```

Here we replace `lm.R` with the name of the file we added. To commit all files, you can use the following:

```
git add *
```

To create a new remote repository of our project on GitHub, we can use the remote function:

```
git remote add origin git@github.com:USERNAME/https://github.com/
USERNAME/PROJECTNAME.git
```

This creates a remote repository and you can push your project to this remote repository with the following lines:

```
git push origin master
```

We will then be able to see the project on the GitHub website on your user account. Using Git with the shell can be confusing in the beginning. But RStudio offers a great UI to work with version control systems such as Git.

Using the shell from Rstudio

RStudio offers us an easy way to open a shell directly in our current working directory by clicking on the gear icon and selecting **Shell...**.

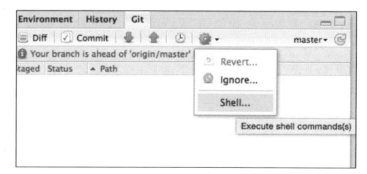

Using Git with RStudio

To use Git with RStudio, we have to set the path to the Git executable in the global options. Therefore, we have to click on **Tools | Global Options...**:

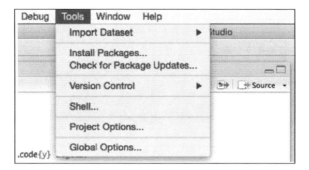

Then, we select the **Git/SVN** tab and click on **Browse...**, and find the place where the Git executables were installed.

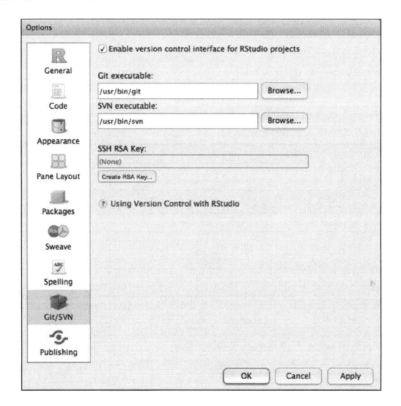

Using RStudio and GitHub via SSH

RStudio also makes it easy to establish a secure connection with `https://github.com/` via SSH. Therefore, we have to create a new SSH RSA key by clicking on **Create RSA Key...**. This will open a new window where we can set a location for the created RSA key to be saved. Normally, we can leave this on the default option.

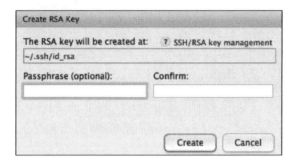

We will then see a new window stating that our public/private RSA key pair has been created, and after closing this window, another will open and show us our public RSA key. We will then have to provide `https://github.com/` with this key. We can do so by logging in to our GitHub account and going to our **Personal settings** page.

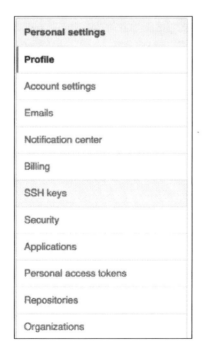

Then, select the **SSH keys** tab and add your public key as a new title.

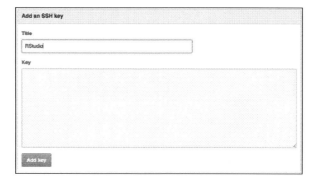

RStudio will now use GitHub via a secure SSH connection.

Creating a new project with Git

Creating a new project with Git is very easy in RStudio. Just create a new project and check the **Create a git repository** checkbox. This will create all the necessary dependencies.

After we've created our new project, we will see a new symbol above the text editor pane, and we can see the `.gitignore` file in our project folder.

Explaining the gitignore file

The `gitignore` file contains files that we do not want to be included in the repository. These files can contain sensitive information such as login information, or are generated on demand. By default, the `gitignore` file contains RStudio-specific files such as our R history.

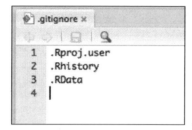

We can add files easily by using the built-in editor by clicking on the **More** button in the Git pane.

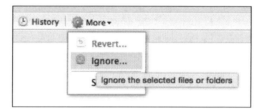

This will open a small editor window, where we can add further entries to our `gitignore` file.

Keeping track of changes

Version control gives us the big advantage of always being able to see what changed in our code. It gives us a good overview of the files that changed, were added, or deleted in our project. RStudio uses three symbols for that:

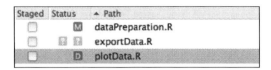

Icon	Icon Name	Description
M	Modified	This means that the content of the file was changed
?	Untracked	This means that the file is new and Git has not seen this file before
D	Deleted	This means that the file was deleted but is still in your repository

We can get a more detailed view when we click on the **diff** button in the Git pane. Here, we can see the changes in the file since the last commit.

If the color is red, it means that the line was removed, and if the line is colored green, it means that it was added to the file.

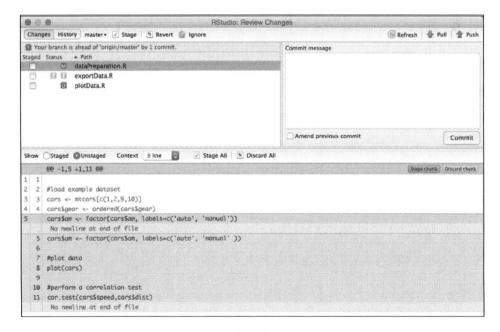

Recording changes

One of the fundamental actions we perform when working with a project in a version control system is *commit*. A commit is a snapshot of the code from our project, at a certain point in time. We can think of it as some kind of backup. When we make a change in our code that causes heavy problems, we can always go back to certain commits, and so, to the version of the code and how it was at time of the commit. Committing files has two steps:

1. **Stage**: We stage a file, and in doing so, tell Git that this change should be included in the next commit. This means that we prepare it for the commit.

2. **Commit**: By this, we actually take a snapshot of the staged files and describe our changes with a message.

We can stage and commit our files in the same menu. To stage a file, we can simply check the box.

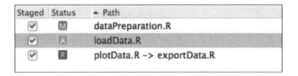

After the files are staged, the icons change. We will now have different icons.

Icon	Description
A	If you stage a new file, it changes from untracked to added. This indicates that Git now knows that you actually want to commit the new file.
R	If you change the name of a file, Git will see it as a deletion and addition of the file with another name.
M	This means that there are staged changes in this file that we will commit the next time.

We can then set the commit message for the next commit. A commit should always contain changes related to a single problem. This will make it easier to follow the development process of our project, and to understand why a certain commit was done.

And so, the commit message should describe the problem related to this commit, and summarize the reasons for the changes. It does not have to include the actual changes made to the code as they are perceived as visual differences in the affected files.

Introducing the Git drop-down menu

When we work with a project that uses Git, RStudio automatically shows us a new symbol right above the text editor pane. This drop-down menu gives us quick access to all the necessary functions needed to work with a version control system.

Undoing a mistake

Because of the principle of commits, it is possible with Git to restore older commits. If we want to undo the changes from the last commit, we can do this with the **Revert** button from the Git window.

If we forgot to add a change to the last commit, we can append it with the **Amend previous commit** function. This will add the new changes we staged to the previous commit, when we press the **Commit** button.

If we do not exactly know where our mistake appeared, or if it did not appear in the last commit, we can take a look at the history of our commits. Click on the **History** button in the Git pane to see the list.

This shows us all our commits, and if we select a certain commit, we can see the actual changes that we committed to the repository there.

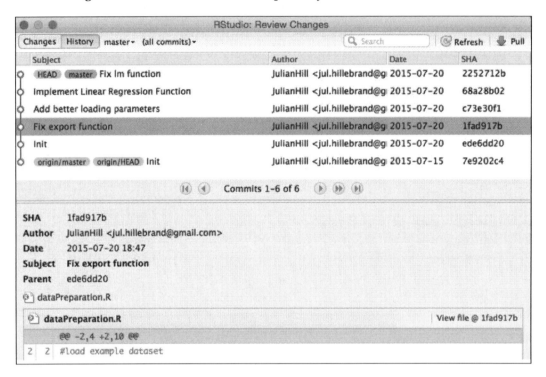

If we found the commit where the mistake appeared, and want to go back in time, we need the SHA key of the commit we want to jump to.

Then we can open a shell and copy the version from the present by using the following line:

```
git checkout <SHA> <filename>
```

Pushing to a remote repository on github.com

Everything we did until now was locally on our computer. Nothing has been pushed to GitHub. We will now upload our project to `https://github.com/`.

First, we have to create a remote repository on `https://github.com/`. This should have the same name as our project, and we can leave all the other fields as they are by default.

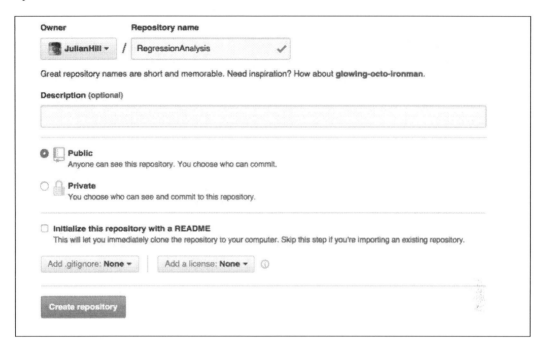

We now have to connect our local repository to this new remote repository and push our changes. Open a shell in our project folder and enter the following:

```
git remote add origin git@github.com:USERNAME/REPOSITORY.git
git push - u origin master
```

Of course, we have to replace USERNAME with our username on `https://github.com/`, and REPOSITORY with the name of our created repository.

We can push the changes we committed to our local repository with the **Push** button in the Git pane.

We do not have to push our code after every commit we make. We should always keep in mind that in this configuration, pushing code means publishing code on GitHub also. So, the code we are pushing *should* work.

After pushing our code, we can find it on our GitHub profile:

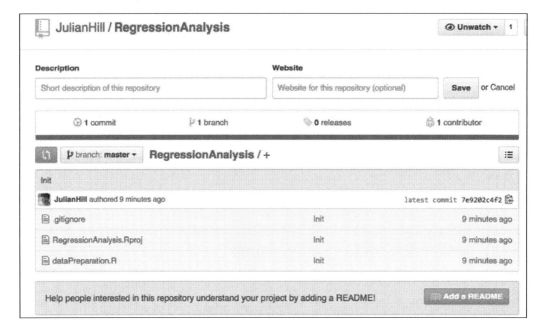

Using an existing GitHub project with RStudio

RStudio offers the ability to check out a project from a version control repository such as `https://github.com/`. A lot of projects that include R code have the `.Rproj` file included, indicating that they are projects created with RStudio. And you can easily check out these project and edit them locally. Of course, we can do this with all kinds of projects, even if they were not created with RStudio.

In the next window, we have to choose **Git**, which is shown in the following screenshot:

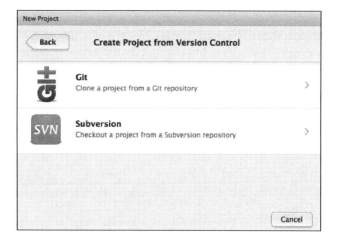

In the next window, we just have to insert the URL of the repository, and the place where we want to save the project:

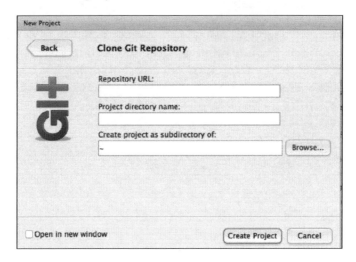

Using branches

A big advantage of Git is that we can not only use it really well for smaller projects, on which just a few people work, but also for much bigger software projects on which several hundred developers work. And so, Git provides a lot of different tools to manage all kinds of different situations.

One of the most important functions is called *Branches*. They give us the ability to try out something experimental or split our commits. The default branch is master. So, you actually have already been using branches, as this branch was where you committed all your changes to.

We can create our own branches with the `checkout` function:

```
git checkout -b <branch name>
```

After we create our new branch, we can see it in the Git pane in RStudio. So, we can actually choose in what branch we want to commit our staged changes.

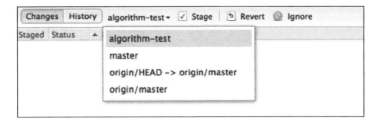

To actually to use the `push` and `pull` functions with this branch, we need to tell RStudio that there is a remote equivalent connected to this local branch. We can do this with the following line:

```
git push --set-upstream origin <branch name>
```

This will enable the functions again, and we can push and pull with our newly created branch.

If we want to go back to the master branch completely, we can use the `checkout` function, again, with the following line:

```
git checkout - b master
```

If we created a branch because we wanted to perform some experiments or test new features, there will come a time when we will actually want to integrate these features in the master branch. Therefore, Git provides the `merge` function.

When we are done within our branch, we switch back to the master branch again:

```
git checkout master
```

Then, we can merge the changes from the branch with the following line:

```
git merge <branch name>
```

After merging the branch, we can actually delete the old branch if we want to. Note that Git only lets you delete a branch when it has been merged with the master branch:

```
git branch -d <branch name>
```

Making a pull request

The pull feature of Git is really useful; especially when we want to collaborate with others on a project. On `https://github.com/`, it is often used to participate in open source projects, and to help in developing them. A pull request is basically an improvement suggestion. So, we can suggest a change, discuss with others about this change, and if it is approved by the project owner, he or she can merge it in the project.

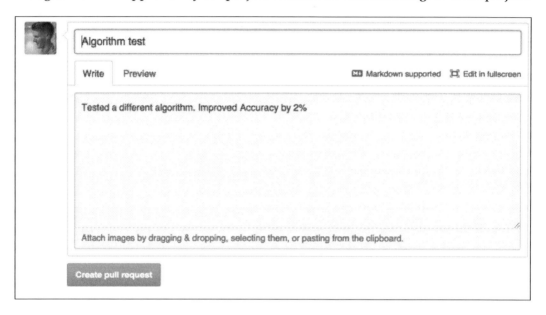

After we create a pull request, it gets a number, and we can see an overview of all the changes that this request includes. Furthermore, we also have the ability to write comments. This gives us the ability to discuss pull request when we work in a team.

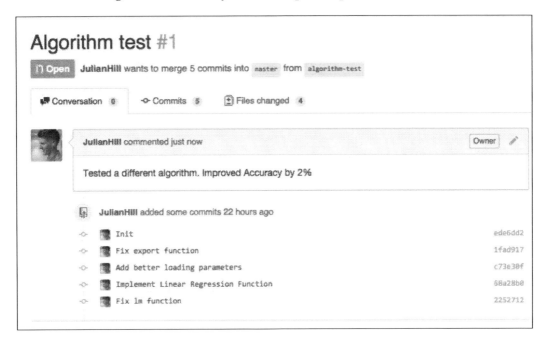

Reviewing and merging pull requests

When we receive pull requests, we should think about whether the changes really make sense and provide value to our project. Therefore, a lot of people recommend the three-steps approach described by Sarah Sharp on her website at http://sarah. thesharps.us/2014/09/01/the-gentle-art-of-patch-review/.

1. **Good or bad idea?**: This should only require a simple yes or no answer. If you do not think that the contribution is a good idea, be gentle to the contributor as he showed a huge interest in your project.

2. **Is this Architecturally Sound?**: In this phase, you look at the architecture of the contribution; if it modifies the right functions in the right way?

3. **Is the contribution polished?**: The last phase is about the non-code parts of the contribution. If it uses the correct wording for the documentation, for example?

If we agree with the contribution, and if it passes all three phases, we can simply click on the **Merge pull request** option and it will be merged with your master branch.

Further resources

Working with Git has the big advantage of having a really huge community providing help for nearly every question that you might have.

Bootcamp, from `https://help.github.com/categories/bootcamp/`, gives you a solid start into the practical world of Git. It gives you further instructions on how to set up a Git and work with the GitHub user interface.

If you want to go deeper into the topic, you should take a look at the official Git website, `http://git-scm.com/`. It provides a very detailed reference on all the functions provided by Git.

Summary

In this chapter, we learned the fundamentals of Git and GitHub. This included the basic terminologies of the different functions, and also how a typical workflow with Git works. We then applied these principles with RStudio and looked at how they are accessible via the graphical user interface.

In the next chapter, you will learn how to use R for your organization by using the RStudio Server.

9
R for your Organization – Managing the RStudio Server

This chapter covers the following topics:

- How to create an Amazon AWS account
- Using the Simple Storage Service, as our data storage system
- Configuring and launching our Elastic Compute Cloud server instance
- Installing the R, RStudio, and Shiny Server on our instance
- Adjusting and managing the RStudio and Shiny server

Managing the RStudio Server

RStudio was originally designed as a web application that was to be run on a Linux-based server. Many RStudio users encounter the desktop version initially, but the server version is essential for easy administration of R and RStudio in organizations allowing users to perform expensive computations on big data, and thus, escaping the limitations of personal computers.

In this chapter, you will learn how to manage the server version of RStudio and Shiny. It may not teach you everything you need to know in order to administer the server for your organization, but it should enable you to help your systems administrator install and manage an R system that effectively serves the needs of your organization.

Using Amazon Web Services as the server platform

Amazon Web Services (AWS) is a cloud-computing platform that combines a collection of dozens of different web services. After the foundation of Amazon in 1994, AWS was created for internal use to manage the massively growing server demands and related services in the year 2002. In 2006, it was officially founded for public usage. Since then, AWS adoption has increased remarkably. Today, it has by far the biggest market share of all cloud infrastructure services, and a huge number of big and famous web services and companies are using AWS. The most popular services are Amazon **Elastic Compute Cloud**, better known as **EC2**, and Amazon **Simple Storage Service**, which is also called **S3**.

Creating an AWS account

Head over to `https://aws.amazon.com` and click on the **Create an AWS Account** button. Every new AWS account includes a bunch of free-of-charge services. In the so-called Free Tier, you get Amazon EC2 for 750hrs/month, 5GB of storage on Amazon S3, and more free of charge services for the first 12 months.

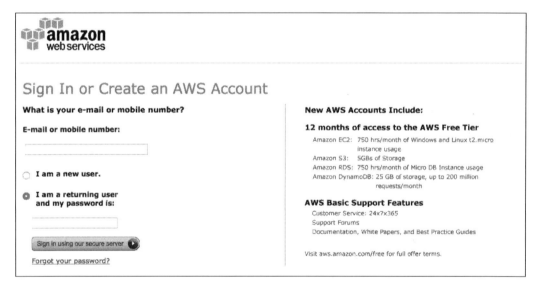

After entering your login credentials, you need to fill out your contact details and enter your payment information. Next, you need to process the identity verification in three steps. Finally, choose a customer support plan and you are ready to go.

After launching the management console, you get the total overview of all AWS services. This may look kind of overwhelming at first glance.

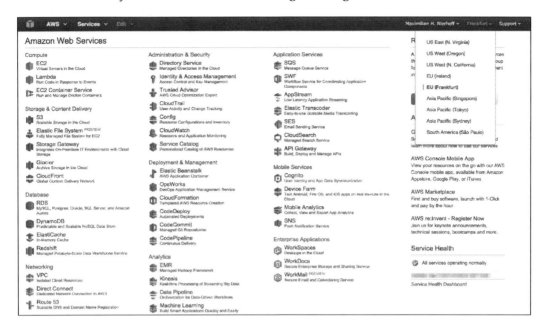

I chose Frankfurt as my server location. Of course, you can select any of the given regions. The different web services are sorted by their possibility of usage and purpose.

As of today, there are the following fields of use, which in turn include various services and tools:

- Compute
- Storage and content delivery
- Database
- Networking
- Administration and security
- Deployment and management
- Analytics
- Application services
- Mobile services
- Enterprise applications

So, there is a service for pretty much any purpose. First, we dedicate ourselves to the scalable cloud storage in the cloud, which is called S3. Then, we need the *Compute* section, which includes the EC2. This service can be seen as a remote server, host, computer, and machine; its specifications are flexible and can be changed easily. In the following sections, you will learn, step by step, how to store your analysis data on an S3 cloud storage system, and how to install and configure the RStudio Server on a virtual cloud server by using EC2.

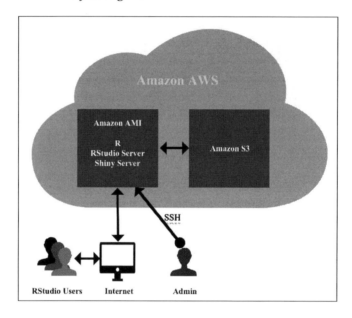

Using S3 to store our data

The Amazon S3 represents our desired way to store big data for our analyses since it is particularly user-friendly. Furthermore, five gigabytes of storage is free. Setting up a so-called S3 bucket is a quick and easy process.

Creating our bucket

To get started, click on **S3** in the AWS dashboard. In the new window, you need to click on the **Create Bucket** button. In a pop-up window, you can enter your desired bucket name; in our case, we choose `mastering-rstudio-data`. It is recommended to choose a descriptive and unique name for your bucket. If you want to set up a logging to get access logs of your bucket, hit the **Create** button and you're done.

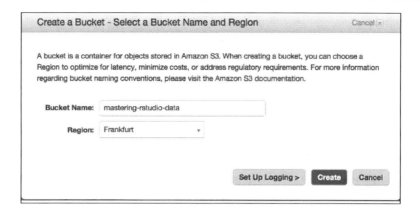

Uploading a dataset to the bucket

We can now upload datasets to our brand new bucket. Furthermore, you can create a meaningful folder structure in your bucket.

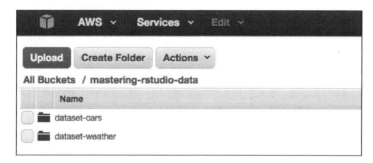

To start a data upload, just hit the **Upload** button. In the pop-up window, you can drag and drop the files that you want to upload, or click on the **Add Files** button to open the files browser on your computer. Next, you can directly upload the chosen data, or you can set some details by clicking the related buttons. If you choose to set some details, you can first decide between standard storage and reduced redundancy storage. Furthermore, you can check if your data should be encrypted.

In the following step, you can set permissions. Now you can, for example, enable your data to be opened and downloaded by everyone. This is necessary if you store images of a website (or is it possible only when you store a dataset which is anyway a public one anyway), but if you store private data, the **Everyone** permission becomes a security issue. Therefore, it is recommended that sensitive data should not be set to **Make everything public**.

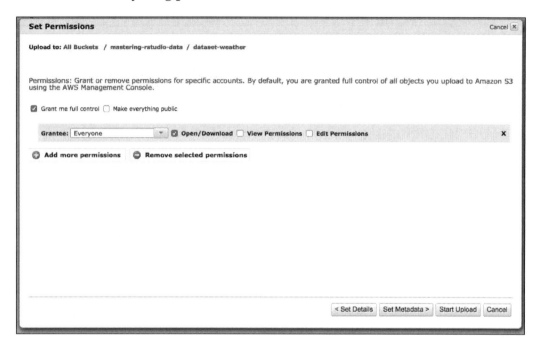

After your data has been uploaded, you can still change and view all your settings by clicking on the **Properties** tab.

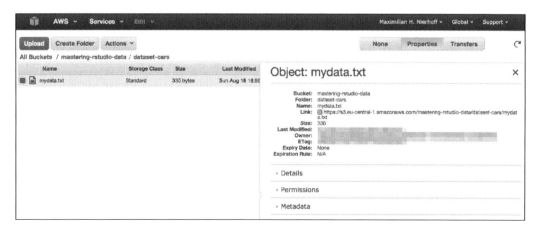

Launching our EC2 instance

Click on **EC2** to get to your EC2 Dashboard. Here, you need to click on the blue **Launch Instance** button. Now, you need to follow a seven-step wizard to launch your instance.

Choosing An amazon Machine Image

The **Amazon Machine Image (AMI)** contains the software configuration (operating system, application server, and applications) required to launch your instance. We choose the Ubuntu Server AMI. This software configuration is also free tier eligible and is the most chosen flavor for RStudio Server installations. Ubuntu is a very stable and user-friendly Linux distribution.

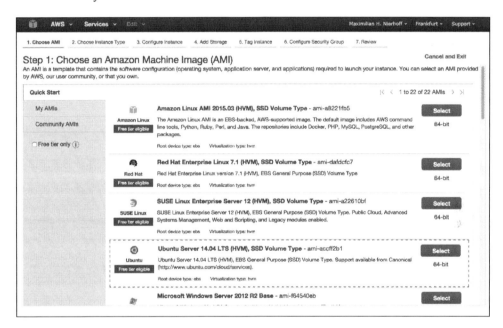

Choosing an instance type

Next, you need to choose the desired virtual server. Amazon offers a wide range of different instance types. Currently, there are five utilization areas with particular specialties:

- General purpose
- Compute optimized
- GPU instances

- Memory optimized
- Storage optimized

These so-called families include, in turn, several instance types with differing combinations of CPU, memory, storage, and network capacity.

We take the first option in the long list, in fact, the t2.micro type of the *General purpose* family. The main reason is that this instance type is the only free tier eligible one. If you are planning to use RStudio Server and AWS professionally for analyzing really big data sets that are also parallelized, it is recommended to launch a bigger instance of the memory optimized or GPU instances families.

You can now also click on the blue **Review and Launch** button to take the shortcut and jump to the last step: the *review*.

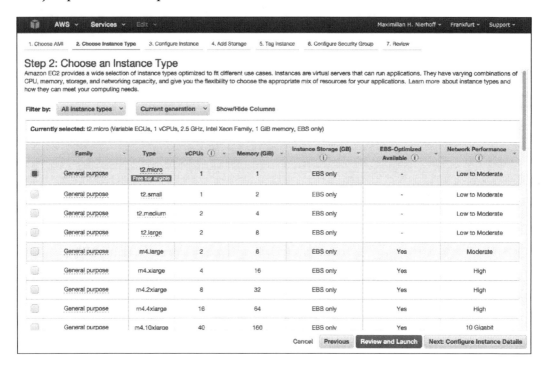

Configuring instance details

The third step of the launching process focuses on configuration options. If you need help, every configuration option offers a question mark icon with explanations and further information. In this step, we first add a new, so-called IAM role and second user data, which installs the R, RStudio, and Shiny server on your micro instance.

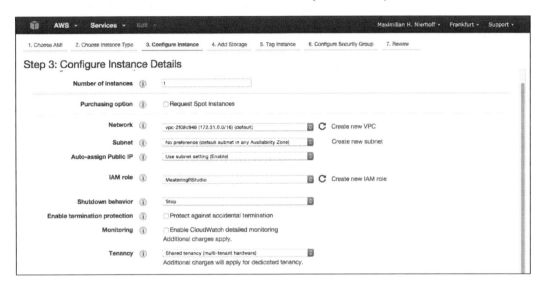

Creating a new IAM role

The reason and purpose of AWS' **Identity and Access Management (IAM)** is stated in the following paragraph:

> *IAM roles for EC2 automatically deploys and rotates AWS credentials for you, removing the need to store your AWS access keys with your application. Select the instance profile that contains the required IAM role. If you created your IAM role using the console, the instance profile has the same name as your IAM role. [...]*

We need to create an IAM role to allow the software we want to install, which are R, RStudio, and the Shiny server, to access the AWS services and make secure API requests. Furthermore, we need this IAM role to read data from the S3 bucket that can store our data and more. As a reminder, in our free account, we also got five gigabytes of free storage for Amazon's cloud storage service called S3.

1. Click on the **Create new IAM role** link text in step 3 of your launching process. This opens a new window, where you can manage all your IAM roles. Next, hit the **Create New Role** button to start the five-step role creation process.

2. First, you need to set your desired role name. In our example, we chose `MasteringRStudio`.

3. Next, we select the role type. In our case, this is **Amazon EC2** in the **AWS Service Roles** tab.

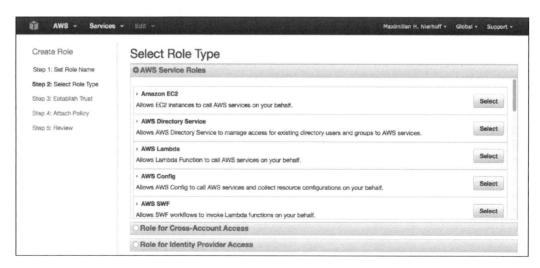

4. The third step is called **Establish Trust**, but it gets automatically skipped since we selected an **AWS Service Role** option in the preceding step.

5. In the fourth step, you can select up to two policies for the role we are creating. We check the **AdministratorAccess** option to give our role full access. Furthermore, we add the policy called **AmazonS3FullAccess**.

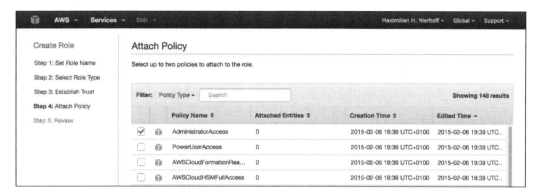

6. The last step represents the review of all the chosen options.

Adding storage

If you'd like to, you can now add additional storage. There is already a fixed storage type called **Root**. This device with a a prefilled size of 8 GB is the installation location for our chosen AMI—the Ubuntu Server. Since we want to use our created S3 bucket to save big data sets, there is no need to change anything here.

Tagging an instance

In this step, you are able to tag your instance. In the screenshot, we gave our instance the name, `RStudio and Shiny Server`, by using the **Name** tags, which represents Amazon's own metadata system. There are a bunch of other tags possible; for our purpose, we do not need to add any other.

Configuring a security group

By defining a security group, you can easily determine the rules that control the traffic of your instance. In fact, the security group acts as a virtual firewall.

We are creating a new security group, which will reflect the required changes that make RStudio and the Shiny server work correctly. Therefore, we are adding two more rules. The first rule opens the port, 8787, for the RStudio Server, and the second one opens the port, 3838, for the Shiny Server. As you can see, the first rule, which comes prefilled, is the SSH one on port range 22. We will explain SSH shortly.

As you can see in the following screenshot, as the source, we chose **My IP** for all three rules. This is only recommended if you have a static IP address. Most companies have a fixed IP address that never changes. But most private users have a dynamic IP address. If this is your case, you need to change the **Source** to **Anywhere**, which makes it possible to access your instance with any IP address. This can be a security problem if you want to analyze sensitive data.

Furthermore, we chose the **Security group name**, `Mastering RStudio`, and a corresponding description.

Reviewing

After all this, we are at the last step: the *review* step. If you selected **Anywhere** as **Source** in the previous step, you will get a warning again. Furthermore, all the settings we made are listed and can be checked. When you are ready to go, you can finally click on the **Launch** button and a new pop-up will appear.

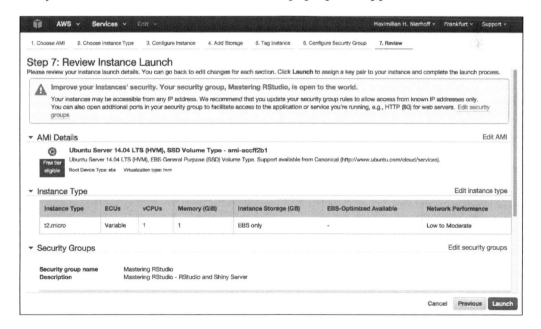

Creating a key pair

So, what is a key pair exactly? Amazon describes it as follows:

> *A key pair consists of a public key that AWS stores, and a private key file that you store. Together, they allow you to connect to your instance securely. For Windows AMIs, the private key file is required to obtain the password used to log into your instance. For Linux AMIs, the private key file allows you to securely SSH into your instance.*

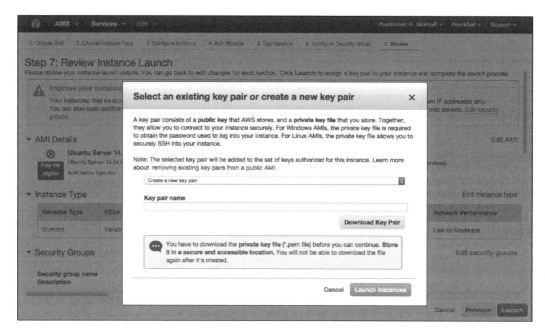

Choose **Create a new key pair** in the selection box, give your key pair a name, and download the key pair by hitting the related button. Now you have a brand new key pair called `Your-Key-Pair-Name.pem` in your download folder.

Launching the instance

After adding your key pair and storing it securely, you are finally truly able to launch the instance. Click on the blue button and you will see some quick processing messages, and within seconds, the **Launch Status** window.

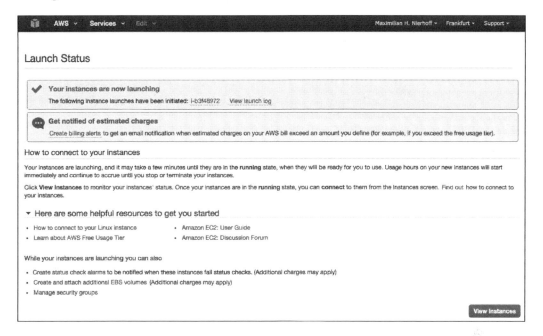

Connecting with the new EC2 instance

Our instance is now launched and running. The next step is to establish a connection with the server in order to complete the desired setup by installing R, RStudio, and the Shiny server.

What is SSH?

Since this a very important topic when you are working with servers in the cloud, we want to give you a brief introduction of SSH. The acronym stands for **Secure Shell** and denotes both, a network protocol, as well as corresponding programs with which you can establish an encrypted network connection with a remote device in a secure manner. Often, this method is used to make a remote command line locally available. Thus, on a local console, outputs of the remote console will be displayed and the local keystrokes will be sent to the remote computer. This can be used, for example, for remote maintenance. The newer version of the SSH-2 protocol provides other functions such as data transfer via SFTP. Usually, SSH uses port 22, and if you remember, we already added the SSH rule during our server configuration.

SSH is not installed by default on computers with the Windows operating system. However, you can download free SSH clients such as PuTTY, MobaXterm, and others. On Linux and Apple Macintosh machines, SSH is installed by default, so you just need the terminal.

Bringing it all together

Remember the created key pair you downloaded before? Next, you need to store this key pair securely, so that it is not be publicly accessible. Use the terminal (also known as shell and console) of your operating system and navigate to the folder where you saved the `Your-Key-Pair-Name.pem` file.

Enter the following line to make sure your private key is not public:

```
chmod 400 Your-Key-Pair-Name.pem
```

Next, we connect via SSH to our created instance. Since we launched an instance with the Ubuntu server as the operating system, the user is just `ubuntu`. Furthermore, you need to copy the Public DNS of your instance, which can be found twice on the EC2 dashboard.

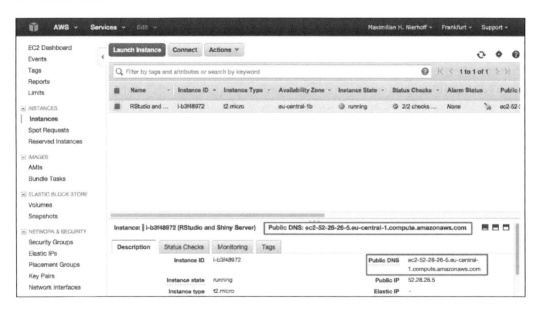

Then bring it all together by typing the following into your terminal:

```
ssh -i Your-Key-Pair-Name.pem ubuntu@<your public DNS>
```

After hitting the *Enter* key, your terminal will print this warning:

```
● ● ●                          1. Default (ssh)
ssh: Could not resolve hostname ec2-198-51-100-1.compute-1.amazonaws.com: nodename nor
  servname provided, or not known
Maximilians-MacBook-Air:~ mhn$ ssh -i MasteringRStudio.pem ubuntu@ec2-52-28-26-5.eu-ce
ntral-1.compute.amazonaws.com
Warning: Identity file MasteringRStudio.pem not accessible: No such file or directory.
The authenticity of host 'ec2-52-28-26-5.eu-central-1.compute.amazonaws.com (52.28.26.
5)' can't be established.
RSA key fingerprint is b0:10:a8:f2:88:dc:48:0b:b8:a5:8e:b6:c2:c8:73:b6.
Are you sure you want to continue connecting (yes/no)? ▮
```

Type `yes`, hit *Enter*, and you will get this response:

```
Are you sure you want to continue connecting (yes/no)? yes
Warning: Permanently added 'ec2-52-28-254-233.eu-central-1.compute.amazonaws.com
,52.28.254.233' (RSA) to the list of known hosts.
```

Now, you are connected to your instance with SSH. Just type in your terminal anytime you want to access your instance:

```
ssh ubuntu@< your public DNS>
```

```
● ● ●                    1. ubuntu@ip-172-31-15-221: ~ (ssh)
Maximilians-MacBook-Air:~ mhn$ ssh ubuntu@ec2-52-28-254-233.eu-central-1.compute
.amazonaws.com
Welcome to Ubuntu 14.04.2 LTS (GNU/Linux 3.13.0-48-generic x86_64)

 * Documentation:  https://help.ubuntu.com/

  System information as of Thu Aug 20 15:05:01 UTC 2015

  System load:  0.34               Processes:           100
  Usage of /:   5.2% of 14.63GB    Users logged in:     0
  Memory usage: 5%                 IP address for eth0: 172.31.15.221
  Swap usage:   0%

  Graph this data and manage this system at:
    https://landscape.canonical.com/

  Get cloud support with Ubuntu Advantage Cloud Guest:
    http://www.ubuntu.com/business/services/cloud

0 packages can be updated.
0 updates are security updates.


Last login: Thu Aug 20 15:05:05 2015 from 37.24.143.126
ubuntu@ip-172-31-15-221:~$ ▮
```

Setting up R, RStudio, and the Shiny Server

Our server is up and running and we are able to communicate with our instance through the Secure Shell. Therefore, it is time to install the R, RStudio, and Shiny servers.

Choosing your RStudio version

There are two different versions of the RStudio Server: the open source version that is free to download, and the Enterprise version, also called RStudio Pro, which represents the paid version and contains some more administrative tools and features. The features are a more effective resource management tool, monitoring functionalities and enhanced security options. We will choose the open source version in the later parts of this chapter.

	Open Source Edition	Commercial License
Overview	• Access via a web browser • Move computation closer to the data • Scale compute and RAM centrally	All of the features of open source; plus: • Administrative Tools • Enhanced Security and Authentication • Metrics and Monitoring • Advanced Resource Management
Documentation	Getting Started with RStudio Server	RStudio Server Professional Admin Guide
Support	Community forums only	• Priority Email Support • 8 hour response during business hours (ET)
License	AGPL v3	RStudio License Agreement
Pricing	Free	$9,995/server/year Academic and Small Business discounts available
	DOWNLOAD RSTUDIO SERVER	DOWNLOAD FREE RSTUDIO PRO EVAL
		🛒 Purchase Now 💬 Contact Sales ⓘ Learn More

Installing base R

Open your terminal and connect with your instance. It is recommended that you use sudo in front of any command, since our instance is an Ubuntu server. Sudo is a command on Unix and Unix-like operating systems, such as Linux or Mac OS X, that is used to launch processes with the privileges of the super user root. Please be patient; some of the upcoming commands can take more than 15 minutes to be ready.

First, we create a user, its password, and a home directory. Now, we add the user with the name, masteringrstudio, create a home directory, and add the password for this user:

```
ubuntu@ip-172-31-15-221:~$ sudo useradd masteringrstudio
ubuntu@ip-172-31-15-221:~$ sudo mkdir /home/masteringrstudio
ubuntu@ip-172-31-15-221:~$ sudo passwd masteringrstudio
Enter new UNIX password:
Retype new UNIX password:
passwd: password updated successfully
ubuntu@ip-172-31-15-221:~$
```

For finishing the user creation process, we need to enter the following command:

```
sudo chmod -R 0777 /home/masteringrstudio
```

Next, we update the Ubuntu software and install base R:

```
# Bringing the Ubuntu software up to date
sudo apt-get update
sudo apt-get upgrade
# Installing the R
sudo apt-get install r-base
```

After this installation, please reboot the whole system by typing `sudo` reboot. After rebooting and reconnecting, you can use R directly within your terminal.

You can easily see that this is not the latest version of R, and we want to have the latest version. Therefore, we need to type the following command to open the so-called sources list of our Ubuntu server:

```
sudo nano /etc/apt/sources.list.d/sources.list
```

Here, you need to add this entry:

```
deb http://<my.favorite.cran.mirror>/bin/linux/ubuntu trusty/
```

Choose a CRAN mirror such as `https://cran.rstudio.com/`, the so-called 0-Cloud. The word, `trusty`, marks the version name of our Ubuntu server. As you may remember, we selected the Ubuntu Server, 14.04 LTS, which is also called Trusty Tahr.

Now, press *Ctrl* + *X* on your keyboard to save and exit this file. Then, you need to confirm with yes again.

In the next step, we need to fetch the secure APT key and feed it to apt-key:

```
gpg --keyserver keyserver.ubuntu.com --recv-key E084DAB9
gpg -a --export E084DAB9 | sudo apt-key add -
```

When this is all done, we can change to the latest R version by the following command:

```
sudo apt-get update && sudo apt-get upgrade
```

But, before we can use the latest version, we need to reboot the server using the already known `sudo reboot` command, and then reinstall the base by typing `sudo apt-get install r-base` into the terminal.

```
ubuntu@ip-172-31-15-221:~$ R

R version 3.2.2 (2015-08-14) -- "Fire Safety"
Copyright (C) 2015 The R Foundation for Statistical Computing
Platform: x86_64-pc-linux-gnu (64-bit)

R is free software and comes with ABSOLUTELY NO WARRANTY.
You are welcome to redistribute it under certain conditions.
Type 'license()' or 'licence()' for distribution details.

  Natural language support but running in an English locale

R is a collaborative project with many contributors.
Type 'contributors()' for more information and
'citation()' on how to cite R or R packages in publications.

Type 'demo()' for some demos, 'help()' for on-line help, or
'help.start()' for an HTML browser interface to help.
Type 'q()' to quit R.

> []
```

Finally, the latest R version is up and running on our server.

Installing RStudio and the Shiny Server

The foundations have been laid; now it is time to install RStudio and the Shiny server on our AWS instance. First, we install the GDebi package installer and another background file:

```
# install prerequisite files
sudo apt-get install gdebi-core
sudo apt-get install libapparmor1
```

Now, we need to get the latest version of RStudio and the Shiny Server. Therefore, we head over to the RStudio website and grab the required commands for our Ubuntu server:

```
wget https://download2.rstudio.org/rstudio-server-0.99.473-amd64.deb
sudo gdebi rstudio-server-0.99.473-amd64.deb
```

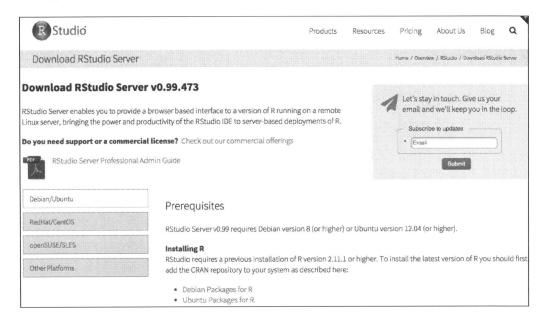

The same procedure applies to the Shiny server installation. Visit the Shiny server page on the RStudio website. Here, we take the open source version again.

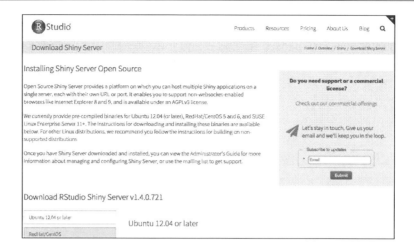

Entering the next commands into the terminal will install the latest version of the Shiny server and the Shiny package:

```
wget https://download3.rstudio.org/ubuntu-12.04/x86_64/shiny-server-
1.4.0.721-amd64.deb
```

```
sudo gdebi shiny-server-1.4.0.721-amd64.deb
```

```
# installing the shiny package
```

```
sudo su - -c "R -e \"install.packages('shiny', repos='https://cran.
rstudio.com/')\""
```

```
1. ubuntu@ip-172-31-15-221: ~ (ssh)
Shiny Server
  Shiny Server is a server program from RStudio, Inc. that makes Shiny applicatio
ns available over the web. Shiny is a web application framework for the R statis
tical computation language.
Do you want to install the software package? [y/N]:y
Get:1 http://eu-central-1b.clouds.archive.ubuntu.com/ubuntu/ trusty-updates/univ
erse libssl0.9.8 amd64 0.9.8o-7ubuntu3.2.14.04.1 [692 kB]
Fetched 692 kB in 6s (75.9 kB/s)
Preconfiguring packages ...
Preconfiguring packages ...
Selecting previously unselected package libssl0.9.8:amd64.
(Reading database ... 79123 files and directories currently installed.)
Preparing to unpack .../libssl0.9.8_0.9.8o-7ubuntu3.2.14.04.1_amd64.deb ...
Unpacking libssl0.9.8:amd64 (0.9.8o-7ubuntu3.2.14.04.1) ...
Setting up libssl0.9.8:amd64 (0.9.8o-7ubuntu3.2.14.04.1) ...
Processing triggers for libc-bin (2.19-0ubuntu6.6) ...
Selecting previously unselected package shiny-server.
(Reading database ... 79147 files and directories currently installed.)
Preparing to unpack shiny-server-1.4.0.721-amd64.deb ...
Unpacking shiny-server (1.4.0.721) ...
Setting up shiny-server (1.4.0.721) ...
Creating user shiny
Adding LANG to /etc/init/shiny-server.conf, setting to en_US.UTF-8
shiny-server start/running, process 2608
ubuntu@ip-172-31-15-221:~$
```

RStudio and the Shiny Server in your browser

All installations have now been completed and it is time to test everything. Take the public DNS of your server and add the port, `:8787`, to open RStudio in your browser. You set this port especially for RStudio traffic during the configuration of the security group of our AWS instance.

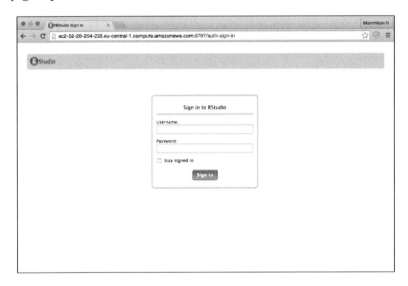

And, et voilà! It works if you see the login screen of the RStudio server after entering the URL of your instance with our opened port, 8787.

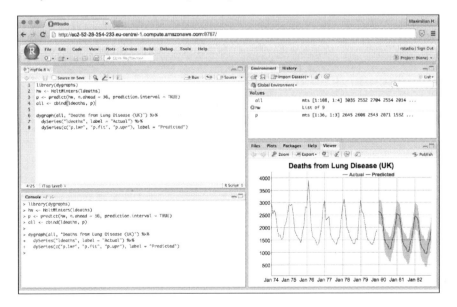

Great, everything has worked! When you add the port, 3838, you will see your brand new and public Shiny server.

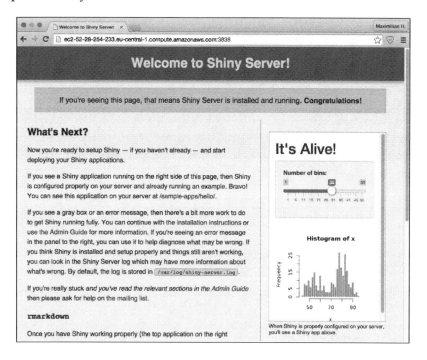

Administrating your RStudio server environment

When you want to use the RStudio server in your organization, there are still several things to do and know in order to manage users, sessions, and the updating of the versions.

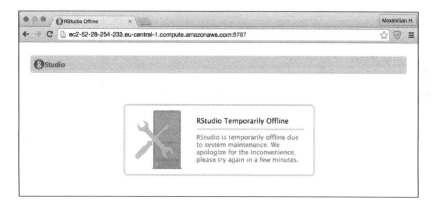

Getting rid of the R memory problem

This is one of the biggest problems most users of instances with only a small amount of RAM are facing—the system is runs out of memory and finally fails.

```
Warning message:
system call failed: Cannot allocate memory
```

Generally, it is no secret that R is a memory hog. In order to prevent this, we need to make some server adjustments and create a so-called `swap` file. Swap space in Linux is used when the amount of physical memory is full. If the system needs more memory resources and the RAM is full, inactive files in memory are moved to the swap space.

Therefore, we will enter this command:

```
sudo swapon -s
```

If the result is empty, we need to assign some swap. With the following commands, we build a swap with a size of 512 MB and activate it:

```
sudo dd if=/dev/zero of=/swapfile bs=1024 count=512k
```

```
sudo mkswap /swapfile
sudo swapon /swapfile
```

To ensure that this file is permanently available, we need to open the `/etc/fstab` file by using `sudo nano` again and adding this line:

```
sudo nano /etc/fstab/
```

```
/swapfile          none      swap      sw          0          0
```

Next, we set the so-called `swappiness` attribute to `10`:

```
sudo echo 10 | sudo tee /proc/sys/vm/swappiness
```

```
sudo echo vm.swappiness = 10 | sudo tee -a /etc/sysctl.conf
```

In the last step, we set the permissions of the swap file to root access only:

```
sudo chown root:root /swapfile
sudo chmod 0600 /swapfile
```

Connecting our S3 bucket with RStudio

Hopefully, you still remember the S3 bucket we created as one of your first steps in this chapter. The idea was to store big datasets in this bucket and read them into RStudio.

Therefore, just install the RCurl library, connect with your stored datasets by using their URL, and you are ready to play with the data:

```
library(RCurl)


myS3Data <- read.table(textConnection(getURL("https://s3.eu-central-1.
amazonaws.com/mastering-rstudio-data/dataset-weather/main.csv")),
sep=",", header=TRUE)
```

Basic RStudio server management

In many situations, it is useful to know which basic commands are available. Since we are using the open source version, the possible commands are limited:

```
# Manually start, stop, and restart the server
sudo rstudio-server stop
sudo rstudio-server start
sudo rstudio-server restart


# Listing all sctive session, suspending options
sudo rstudio-server active-sessions
sudo rstudio-server suspend-session <pid>
sudo rstudio-server suspend-all


sudo rstudio-server force-suspend-session <pid>
sudo rstudio-server force-suspend-all


# Taking the server on- and offline
sudo rstudio-server offline
sudo rstudio-server online
```

Also, if you want to upgrade to a newer version of the RStudio server, the command is really simple:

```
wget <rstudio-download-URL>
sudo gdebi <lastest-rstudio-server-package.deb>
```

To add new users, just use the following already-known commands:

```
sudo useradd user2
sudo mkdir /home/user2
sudo passwd user2
sudo chmod -R 0777 /home/user2
```

Managing the Shiny Server

We have already seen that our Shiny server runs under the port, 3838. When you use the URL, `http://<your-public-DNS>:3838/sample-apps/hello/`, you will see that the server is working properly. We can now host Shiny apps and interactive documents.

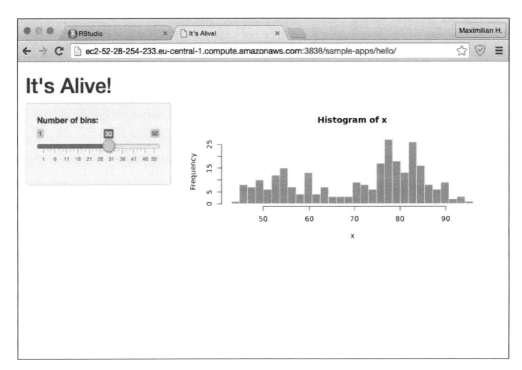

Since the default configuration is set to serve all applications in the directory, `/serv/shiny-server`, every new app or markdown file will be placed into the directory, `/serv/shiny-server/the-new-app`. Thus, the related URL is `http://<your-public-DNS>:3838/the-new-app`.

But, we can also change the setting that users have for their own Shiny apps folder, and the related URL will look like this `http://<your-public-DNS>:3838/user-name/the-new-app`. To apply this, we need to navigate to the Shiny configuration file:

```
sudo nano /etc/shiny-server/shiny-server.conf
```

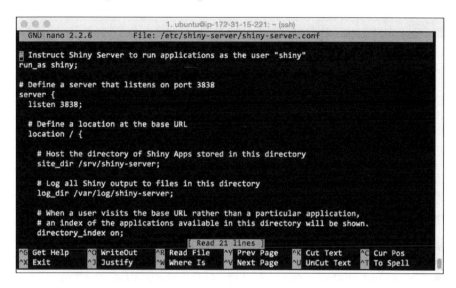

In this file, we flesh out the location file a bit:

And at last, we restart the Shiny server to apply the changes we made. Now, you can create a Shiny app in the RStudio server and run this app directly on the Shiny server with your user.

Basic commands for the Shiny Server

The basic commands to administrate the Shiny server are self-explanatory and very similar to the RStudio server ones. If you are using Ubuntu 12.04 to 14.04, the commands are:

```
sudo start shiny-server
sudo stop shiny-server
sudo restart shiny-server
sudo reload shiny-server
status shiny-server
```

Summary

In this chapter, you learned, step by step, how to create an AWS account to set up and launch your EC2 instance, and how to use S3 cloud storage to save your data. Next, you learned, in detail, how you can use the terminal to communicate with your EC2 instance via SSH. In this manner, we then installed and fully set up R, RStudio, and the Shiny server. Then, you learned how to manage and administrate both RStudio and the Shiny server.

Generally, there are, of course, several other good services besides Amazon AWS, such as Digital Ocean, Heroku, and others, where you can set up and launch the RStudio server in nearly the same manner and time. And, since some time, the famous concept of containerization in terms of Docker, with the related RStudio image named rocker, marks a possible AWS and hosting alternative in combination with Docker hosting services such as tutum, StackDock, dotCloud, and many others.

In the upcoming chapter, you will discover how to extend your RStudio usage with some tricks. Furthermore, we will discover all the places from where you can get help, and lastly, we will check all the known resources and blogs to stay up to date in the cases of R and RStudio.

10
Extending RStudio and Your Knowledge of R

This chapter covers the following topics:

- How to extend RStudio by customizing your Rprofile
- Finding help by using the best Q&A site for R
- Learning more about packages and R by using specialized pages
- Refreshing and deepening your R knowledge with MOOCs, tutorials, and more
- Staying up to date in the R world

Extending RStudio, finding answers, and more

In this chapter, which is the final chapter of this book, we want to show, on one hand, how to expand RStudio functionalities, and on the other, how to individualize the IDE itself. Furthermore, we want to present the most common opportunities to get R and RStudio-specific help. In this chapter, you will find an overview of how and where you can deepen your R and RStudio knowledge even further. Finally, this part of the book includes a list of known sources to stay up to date in terms of R in general, and of course, RStudio.

RStudio environment customizations

Already in the first chapter, we showed you how to set up RStudio with the built-in settings so that it corresponds, practically and visually, with your wishes and preferences. But, there are also other options that cannot be set within the RStudio GUI since they are general R settings. An example of this is the **Rprofile**. But everything you determine in your personal Rprofile will also be executed in RStudio.

Customizing the Rprofile

You may have never heard of the so-called Rprofile before. In fact, at first glance, it is just a normal text file, which can be found in the R home directory. But it could also be possible that you do not have such a file.

The customization of Rprofile is an interesting way to load personally stored functions, options, scripts, the preferred CRAN mirror, and so on, for your R sessions at every startup of R, respectively RStudio.

Where to find your Rprofile

For Windows environment to change your Rprofile on Windows, navigate to the ...\R\R-Version\etc folder and edit the file, `Rprofile.site`. Next, restart R and you are done.

For Mac and Linux, first you need to create the Rprofile file. Create a new file named `Rprofile.txt`. This can be done with any text editor. Open your terminal and enter the following: `cp Rprofile.txt .Rprofile`. By doing so, the profile file becomes invisible, which is the standard case for such files. Then, restart R.

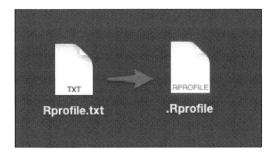

Adding custom functions

Since the possible features that you can integrate into your personal Rprofile are endless, in the following sections, we will discuss only a few examples.

The first and last functions

As the name implies, by using these functions, it can be defined what happens first, and what happens at the end of your R session. For example, you can define that some libraries should be loaded at the startup, and further, write a custom startup message:

```
.First <- function(){
library(ggplot2)
library(stats)
library(htmlwidgets)
library(shiny)

cat("\nHey there, welcome back! Let's write some great R code.")
}
```

```
Hey there, welcome back! Let's write some great R code.
>
```

In the same way you, can deal with the .Last function. For example, save your whole R command history and print a goodbye message:

```
.Last <- function(){

  if (!any(commandArgs()=='--no-readline') && interactive()){
     library(utils)
     try(savehistory(Sys.getenv("R_HISTFILE")))
        }

cat("\nIt was a long day. Goodbye at ", date(), "\n")
}
```

More ideas for your Rprofile

Add a local CRAN mirror:

```
local({r <- getOption("repos")
      r["CRAN"] <- "https://cran.rstudio.com/"
      options(repos=r) })
```

Easy debugging:

```
# turn debugging on or off
# place "browser(expr = isTRUE(getOption("debug"))) # BROWSER" in your
function
# and turn debugging on or off by bugon() or bugoff()
bugon <- function() options("debug" = TRUE)
bugoff <- function() options("debug" = FALSE) #pun intended
```

Preceding example is taken from: http://stackoverflow.com/posts/7107100/revisions.

Using aliases:

```
#ht==headtail, i.e., show the first and last 10 items of an object
ht <- function(d) rbind(head(d,10),tail(d,10))

# Show the first 5 rows and first 5 columns of a data frame or matrix
hh <- function(d) d[1:5,1:5]
```

Preceding example is taken from: http://stackoverflow.com/posts/8676073/revisions.

Set a proxy for your web requests:

```
Sys.setenv(http_proxy="http://XXX.xxx.x.xxx:xx/")
```

As already stated, you can almost define and set everything that you can imagine in your personal Rprofile. However, where a lot of light is, there is also shade. If you often collaborate with other people on R projects, or when you share your R scripts elsewhere, a big problem can arise with an intensely customized Rprofile: reproducibility. There can be several settings that you have added, which other users do not see, and your scripts may fail.

You can check this if you start R in your terminal with the command, `--no-init-file`. If your scripts are still working, you can share them without having to worry.

R help is on the way

Whether beginner or professional, every R user needs help one day and wants to ask specific questions. Also, the inbuilt R help and documentation are really great; there are several more ways to get help from other users. Thanks to the ever growing popularity of R, there are now a variety of all kinds of forums, websites, FAQs, and help pages. Of course, there are endless groups and places on the well-known social networks, but we will focus on autonomous pages in the following. Let's start with the question and answer sites.

Getting questions and answers

The biggest question and answer network is surely **Stack Exchange**. There are currently 148 different questions and answers sites under its roof.

Stack Overflow (Stack Exchange)

The official site for Stack Overflow is `http://stackoverflow.com/`. The most popular question and answer page for all kinds of programmers is Stack Overflow. This page is part of Stack Exchange, a big question and answer network. In addition to the logical possibility of asking questions and giving answers, you can also vote for great answers or down vote not so good ones. Furthermore, you can earn badges, get a better reputation score, and avail of several other user privileges and tools, the more votes you get for your answers.

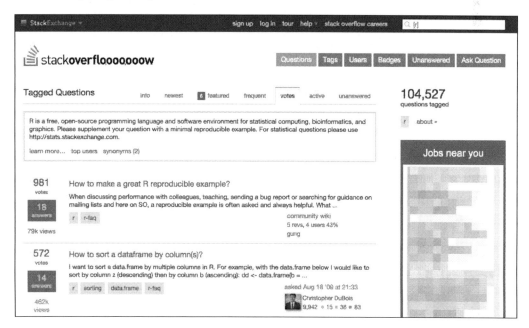

If you want to add a question about a special topic, the inbuilt tag system of Stack Overflow is a great tool. Of course, by using tags, you can also find the topics you like the most and give answers to open questions. A useful tag might be the `r-faq` tag:

> *The r-faq tag is created to group a limited number of questions discussing problems that come up regularly on the R tag. It is not the official FAQ on R for SO, but should serve as an interesting source of information on common problems.*

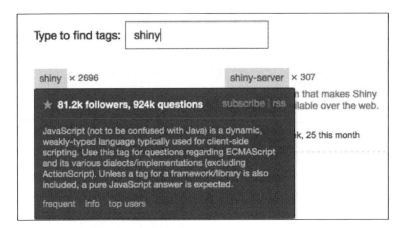

Stack Overflow also offers two R chat rooms, a standard R chat room for discussions, and a public one for all R related questions.

Data Science (Stack Exchange)

The official site for Data Science is `http://datascience.stackexchange.com/`. Another useful question and answer page of the Stack Exchange empire is the still relatively new Data Science page. This page works the same as Stack Overflow, but is purely focused on Data Science topics, which most often includes R.

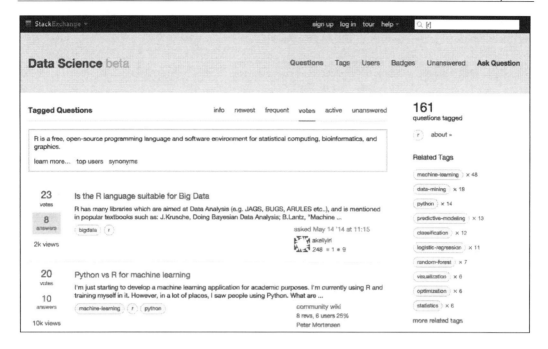

Cross Validated (Stack Exchange)

The official site of cross validated is `http://stats.stackexchange.com/`. Another relevant question and answer site of Stack Exchange for R users is called Cross Validated. The focus of this page lies on statistics, machine learning, data analysis, and other related topics. Again, R is well represented on this site. In fact, it is very similar to the Data Science page.

The perceived difference is, in my opinion, that Cross Validated is more theoretical while the Data Science site is more practical.

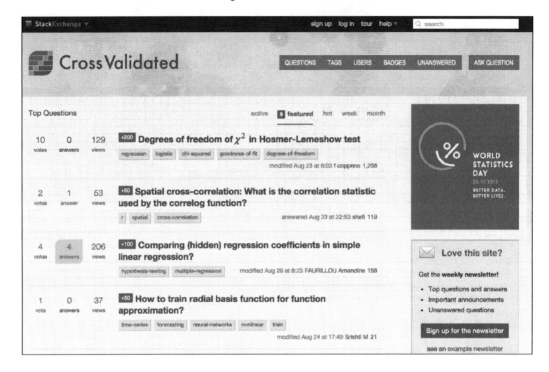

Open Data (Stack Exchange)

The official site for Open Data is at `http://opendata.stackexchange.com/`. Last but not least, there is another interesting Stack Exchange page, which is called Open Data. Of course, this page is not directly connected to R. But it might be very interesting for nearly all R users, since data is the oil for most of our scripts and analyses.

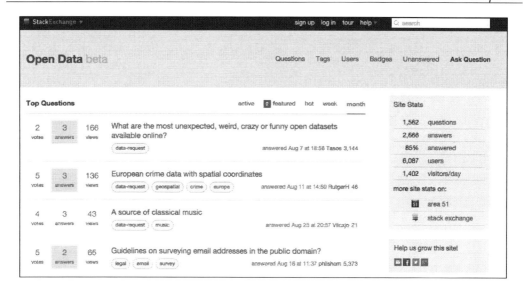

R mailing lists – R-help

Another way to get help is by joining the R mailing list called R-help. R mailing lists are a part of the R project. Currently there are six different mailing lists:

- R-announce
- R-help
- R-package-devel
- R-devel
- R-packages
- Special Interest groups

In our context, of course, the help mailing list is the most interesting. The R project writes the following about this list:

> *The 'main' R mailing list, for discussion about problems and solutions using R, announcements (not covered by 'R-announce' or 'R-packages', see above), about the availability of new functionality for R and documentation of R, comparison and compatibility with S-plus, and for the posting of nice examples and benchmarks. Do read the posting guide before sending anything!*

> *This has become quite an active list with dozens of messages per day. An alternative is to subscribe and choose daily digests (in plain or MIME format). Use the web interface for information, subscription, archives, etc.*

Source: `https://www.r-project.org/mail.html`

Reddit

The official site for Reddit is at `https://www.reddit.com/r/rstats/`. Reddit is a well known website that acts like a bulletin board system. The content is divided into different topic ranges called **subreddits**. And, there is also an R related subreddit. The page works comparable to Stack Overflow because users can up or down vote questions and answers. Often, longer discussions arise.

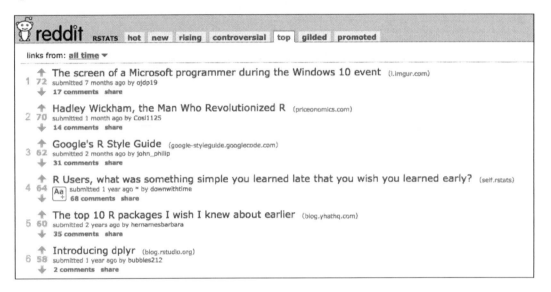

The Stack Exchange sites, the mailing list R-help and the `rstats` subreddit are the best-known and highly frequented sources to ask questions and give answers. Of course, there are probably hundreds of forums and sites where you can get help, and where contributors are more or less discussing the subject of R.

How to ask questions correctly

No matter which page you use to ask your question, in general, it is important to ask your R question the right way. There are only a few details that are better to include in order to get a confident answer.

1. Which R version and operating system are you using? Just use the `sessionInfo()`, or the similar `devtools` function, `devtools::session_info()` to get and post your system information:

    ```
    > sessionInfo()
    R version 3.2.0 (2015-04-16)
    Platform: x86_64-apple-darwin13.4.0 (64-bit)
    Running under: OS X 10.10.5 (Yosemite)
    ```

```
locale:
[1] de_DE.UTF-8/de_DE.UTF-8/de_DE.UTF-8/C/de_DE.UTF-8/de_DE.UTF-8

attached base packages:
[1] stats     graphics  grDevices utils     datasets  methods
[7] base

loaded via a namespace (and not attached):
 [1] rversions_1.0.2  tools_3.2.0       rstudioapi_0.3.1 curl_0.9.2
 [5] Rcpp_0.12.0      memoise_0.2.1    xml2_0.1.1
git2r_0.11.0
 [9] digest_0.6.8     devtools_1.8.0
```

2. Tell readers the goal of your code and give them relevant context information.

3. Specifically describe your problem. Persons who want to help you should be able to reproduce your problem in order to find a solution.

4. Instead of posting your whole R script, isolate the functions that may have cause your problem. But be sure to have the complete scripts available if people request them.

5. Provide information on your dataset or post similar sample data.

6. Be polite and friendly because you would want that readers like to help you.

Learning more about packages, functions, and more

Often you just need to know how to use this special function, or you want a particular R package. Here you do not necessarily need to use the question and answer sites, because they are also a bunch of resources for searching CRAN packages and R documentations.

R FAQs

The R Project itself offers the most detailed general R FAQ and also two specific ones for Windows and Mac OS users (https://cran.r-project.org/faqs.html).

R and CRAN documentations

The page R documentation serves in-depth options to search for functions, packages, and more. The page aggregates all packages from CRAN, GitHub, and Bioconductor. (http://www.rdocumentation.org/).

Another page where you can search for CRAN packages only and related information is called **crantastic**, which can be found at http://crantastic.org/. Since there are currently more than 7,000 different packages, and the CRAN pages do not provide a comfortable search function, pages like these are a great help:

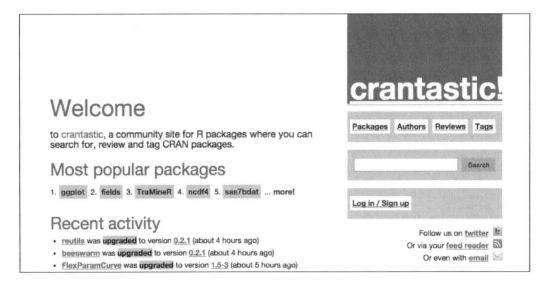

The next address for discovering CRAN packages is called **CRANberries** by Dirk Edelbüttel. Here you can find all information about new, updated, and removed R packages. In particular, this page shows the difference between the old and new package version (http://dirk.eddelbuettel.com/cranberries/).

R search engines

There are also several R specific search engines out there that do their purpose, but are visually a bit old fashioned:

1. **R Site Search** (`http://finzi.psych.upenn.edu/search.html`): This searches help files, mailing archives, and more.

2. **Gmane's R-lists** (`http://dir.gmane.org/index.php?prefix=gmane.comp.lang.r`): This page mirrors the R project mailing lists, news, and RSS feed.

3. **The Nabble R Forum** (`http://r.789695.n4.nabble.com/`): Here you can browse tons of R related messages.

4. **R Seek** (`http://rseek.org/`): This is a very simple search page for everything R.

5. **Bonus**: You can also add a CRAN search engine to your browser.

The following example is for the Chrome browser:

1. Paste `chrome://settings/searchEngines` into your location bar and hit enter.

2. Scroll down until the input boxes show, enabling you to add a search engine.

3. For adding a new search engine, put CRAN.

4. For keyword, put R, rstats or CRAN, but R is super easy to type, though it may not be optimal for you.

5. For URL with `%s` in place of query, type in the following: `https://www.google.com/search?as_q=%s&as_epq=&as_oq=&as_eq=&as_nlo=&as_nhi=&lr=&cr=&as_qdr=all&as_sitesearch=cran.rstudio.com&as_occt=any&safe=images&as_filetype=&as_rights=&gws_rd=ssl`.

Source: (`http://rud.is/b/2015/08/07/adding-a-cran-search-engine-to-chrome/`)

RStudio cheat sheets

The official site for RStudio cheat sheets is `https://www.rstudio.com/resources/cheatsheets/`. RStudio itself offers a bunch of very useful cheat sheets that can be downloaded as a PDF document. They are also available in a few other languages. Currently, the following sheets are available:

- **The Shiny Cheat Sheet**: This contains the Shiny package

- **The Data Visualization Cheat Sheet**: This contains the `ggplot2` package

- **The Package Development Cheat Sheet**: This contains the `devtools` package
- **The Data Wrangling Cheat Sheet**: This contains the `dplyr` and `tidyr` packages
- **The R Markdown Cheat Sheet**: This contains the `rmarkdown`, `knitr` packages
- **R Markdown Reference Guide**: This contains markdown syntax, as well as options for knitr chunks and Pandoc.

Sharing your R code

Whenever you need help, you might want to be sharing your R code. Of course, you can just copy and paste it to one of the aforementioned help pages. But there are also other, more flexible ways. An example for this is R-Fiddle. Just go to `http://www.r-fiddle.org/` and type in something or paste your script. Then you can save, embed, and share it. Due to the inbuilt console and the option to show all graphs, it is like a light version of RStudio for your browser.

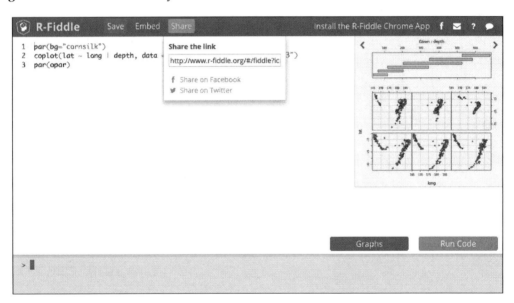

For completeness' sake, other online R consoles and environments are listed as follows:

- DataJoy (`https://www.getdatajoy.com/`)
- Jupyter (`https://try.jupyter.org/`)
- codingground (`http://www.tutorialspoint.com/r_terminal_online.php`)

Improving your R knowledge

R is more popular than ever. It has been the go-to language for many statisticians and analysts since a long time. But, the popularity of this programming language has skyrocketed due to the advent of the now ubiquitous topic areas of Data Science, big data, and Machine Learning. Therefore, it is only natural that more and more people also want to learn R. Thus, there are now a large number of different types of learning opportunities.

Learning R interactively

Learning by doing is the best possible way for many people to learn something new. Because of that, there are several different platforms where you can learn R interactively. This means directly in your browser or in R/RStudio. The following examples can be started whenever and wherever you like.

Try R

The official site for try R is `http://tryr.codeschool.com/`. Try R by Code School offers a very basic but entertaining and visually appealing course to get started with R. Everyone who is interested in R and wants a first experience is certainly in good hands here. This course is free.

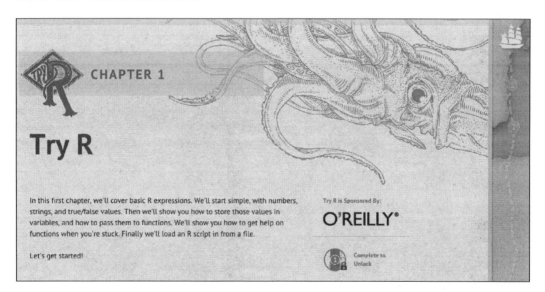

DataCamp

The official site for DataCramp is `https://www.datacamp.com/`. DataCamp is one of the bigger platforms on which you can learn R programming interactively. All given lectures can be done in your browser. Currently, they offer 14 courses from a beginner to professional level with topics ranging from R introduction over data manipulation with the `dplyr` package, to a Kaggle R tutorial on machine learning. You can start for free, or pay a subscription fee if you want to gain access to all courses and features.

Leada

The official site for Leada is `https://www.teamleada.com/`. Leada is another platform that offers several courses on R, but it also has courses on SQL and Python. Currently, there are three R introduction courses: one for machine learning, one for A/B testing, and one for the R Bootcamp. However, Leada is only partly interactive, or in their own words, Leada lessons are meant to interactively teach you in your own environment.

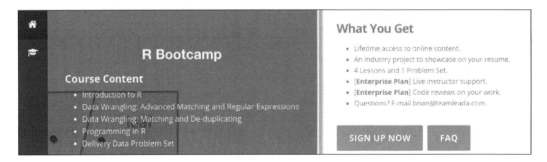

Swirl

Swirl is an innovative and interactive way to learn R programming directly in your R console. You just need to install the `swirl` package and follow the introduction. Currently, you can load eight different courses ranging from a basic to an advanced level. The package and its courses are free of charge.

```
Console  ~/Desktop/Book/Chapter-10/
> library(swirl)

| Hi! Type swirl() when you are ready to begin.

> swirl()

| Welcome to swirl!

| Please sign in. If you've been here before, use the same name as you
| did then. If you are new, call yourself something unique.

What shall I call you? Maximilian

| Thanks, Maximilian. Let's cover a few quick housekeeping items before
| we begin our first lesson. First of all, you should know that when
| you see '...', that means you should press Enter when you are done
| reading and ready to continue.
```

Attending online courses

Massive open online courses, also called MOOC, are on everyone's lips. Instead of learning at your own pace, you mostly take part in timely limited quizzes and other challenges with a strict deadline. Some courses offer certificates, if you want to pay a fee.

Coursera

The official Coursera is `https://www.coursera.org/`. Coursera is one of the biggest players in the MOOC world. This platform works with a huge number of institutions from all over the world to deliver courses at a university level on nearly any topic you can imagine.

Johns Hopkins University – Data Science Specialization

The Data Science Specialization of the *Johns Hopkins University* is an extremely successful example of an MOOC program. Back in February 2015, already almost 1.8 million people were enrolled.

> *This specialization covers the concepts and tools you'll need throughout the entire data science pipeline, from asking the right kinds of questions to making inferences and publishing results.*
>
> *– https://www.coursera.org/specializations/jhudatascience*

In total, there are nine courses and a capstone project. All tasks related to programming must be done with R. All courses must be completed within four weeks, but the capstone project takes eight weeks.

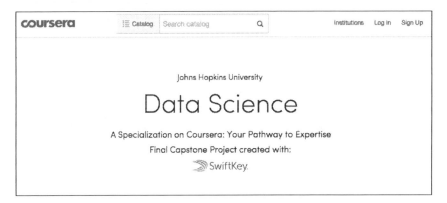

Johns Hopkins University – Genomic Data Science

The third relevant specialization is called **Genomic Data Science**. It consists of seven different courses and a capstone project. The duration for each course is, again, four weeks. R does not play the leading role this time, but is a used tool for these courses.

> *This specialization will teach you to understand, analyze, and interpret data from next-generation sequencing experiments. You will learn common tools of genomic data science, including Python, R, Bioconductor, and Galaxy.*
>
> *– https://www.coursera.org/specializations/genomics*

Udacity

Udacity is another heavyweight in the world of MOOCs. However, unlike Coursera, this platform works together with many large and reputable companies such as Facebook, Google, AT&T, and more. Udacity offers so-called **Nanodegree** programs. The Data Analyst Nanodegree includes a bunch of lessons, all more or less with the involvement of R. To complete it, you need to invest more than ten hours per week and the Nanodegree takes more than nine months minimum. The lessons are certainly quite challenging and interesting, but you have to pay a monthly subscription fee of $200. In their own words, this Nanodegree program is the most efficient curriculum to prepare you for a job as a Data Analyst. You will learn to:

- Wrangle, extract, transform, and load data from various databases, formats, and data sources

- Use exploratory data analysis techniques to identify meaningful relationships, patterns, or trends from complex data sets

- Classify unlabeled data or predict into the future with applied statistics and machine learning algorithms

- Communicate data analysis and findings well through effective data visualizations

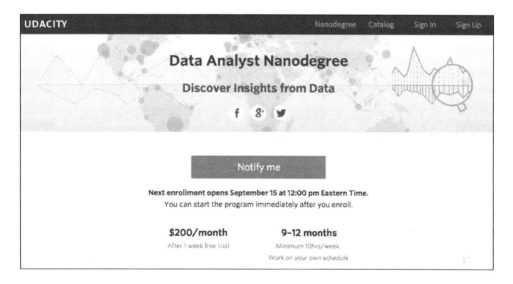

Other MOOC courses, related platforms, and programs

Some other remarkable courses of MOOC's platforms and universities are:

- Stanford University offers Statistical Learning, all computing in this course is done in R (`http://online.stanford.edu/course/statistical-learning`)

- The MOOC platform, edX, offers several courses with R involvement; to be mentioned specially are Statistics and R for the Life Sciences held by Harvard University and the relatively new course, Introduction to R Programming, held by Microsoft (`https://www.edx.org/`).

- Statistics.com also offers a huge number of coursers that involve the usage of R, such as data mining or mapping with R and more (`http://www.statistics.com/`).

- RStudio itself offers several tutorials on R, Shiny, R Markdown, and related software (`https://www.rstudio.com/resources/training/online-learning/`).

We can only display a limited range of learning opportunities here. There are, of course, many, many more courses and similar programs. Beyond that, you can discover an endless number of written tutorials and guides about R in general, or regarding specific topics such as machine learning, artificial intelligence, and so much more. The same goes for books and videos.

Staying up to date in the R world

Our world is in constant motion; constantly, there are new developments, techniques, methods, and tools. Of course, the same applies to the R World. If you do not want to lose the connection, you need to stay up to date. Fortunately, there are some great resources on the topic of R and its news.

R-Bloggers

The official site for R-Bloggers is `http://www.r-bloggers.com/`. The R-bloggers website is an absolute must-read for every R user and fan. This website aggregates the blog posts of more than 570 different blogs. Here, you really learn everything new and worth learning. The variety of articles includes general to specific R news, announcements, and researches. Furthermore, you can read posts ranging from a simple to a highly professional level.

In short, R-Bloggers presents a wild and very entertaining potpourri that you would not want to miss. Since this page aggregates really all important R blogs, there are no other remarkable blogs to stay up to date at the moment.

The R Journal

The official site for R Journal is `http://journal.r-project.org/`. The R journal is virtually a periodic magazine of the R project. It appears in the PDF format and includes a multitude of research articles, which are on a higher scientific level. Because of that, it clearly differs from most normal blog postings. Besides this, there is also a news and notes area.

Summary

In the beginning of this chapter, you learned how to use a custom Rprofile to boot RStudio so that everything important is already been set for you. Then we discovered that everything revolved around the topic of getting help. We listed several go-to platforms where you can ask your R-related questions. Furthermore, we showed how to ask questions correctly, in order to get useful answers. After that, we took care to draw up a meaningful list with platforms, webpages, and tools to help you to refresh and deepen your R knowledge further. Finally, we checked the resources to stay up to date in the R world.

Since this is the last chapter, we hope that you enjoyed the book and are now truly able to master RStudio and its special features.

Index

layers, adding with geoms 92, 93
parameters, modifying 96
Qplot() function 89
stats layers, using 100-102
used, for creating first graph 89-91
using 88
ggthemes 105
ggvis package
about 108
first graphic 108, 109
interactive ggvis graphs 110, 111
used, for interactive R Markdown
documents 167-169
Gist
Shiny application download option,
offering 152, 153
Git
branch 243
commit 243
configuring 242
diff 243
dropdown menu 251
fetching 243
gitignore file 248
installing, on Linux 242
installing, on Windows 242
merging process 243
mistake, undoing 251, 252
Pull 243
pushing process 243
remote repository on GitHub,
pushing 253, 254
repository 243
resources 260
URL 241, 260
used, for creating new project 247
using, via shell 244
using, with RStudio 245
GitHub
and RStudio, using via 246, 247
remote repository, pushing to 253, 254
Shiny application download option,
offering 153
URL 242-258

gitignore file 248
Google Analytics 197-199
Google API application
creating, URL 198
Google Sheets 202
googleVis package 171
Grammar of Graphics
about 88
applying, with ggplot2 88
grammar of graphics plot 89
graphic system, R
about 73
graphic devices 74
graphs
creating, with economist theme 106
creating, with wall street journal theme 107
grid layout 136, 138

H

Help pane 16, 21
History pane 14-16
HTML widgets
about 114, 172
dygraphs 115
Leaflet 116
rbokeh 117

I

icons
URL 186
Identity and Access Management (IAM)
role, creating 269-271
installation
devtools 211
Git 242
Git, on Linux 242
Git, on Windows 242
roxygen2 package 227, 228
shinydashboard 182
**integrated development environment
(IDE) 1**

Thank you for buying
Mastering RStudio – Develop, Communicate, and Collaborate with R

About Packt Publishing

Packt, pronounced 'packed', published its first book, *Mastering phpMyAdmin for Effective MySQL Management*, in April 2004, and subsequently continued to specialize in publishing highly focused books on specific technologies and solutions.

Our books and publications share the experiences of your fellow IT professionals in adapting and customizing today's systems, applications, and frameworks. Our solution-based books give you the knowledge and power to customize the software and technologies you're using to get the job done. Packt books are more specific and less general than the IT books you have seen in the past. Our unique business model allows us to bring you more focused information, giving you more of what you need to know, and less of what you don't.

Packt is a modern yet unique publishing company that focuses on producing quality, cutting-edge books for communities of developers, administrators, and newbies alike. For more information, please visit our website at www.packtpub.com.

About Packt Open Source

In 2010, Packt launched two new brands, Packt Open Source and Packt Enterprise, in order to continue its focus on specialization. This book is part of the Packt Open Source brand, home to books published on software built around open source licenses, and offering information to anybody from advanced developers to budding web designers. The Open Source brand also runs Packt's Open Source Royalty Scheme, by which Packt gives a royalty to each open source project about whose software a book is sold.

Writing for Packt

We welcome all inquiries from people who are interested in authoring. Book proposals should be sent to author@packtpub.com. If your book idea is still at an early stage and you would like to discuss it first before writing a formal book proposal, then please contact us; one of our commissioning editors will get in touch with you.

We're not just looking for published authors; if you have strong technical skills but no writing experience, our experienced editors can help you develop a writing career, or simply get some additional reward for your expertise.

Data Manipulation with R

Second Edition

ISBN: 978-1-78528-881-4   Paperback: 130 pages

Efficiently perform data manipulation using the split-apply-combine strategy in R

1. Perform data manipulation with add-on packages such as plyr, reshape, stringr, lubridate, and sqldf.

2. Learn about factor manipulation, string processing, and text manipulation techniques using the stringr and dplyr libraries.

3. Enhance your analytical skills in an intuitive way through step-by-step working examples.

Big Data Analytics with R and Hadoop

ISBN: 978-1-78216-328-2   Paperback: 238 pages

Set up and integrated infrastructure of R and Hadoop to turn your data analytics into Big Data analytics

1. Write Hadoop MapReduce within R.

2. Learn data analytics with R and the Hadoop platform.

3. Handle HDFS data within R.

Please check **www.PacktPub.com** for information on our titles

R Statistical Application Development by Example Beginner's Guide

ISBN: 978-1-84951-944-1   Paperback: 344 pages

Learn R Statistical Application Development from scratch in a clear and pedagogical manner

1. A self-learning guide for the user who needs statistical tools for understanding uncertainty in computer science data.

2. Essential descriptive statistics, effective data visualization, and efficient model building.

3. Every method explained through real data sets enables clarity and confidence for unforeseen scenarios.

Learning RStudio for R Statistical Computing

ISBN: 978-1-78216-060-1   Paperback: 126 pages

Learn to effectively perform R development, statistical analysis, and reporting with the most popular R IDE

1. A complete practical tutorial for RStudio, designed keeping in mind the needs of analysts and R developers alike.

2. Step-by-step examples that apply the principles of reproducible research and good programming practices to R projects.

3. Learn to effectively generate reports, create graphics, and perform analysis, and even build R-packages with RStudio.

Please check **www.PacktPub.com** for information on our titles

Made in the USA
Lexington, KY
19 December 2016